Power and Contestation

About the authors

Nivedita Menon, Professor at Centre for Comparative Politics and Political Theory, Jawaharlal Nehru University, Delhi, is the author of *Seeing like a Feminist* (2012) and *Recovering Subversion: Feminist Politics Beyond the Law* (2004). She also has two edited volumes *Gender and Politics in India* (1999) and *Sexualities* (2007); and a book co-edited with Aditya Nigam and Sanjay Palshikar *Critical Studies in Politic. Exploring Sites, Selves, Power* (2013). An active commentator on contemporary issues on the blog kafila.org, she has also translated fiction and non-fiction from Hindi and Malayalam into English. She has been active with non-funded, non-party citizens' forums in Delhi on issues of secularism, workers' and women's rights, sexuality, and in opposition to the nuclear bomb.

Aditya Nigam is Professor at the Centre for the Study of Developing Societies, Delhi. He was a political activist for two decades before he joined academics. Nigam has published widely on issues relating to Marxism, secularism, nationalism and radical politics. He is the author of *The Insurrection of Little Selves: The Crisis of Secular Nationalism in India* (2006), *After Utopia: Modernity, Socialism and the Postcolony* (2010), and *Desire Named Development* (2011). He is also co-editor, with Nivedita Menon and Sanjay Palshikar, of *Critical Studies in Politic. Exploring Sites, Selves, Power* (2013).

Apart from writing regularly on contemporary issues on kafila.org, he is also one of the editors of *Pratiman – Samay, Samaj, Sanskriti*, the Hindi social science journal published by CSDS.

Power and Contestation
India since 1989
With a new Epilogue

Nivedita Menon • Aditya Nigam

Orient BlackSwan

POWER AND CONTESTATION

ORIENT BLACKSWAN PRIVATE LIMITED

Registered Office
3-6-752 Himayatnagar, Hyderabad 500 029, Telangana, India
email: centraloffice@orientblackswan.com

Other Offices
Bangalore, Bhopal, Chennai, Ernakulam, Guwahati, Hyderabad,
Jaipur, Kolkata, Lucknow, Mumbai, New Delhi, Noida, Patna

With a new epilogue, © 2014
© Nivedita Menon and Aditya Nigam 2007
This edition of Power and Contestation: India since 1989 is published by
arrangement with Zed Books.

First published in India by
Orient Blackswan Private Limited 2008
This edition 2014

ISBN 978 81 250 5619 5

Printed in India at
Yash Printographics
Noida

Published by
Orient Blackswan Private Limited
1/24 Asaf Ali Road
New Delhi 110 002
email: delhi@orientblackswan.com

Licensed for sale only in India, Pakistan, Nepal, Bhutan, Bangladesh, Sri Lanka
and the Maldives; not for export.

The external boundary and coastline of India as depicted in the map in this
book is neither correct nor authentic

Contents

Acknowledgments | vi
Abbreviations | vii Timeline | x
India at a glance | xiii Map | xiv
Introduction: a genealogy of the 1990s | 1

1 The recalcitrance of caste | 15
2 Politics of Hindutva and the minorities | 36
3 Globalization I: accumulation by dispossession | 61
4 Globalization II: new economies of desire | 83
5 Old Left, New Left | 103
6 When was the nation? | 135
7 India in the world | 166
Conclusion: a heterogeneous present | 176
Epilogue June 2014 | 182

Notes | 210
Bibliography | 229
Index | 256

Acknowledgments

We are grateful to Nick Guyatt, the series editor; Ellen McKinlay, Commissioning Editor, Zed Books; the two anonymous readers and our friend Mary John for their careful reading of the first draft of this book. Their thoughtful suggestions have been invaluable.

We also thank Sujit Deb and Avinash Jha of the library of the Centre for the Study of Developing Societies, Delhi, without whose enthusiastic support beyond the call of duty, our task would have been much more difficult.

Abbreviations

AAP	Aam Admi Party
ADB	Asian Development Bank
AFSPA	Armed Forces Special Powers Act
AGP	Asom Gana Parishad
AIADMK	All India Anna Dravida Munnetra Kazhagham
AIBMM	All India Backward Muslim Morcha
AIPRF	All India People's Resistance Forum
AITUC	All India Trade Union Congress
APCLC	Andhra Pradesh Civil Liberties Committee
APDR	Association for the Protection of Democratic Rights
APHC	All Party Hurriyat Conference
BJP	Bharatiya Janata Party
BSP	Bahujan Samaj Party
CAG	Comptroller and Auditor General
CITU	Centre of Indian Trade Unions
CMM	Chhattisgarh Mukti Morcha
CMSS	Chhattisgarh Mines Shramik Sangh
CNDP	Coalition for Nuclear Disarmament and Peace
CPI	Communist Party of India
CPI(M)	Communist Party of India (Marxist)
CPI(Maoist)	Communist Party of India (Maoist)
CPI(ML)	Communist Party of India (Marxist-Leninist)
CSWI	Committee for the Status of Women in India
DMK	Dravida Munnetra Kazhagham
EP	Ekta Parishad
HM	Hizb-ul-Mujahideen
IIM	Indian Institute of Management

IIT	Indian Institute of Technology
INTUC	Indian National Trade Union Congress
IRC	Independent Review Committee
JKLF	Jammu and Kashmir Liberation Front
JTSA	Jamia Teachers Solidarity Association
JVC	Justice Verma Committee
SSP	Kerala Shastra Sahitya Parishad
KSU	Khasi Students' Union
LF	Left Front
MBCs	Most Backward Classes
MCC	Maoist Communist Centre
MKSS	Mazdoor Kisan Shakti Sangathan
MNC	Multinational Corporation
MP	Member of Parliament
MPLF	Manipur People's Liberation Front
MUF	Muslim United Front
NC	National Conference
NCL	National Centre for Labour
NDA	National Democratic Alliance
NESO	North East Students' Organization
NHDC	Narmada Hydroelectric Development Corporation
NHPC	National Hydro Power Corporation
NIMZs	National Investment and Manufacturing Zones
NNC	Naga National Council
NREGA	National Rural Employment Guarantee Act
NSCN	National Socialist Council of Nagaland
NTUI	New Trade Union Initiative
NVP	Narmada Valley Project
OBC	Other Backward Classes, used to refer to lower castes other than Dalits
PIL	Public Interest Litigation
PLA	People's Liberation Army

PMM	Pasmanda Muslim Mahaz or the Backward Muslim Front
POK	Pakistan Occupied Kashmir
POTA	Prevention of Terrorist Activities Act
POW	Progressive Organization of Women
PRIs	Panchayati Raj Institutions
PUCL	People's Union for Civil Liberties
PUDR	People's Union for Democratic Rights
PWG	People's War Group
RSS	Rashtriya Swayamsevak Sangh
RTI Act	Right to Information Act
SASB	Shri Amarnath Shrine Board
SC	Scheduled Castes (the administrative category for Dalits)
SEZ	Special Economic Zone
SJM	Swadeshi Jagaran Manch
SP	Samajwadi Party
SSP	Sardar Sarovar Project
ST	Scheduled Tribes (the administrative category for Adivasis/Tribals)
TISCO	Tata Iron and Steel Corporation
UF	United Front
ULFA	United Liberation Front of Asom
UNLF	United National Liberation Front
UPA	United Progressive Alliance
VHP	Vishwa Hindu Parishad
WDP	Women's Development Programme
WRB	Women's Reservation Bill

Timeline

Major country-level landmarks in India since Independence

This timeline is meant only as an aid for those with little familiarity with Indian history and politics. It is necessarily limited and schematic, focusing only on some formal political events at the national level.

1947–89

August 15, 1947 India attains Independence from British rule.

January 26, 1950 The new Constitution of the Indian Republic comes into force.

1967 Defeat of the Congress in nine states (including two Left-led governments).

The Maoist revolt (Naxalbari – the rebellion of idealist elite youth).

1969 Split in ruling Congress (1969) and the "radical" turn in Congress – bank nationalization, *garibi hatao* (End Poverty) policy.

1971 Bangladesh attains Independence from Pakistan, in which India sends troops to aid Bangladesh.

1973–74 Gujarat student agitation known as the Nav Nirman movement.

Bihar movement led by Gandhian leader Jaya Prakash Narayan, which eventually spreads all over northern India.

Railway strike.

Allahabad High Court judgment on corruption in electoral practices against PM Indira Gandhi – leading to the declaration of Emergency.

1975–77 The government declares a state of Emergency, which lasts till March 1977. In this the government receives full backing of the Soviet bloc.

1977–79 Defeat of Congress. Janata Party government comes to power, and restoration of democracy.

July 1979   Collapse of Janata government.

1980–90   The return of Indira Gandhi (1980) inaugurates another decade of Congress rule. A decade full of turbulence marked by terrorism in Punjab and the rise of "separatist" movements.

June 1984   "Operation Bluestar" – the Indian Army moves into the Amritsar Golden Temple to "flush out" terrorists, involving a major gun battle and large-scale destruction of the Sikh place of worship.

31 October 1984   Indira Gandhi assassinated by Sikh bodyguards, Rajiv Gandhi becomes caretaker prime minister. Large-scale Congress-sponsored massacre of Sikhs.

December 1984   The Congress Party under Rajiv Gandhi sweeps the general elections under the impact of a sympathy wave combined with a Hindu backlash against Sikh "terrorism."

1986   Government passes Muslim Women (Protection of Rights on Divorce) Act 1986, overturning the Supreme Court judgment on Shah Bano.

1987   India deploys the Indian Peace Keeping Force (IPKF) in Sri Lanka, which turns out to be another misadventure.

1989 onwards

1989   Defeat of the Congress following widespread allegations of corruption. National Front government under V. P. Singh, supported by the Left and the Right, takes power.

1990   Mandal Commission report implemented. Indian troops withdrawn from Sri Lanka.

1991   National Front government falls as BJP withdraws support over the first major attempt at demolition of the Babri Masjid. Congress returns to power.

Rajiv Gandhi assassinated by a Sri Lankan Tamil suicide bomber.

Structural adjustment program initiated.

1992   Babri Masjid demolished through Hindu right-wing mass mobilization.

1996   Congress defeated once again in general elections. BJP emerges as single largest party in parliament but unable to garner support. The United Front government supported by the Left takes power.

1998 Right-wing BJP-led National Democratic Alliance takes power at Center.
India explodes nuclear device.
February 2002 Gujarat carnage.
April 2004 Defeat of NDA. United Progressive Alliance government supported by Left and social movements comes to power.

India at a glance

Area (sq. km)	3,166,000
Population (million)	1,027
Population living in rural areas, as per the 2001 Census (%)	72.2
Number of States and Union Territories	35

Biggest cities: Mumbai (formerly Bombay), Delhi, Kolkata (formerly Calcutta), Chennai (formerly Madras), Bangalore, Hyderabad

Literacy rate: 2001:
Total	65.38
Male	75.85
Female	54.16
Male–female gap	21.7

Note: Literacy rate represents the number of literate persons as a percentage of the total population.
Source: Census of India, 2001

Number of official languages	23

Government of India uses both Hindi and English for official purposes.

Human Development Indicators:
1 Human Development Index Rank	127
2 Human Poverty Index (Rank)	53
3 Population living below $1 a day, 1990–2001 (%)	34.7
4 Population living below $2 a day, 1990–2001 (%)	79.9
5 Population living below the national poverty line, 1987–2000 (%)	28.6

Source: Human Development Indicators, 2003, UNDP

Sex ratio (women per 1,000 men)	933

Religious community-wise break-up (%):
Hindu	85
Muslim (world's second largest population after Indonesia)	13.4
Christian	2.3
Sikh	1.9
Buddhist	0.8
Population classified as Scheduled Tribes	8.2
Population classified as Scheduled Castes (Dalit)	16.2

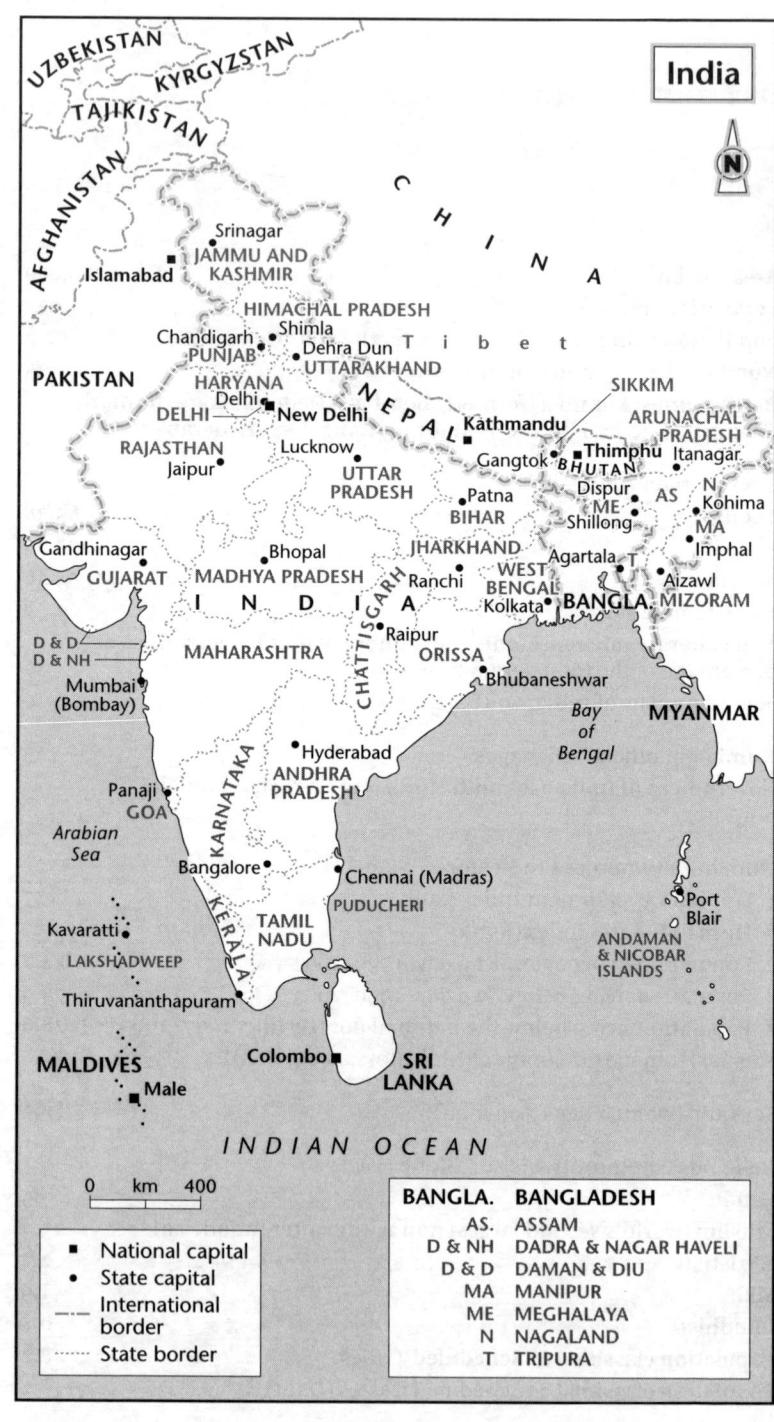

Introduction: a genealogy of the 1990s

India, looked at from the West, appears as a predictable cascade of contrasting images of which it is impossible to make any sense: slums and skyscrapers, call centers and illiteracy, Bollywood and anti-Valentine's Day protests, McDonalds and farmers' suicides.
Suketu Mehta is despairing: "Bombay is the future of urban civilization on the planet. God help us" (Mehta 2004: 3). His book on Bombay, *Maximum City*, written while living for a short period in India, produces that familiar patchwork so deftly (gangsters and tough cops, mini-skirt-wearing socialites, close encounters with human shit) that it leaves the reviewer of *The Economist* exhausted: "Mr Mehta paints a picture of an India that is so vast, complex and confusing as to defy generalisation, and facing such a terrifying array of problems that it forbids optimism." And yet, Indians show "dauntless optimism." How can this be? "To many foreigners it seems almost unseemly: how can a country talk so proudly when so many of its people – 260m at the government's count – live below the poverty line?"[1]
Thomas Friedman, on the other hand, is ebullient. "You know, you know you're in Bangalore, you know you're in the Silicon Valley of India ... when you go to play golf and the caddy on the first tee says you can either aim at the Microsoft building or the IBM building. You know you're at Bangalore when you see the Pizza Hut advertisement says 'gigabytes of taste.' And you know you're at Bangalore when you see street signs sponsored by Texas Instruments. This is one hot town ... it's producing a lot of energy, and it's going to be a real challenge to American workers."[2] Watch out, says Friedman, you know what it is like to be in India? "Shake a champagne bottle for about 15 minutes and take off the cork. You don't want to get in the way of that cork!"[3]
That's funny, because if you're "*in* India," then you're the cham-

2 | Introduction

pagne, *you* gush out with the cork – it's the cork that's in your way, not you that's in the way of the cork. This characteristic Friedmanesque flourish is, in this context, rather more than a mixed metaphor. It is revealing of what Mahmood Mamdani (2007) has identified as a "denial of a history and a politics" – what we might term the denial of an "inside" – to the non-West. There it is, mysterious and inscrutable, its intriguing surfaces always (only) available to be gazed upon from the outside.

Read that sentence from the review of *Maximum City* again. Is there any part of the world today – the USA, Canada, Europe – that is not "so ... complex and confusing as to defy generalisation, and facing such a terrifying array of problems that it forbids optimism"? And yet you can be certain that the particular collections of phrases above would be used – from a Western perspective – only for Asia, Africa, South America.

This book is an attempt to introduce general readers to the vast body of scholarship on India that does behave as if India has a politics and a history. The focus is on the period since 1989, but while 1989 is a critical turning point in India's contemporary history, it is so for reasons very different from the global ones that relate to "end of the cold war." Undoubtedly, there are important points of intersection between historical developments in India and those at the global level. As the subsequent chapters will show, however, there are significant internal conflicts and logics that have propelled these developments. Sometimes these are of all-India or "national" significance but, often enough, they are part of other smaller stories, not all of which tie up together into one neat narrative. We have therefore tried to tell these smaller stories even if that seems to deprive us of the coherence of a larger framework, leaving us with a more fragmentary account of India's present history. In this sense we write from what we call a post-national perspective, one that seeks out political tendencies that work "under" the nation, resisting inclusion into the "larger" national identity, insisting on space/time trajectories that do not mesh with progressivist dominant narratives of nation and history.

Inevitably, the story is told with a particular slant, as all stories are. The slant arises from the (severe!) constraints of space as well as from the intellectual and political perspective of the authors and their geographical location in Delhi. If readers are looking for a comprehensive account of all the trends shaping power and contestation since 1989, they will be disappointed. What they will find, though, is a selective account of themes that appear, from what we term our specific "New Left" perspective, to be significant. We explain what we mean by the New Left in more detail in Chapter 5, but briefly, from this point of view, *power* is the axis constituted by Nation and Capital, while *contestations* are of two kinds – one demanding inclusion within, the other running counter to these entities.

Our perspective is also, from the outset, feminist. Thus, while the women's movement (or more accurately, women's movements) in India are articulate, visible, effective, and rich with internal debate, we have chosen not to restrict this aspect to a separate chapter. Rather, feminist analysis is a thread running through the book, our attempt being to allow a critical grasp of gendered power relations to challenge orthodoxies of all kinds.

Collapse of the "Nehruvian consensus"

The political conjuncture of the years 1989–92 constitutes a truly ruptural moment in contemporary Indian history. At one level, it saw the complete collapse of the "Nehruvian consensus" – a consensus that combined three key features:

- a vision of a self-reliant economy based on an import-substituting industrialization strategy;
- a broadly secular polity; and
- a non-aligned foreign policy that not only steered clear of international military alliances but was also anti-imperialist, especially vis-à-vis the USA, even if inconsistently so.

At another level, this moment inaugurated what seems like an irreversible decline of the Indian National Congress that had ruled the country almost continuously barring three years (1977–79), since Independence in 1947, ushering in an era of coalition politics at the Center. From another angle it could also be said to have ushered in an era of instability, considering that in the seventeen years since then, there have been seven coalition governments at the Center.

As we shall see below, however, the consequences of this instability were not altogether negative, for some social groups discovered immense liberatory possibilities in this moment. Scholars have focused on different aspects of this conjuncture and referred to the period inaugurated by it variously as a "post-Congress polity" or a "globalizing economy" or one marked by the rise of the Hindu Right. All these descriptions point to certain important features of this period but their relation to the specific conjuncture needs to be understood. It should be emphasized that this political moment actually condenses within it a whole array of other social conflicts and developments and we may justifiably call it, after Louis Althusser, an *overdetermined* conjuncture, that is to say one where many different social conflicts merge into an explosive unity. Compressed within these four years are almost apocalyptic events in the life of the country:

- The irreversible decline of the Congress and the emergence of an era of coalition politics begun by its defeat in the 1989 elections.
- The implementation of the Mandal Commission recommendations in 1990, providing for affirmative action for lower castes (OBCs – Other Backward Classes) and the violent battles fought around it that have permanently changed the nature and language of Indian politics. Further, we see the consolidation, around this event, of a wide range of regional, lower-caste political parties, which emerged thereafter as significant players in national politics.
- The assassination of Prime Minister Rajiv Gandhi, in 1991, by a Sri Lankan Tamil suicide bomber in the southern state of Tamil Nadu – a consequence of the perceptions of India's role in Sri Lanka where the Indian Army had been stationed. The "Indian Peace Keeping Force" as it was called, was meant to assist the government of Sri Lanka in handling Tamil insurgency and turned out to be, ultimately, a complete misadventure.
- The initiation of the structural adjustment program, under the auspices of the International Monetary Fund and the World Bank after India went in for an IMF loan. This development was, of

course, facilitated by the collapse of the socialist bloc, especially the Soviet Union, which deprived the country of one of its traditional trading partners and supporters. More importantly, the collapse of the Soviet Union in itself became the major argument for pushing through neoliberal reforms, delegitimizing the voice of left-wing opponents.

- The rapid rise of the Hindu nationalist Bharatiya Janata Party (BJP) as a major claimant for political power at the Center and the unexpectedly successful mass mobilization by Hindu rightwing organizations leading to the demolition, in 1992, of the Babri Masjid, a 400-year-old mosque in the town of Ayodhya in Uttar Pradesh. This event also initiated a new phase of sectarian violence and the targeting of minorities, especially Muslims. Symbolically, it constituted the signal event that marked the defeat of secularism and secular nationalism, at least temporarily, and the transformation of public discourse in the media and elsewhere.
- The beginnings of the media explosion that was to gather momentum through the 1990s and 2000s. This period marks the beginning of the end of the state-run media and the advent of a whole series of new media technologies that radically transformed the nature and form of politics and the terrain of social and cultural life in this period.

These different conflicts and tendencies coming together in this conjuncture did not appear overnight. Indeed, they had been developing over a long time, accelerating over the decade of the 1980s. What is crucial about this moment is precisely that they are condensed here into a situation that was potent with innumerable possibilities and dangers.

The long 1980s – after the Emergency

In March 1977, India came out of the trauma of nineteen months of authoritarian rule, presided over by Prime Minister Indira Gandhi, during which all constitutional rights and civil liberties had been abrogated, the freedom of the press all but annihilated and political opponents of the regime thrown into prison. The period, known in Indian political vocabulary as "the Emergency" after the specific constitutional provision that allowed for the suspension of democratic institutions and procedures under certain extreme circumstances, extended from June 1975 to March 1977. The lifting of the Emergency, following the electoral defeat of the ruling Congress Party, led to a veritable explosion of long accumulated democratic aspirations. It can also be argued that the very fact that Mrs Gandhi preferred to hold elections and seek democratic legitimation rather than opting for the route taken by many other third world dictators, demonstrates how deep were the roots that democracy had struck in India.

The Janata Party (JP) that had defeated the Congress at the elections had emerged out of the merger of a large number of disparate parties, from the socialists to the Hindu nationalist Jana Sangh (the earlier avatar of the BJP), united on the single issue of defeating the Emergency regime of the Congress. The JP brought a large number of lower- and middle-caste peasants/farmers into parliament – more than the parliament had ever had before (Corbridge and Harris 2000: 89). At one level, it was a conflict between this segment and the predominantly upper-caste, right-wing Jana Sangh that brought about the downfall of this government in a little over two years. But at another level, it was the attempt by the Jana Sangh and its fascistic mother organization, the Rashtriya Swayamsevak Sangh (RSS) to seize control of the JP-led state governments that really precipitated the crisis.

Throughout the period of the JP rule though, it should be borne in mind, there were major upheavals and mass struggles, as the accumulated democratic desire dammed by the Emergency burst forth in different ways: militant working-class struggles for wage revisions and restoration of trade union rights, students' movements and, to cap it all, a widespread police revolt against abysmal working and living conditions, which enveloped the police force of seven JP-ruled states. The police revolt in May 1979 was soon followed by a rebellion in the ranks of the Central Reserve Police. Such militant expression of widespread accumulated discontent, and the inability of the JP government to handle it, gave the impression of a dangerous drift, a galloping anarchy, especially to the vocal middle classes. It was in that context that the Congress seemed to appear to many to be the only force that could restore a semblance of order and stability.

The Congress thus returned to power in January 1980, in an atmosphere of deep cynicism and apathy bred by two and a half years of Janata rule. In retrospect, however, it seems the cynicism and apathy that engulfed urban middle-class India around this time also had to do with the emergence of what the popular news magazine *India Today* called "peasant power" and its spectacular demonstration through huge rallies in the heart of Delhi, the capital of urban India. Rustic, unsophisticated, and untrained in the ways of the old Nehruvian generation of parliamentarians, these new and powerful leaders were clearly making a bid for power. But the picture was far more complicated than it might appear, for this was not simply a rural versus urban divide: condensed into this assertion of "the rural" were also the aspirations of an emergent vernacular elite that was at the same time predominantly lower- and middle-caste. These were the populist leaders of OBC castes that the Mandal Commission was to empower a little over a decade later.

To this new brand of vernacular leaders, then, the ideological battles between the Left and the Right might have appeared, says political theorist Sudipta Kaviraj, as insubstantial differences within a modernist bloc of privilege. Most observers and analysts on the Left, however, seem to have missed not only this very significant fact of cultural exclusion from the institutions of the Nehruvian period, steeped as they were in the normative world and etiquette of Western modernity; they also seem to have been completely oblivious of the lower-caste dynamics of this new assertion. Thus they saw merely the class aspect of this assertion and labeled these sections "kulaks" or "rich peasants," missing the point of this upsurge altogether.

Let us return to our narrative. In 1980 the Janata government had collapsed and Indira Gandhi had returned to power. Throughout the decade to follow, her party continued to be in command of the situation, even though she herself fell to assassins' bullets shortly before her five-year term was over. Her assassination was followed by large-scale anti-Sikh pogroms in many parts of the country – with the epicenter in Delhi. Led by Congress leaders, this bloodbath helped the party gather the Hindu backlash around it – so much so that even the RSS was momentarily to desert the "revisionist BJP" and rally around the Congress. And thus, in the midst of this blood and mayhem, Indira Gandhi's elder son Rajiv Gandhi acceded to prime ministership.

Rounding up the highlights of the decade, *India Today* noted in its first issue of 1990 that though the 1980s were years of formal Congress dominance, "they were also years when the grip and authority of the Centre over the country's several constituents steadily weakened." The specter that the Center may not hold faced Indians time and again, the report said, as the politics of separatism, terrorism, communalism, and corruption flourished, putting the "entire political fabric" under unprecedented strain.[4] On her return to power Indira Gandhi and the Congress had to deal, among other things, with two major secessionist movements, one in the north-eastern state of Assam and the other in the northern state of Punjab. The situation in Punjab was largely of the Congress Party's own making, escalating what was essentially an issue of greater state autonomy into a violent separatist movement using terrorist tactics. Four years later, on October 31, 1984, Mrs Gandhi was shot by her own Sikh armed bodyguards.

The accession of Rajiv Gandhi to prime ministership became an important turning point in more than one sense. As has been often noted, he and his entourage, dubbed the "computer boys," had neither any connection with the anti-colonial nationalist traditions of the Congress Party, nor any grounding whatsoever in politics. They generally gave the impression of being a group of impatient reformers who wanted to run the country in the manner of CEOs of corporate houses. This group, drawn from among Rajiv Gandhi's old schoolmates, was basically fired by the idea of the new technological revolution powered by computers and microchip technology. "Preparing India for the twenty-first century" was Rajiv's pet slogan. And to that end they wanted to rapidly bypass the bureaucracy – of the government as well as that of the Congress. In retrospect, however, what seemed like their major shortcoming was probably also their major strength. The fact that they were not constrained by many of the articles of faith of the old nationalist elite enabled them to push through some of the most significant changes that made possible the introduction of new technologies, which eventually became an important vehicle for the transformation of life in the 1990s and thereafter. The case of the Telecom Commission, set up in early 1989, best exemplifies this style. Headed by Satyen Gangaram Pitroda (generally known as Sam Pitroda), a US-based businessman and a close confidant of Rajiv Gandhi, the Telecom Commission was set up "in the teeth of fierce opposition from the bureaucracy." Pitroda explained that this was necessary because "The way telecommunications is changing, it is essential to have a flexible organization that can respond to changes." The commission eventually heralded a fundamental transformation of the telecom scenario. In a country where there were a mere 4 million phone lines for a population of 800 million, Pitroda emphasized the setting up of a wide network of public phones – and given the low literacy and numeracy levels, he proposed that instead of automated machines, there be human beings handling these.[5] Within a couple of years, all over urban India there was a wide network of what are called PCOs (public call offices) with facilities for long-distance calls as well. This became the basis, it is now recognized, of India's telecom revolution.

The years of Rajiv Gandhi's rule also saw the acceleration of the liberalization of the Indian economy – especially the dismantling of the import-substituting model of industrialization and the rapid opening up of international trade. This regime was responsible, in large measure, for making the 1980s the decade of consumption-led growth. Through the 1980s, the economy maintained a growth rate of 5.5 percent, with industry growing at an annual rate of 6.6 percent and the consumer durables sector itself growing at over 14 percent annually. This also signaled the coming of age of the Indian middle class, whose pent-up consumerist desire was tapped by the new regime to power the new growth of the economy. In the good old days of the Nehruvian consensus, this would have been scandalous: the entire idea of nation-building of that period was predicated upon curtailing present consumption and encouraging savings to finance the development of the capital goods sector.

The other major change since the days of Nehruvian nationalism was the new imagination ushered in by the Rajiv Gandhi regime, which has been described as that of the "global nation" as opposed to the idea of the territorial nation that recognized as its citizens only those who lived within its borders (Nigam 2004). In earlier days the diaspora had been the cause of much consternation for the nationalists, who saw in it what they called the "brain drain" – demonstrating an unfortunate lack of patriotic commitment to the nation. In the new dispensation, however, the diasporic Indians who had left the country and settled elsewhere, especially in the West, were seen as the resources to be harnessed for the new economic model. These diasporic Indians, referred to as Non-Resident Indians (NRIs), were seen as people with resources for investing in the country's economy, and as earners of precious foreign exchange. More importantly, however, they were now considered as "brain banks" whose skills and knowledge could be harnessed for the development of the country to "take it into the twenty-first century."

When Rajiv Gandhi took over power after his mother's death, he had appeared to the public at large as a relatively unblemished figure who was sincere and was out to clean up India's public life. His speech to the Congress session in 1985, where he launched a frontal attack against powerbrokers in the party, helped enhance this image and he was soon being referred to in the media as Mr Clean. Within a couple of years, however, this Rajiv died a quiet death at the hands of the other Rajiv whose regime, in popular perception, was now mired in a whole series of scandals and corrupt defense deals. Emblematic of these was the "celebrated" Rs1,700 crore (1 crore = 10 million) Bofors gun deal in 1986, in which people close to Rajiv Gandhi were suspected to have received kickbacks. The Bofors matter first came to light on April 16, 1987, when Swedish Radio reported that Swedish arms manufacturer A. B. Bofors had paid bribes to Indian politicians and key defense figures to swing the contract in their favor. Even though Rajiv Gandhi denied that anybody had received such pay-offs, in the public perception he himself was not free of suspicion. As recently as July 2006, more than eighteen years later, a member of Rajiv's inner circle, Arun Singh (then defense minister) said in a television interview that he was sure somebody had made money on the deal, though he was not sure it had been Rajiv himself.

Long before the controversies over the defense deals broke out in public, widespread resentment against Rajiv Gandhi's brash and abrasive style had been building up. What were initially seen as the angry outbursts of an honest and clean reformer against the wheeler-dealing of his politically savvy colleagues, now seemed to the public at large as intemperate attacks on respected leaders – both in the opposition as well as in his own party. All this rapidly alienated him from a large cross-section of people, especially now that the new regime seemed to be immersed in high-level corruption of a sort that compromised national security. It was against this background that the entire opposition united to oust the Rajiv-led Congress regime in 1989. Demands for the resignation of the government started to become strident after the Comptroller and Auditor General's (CAG) report tabled in parliament confirmed serious irregularities involved in the decision to acquire the Bofors guns. Seventy-three opposition members of parliament eventually resigned in protest against the government's refusal to quit. As Atal Behari Vaypayee, BJP leader, put it, soon after the resignations, "From left to right, we have all come together against a common enemy" (Gupta and Roy 1989: 24). Thus was the stage set for the entire opposition to fight the elections in tandem and for the National Front government to take power with outside support from both the Right and the Left.

This year, 1989, was also marked by brutal corporate wars. The rise of Dhirubhai Ambani and his Reliance Industries in this period is illustrative of a change that had already taken hold of India's corporate sector: cut-throat competition and large-scale corporate takeovers on the one hand, and booming stock markets amid serious political upheavals on the other. Reliance Petrochemicals' Rs575 crore public issue was a thumping success and underlined the appearance of another kind of middle-class investor. The mode of household savings among large sections of the middle class switched from holding bank accounts and purchasing savings certificates to capital markets. In a sense, in this decade "the Indian middle class announced its arrival." If, in 1980, there were just about 2 million small investors in stock markets, by 1989 there were 10 million (Vasuki and Taneja 1990: 65). This transformation should be read as a sign of many others, important as it was in itself.

Enter the 1990s

This brings us right into the period with which the rest of this book will be dealing. Each of the separate chapters will take up different aspects of this extremely important and eventful period. One broad point, however, needs to be made here, conceptually speaking, which seems to us to be crucial in understanding the difference between the 1980s and the 1990s.

The end of the Emergency, as we have already noted, saw an explosion of accumulated democratic aspirations. This was manifested in many ways. First, it gave an opportunity to different kinds of marginalized forces to regroup and to make a decisive bid for power. The formation of the JP government was, in this respect, despite being a failed experiment, an important milestone in their long-term struggle for recognition. Second, the post-Emergency dispensation provided the opportunity for various mass struggles and movements to emerge in a context where outright repression had been de-legitimized as an appropriate response. Third, it led to a deep reflection on the entire experience and the need to develop adequate constitutional safeguards to prevent such a situation from happening again. Both the judiciary as an institution, as well as individual judges and lawyers, played an important role in this respect. In fact, they formed probably the most crucial component of the civil liberties and democratic rights movement that was subsequently to emerge as the voice of conscience of Indian democracy. Fourth, this period saw a veritable explosion of the media – especially a whole range of newspapers, news magazines, and journals that gave voice to all that had been suppressed during what came to be referred to popularly as the "dark days" of the Emergency. The media emerged as important watchdogs of democracy and freedom of expression. And central to the idea of democracy that can be seen to be at work in the new, self-defined role adopted by these institutions, was a concern with "the people" – the faceless and the voiceless who had had to bear the brunt of the Emergency in large parts of the country.

In other words, the judiciary and the media emerged in the aftermath of the Emergency as the sentinels of democracy – a role that was to be rapidly reversed in a matter of a little over a decade. It is not that these institutions are now advocating authoritarianism; they are in fact engaged in the very different enterprise of *redefining* democracy. By the beginning of the 1990s, these two institutions were to emerge as the standard bearers of a whole new transformation of common sense that seeks to reduce democracy – rather, to redefine it – as a set of abstract rules *sans* politics and people. Another way of marking this shift could be by referring to a new and deep conflict that has probably always been present in India, and perhaps in all post-colonial societies. Political theorist Partha Chatterjee calls this a conflict between modernity and democracy, where modernity is about rights and sanitized public spaces evacuated of all the messiness that accompanies democratic practices and politics. Democracy, on the other hand, Chatterjee suggests, comes alive at the point where politics meets the popular. Chatterjee gives the name "civil society" to the realm of modernity and the domain of rights of which, of late, the courts and the media seem to have emerged as the champions. As opposed to this, he suggests the term "political society" to refer to the domain of democracy and the popular. Our use of these terms in the book will broadly follow Chatterjee's nomenclature and we hope it will become clear to the reader, as we go along, why this distinction is so critical to an understanding of contemporary Indian politics.

In the first four chapters, we have tried to map the contours of what we think are the three signal moments of the conjuncture of the early 1990s. In Chapter 1, we discuss the revolt of the lower castes that becomes manifest in 1990, around the implementation of the Mandal Commission Report on affirmative action for the backward castes. Chapter 2 focuses on the politics surrounding the second moment, Hindutva (the politics of Hindu nationalism) in India, and the intra- and inter-community dynamics produced by it. Chapters 3 and 4 focus on different aspects of the processes grouped under the rubric of "globalization." Chapter 3 focuses on the accelerated process of "accumulation by dispossession" and the larger question of the development model to which it is linked. We argue, however, that this is not the only story unfolding with "globalization" and that there are other new arenas opening up in interesting ways. We have called these the "new economies of desire," and we explore them in

Chapter 4. In Chapter 5, we present some instances of the processes of production of the Indian nation-state as one illustration of what we think is the historical impossibility of the project of attaining nationhood once and for all. Chapter 6 looks at the strivings for transformation and the state of the Left – both the mainstream institutional Left as well as what we call the "New Left." In Chapter 7, we take a quick look at the Indian elites' changing perceptions of India's role in the world – this is one aspect of power where the contestations are purely between different sections of the elite, "people" figuring only in more quotidian ways as they routinely cross borders legally and illegally. Finally, in the Conclusion, we remark on the extreme heterogeneity of the present moment in India, where the left-of-center UPA coalition represents the contested space claimed both by the "globalizing" elites and alternative, left-wing voices and visions.

1 | The recalcitrance of caste

The "backward castes" in power

The period since the mid- to late 1980s has seen a dramatic collapse of old political formations and parties, which had dominated politics in the Nehruvian era.[1] Even the movements of that period, right up to the mid-1970s, were largely movements around economic issues and questions of corruption, black-marketeering, hoarding, and food shortages. Through the decade of the 1980s, there was a gradual erosion of the Nehruvian secular-nationalist imagination, and one of the factors responsible for it was the "re-emergence" of caste in public discourse.

The watershed, in this respect, was the implementation of the famous Mandal Commission Report and the agitation against it. "Mandal" has since become something of a metaphor in contemporary Indian politics. The commission, which was instituted in 1978, during the Janata Party government, under the stewardship of B. P. Mandal, a socialist leader from a "backward caste," was given the task of looking into the question of "backwardness" of certain castes and suggesting remedies for its redressal. For about a decade after the commission submitted its recommendations in 1980, the report lay in cold storage after the Congress, under the leadership of Indira Gandhi (and subsequently of her son Rajiv), returned to power. It was implemented under extremely contentious circumstances in 1990 by V. P. Singh as prime minister. Its main recommendations included 27 percent reservations in educational institutions and public employment for these "Other Backward Classes" or OBCs.

The alternative political formations that took power, first in the form of the Janata Party in 1978 and in 1989 as the National Front, were primarily formations of the lower-caste peasantry. This was a revolt that had been brewing over the past decades. The implementation of the Mandal Commission Report was thus not a simple governmental intervention; it was an intervention of this new formation in power seeking to make a claim to representation in the bureaucracy and other public institutions. As soon as the government announced its decision to implement the commission's recommendations, all hell broke loose. There were widespread violent agitations all over north India, with the sons and daughters of "respectable families" taking to the streets. It was an unprecedented sight to see these young people, generally cynical about all political activity, taking to road blockades, demonstrations, picketing, and other such activities. Many of them even committed public self-immolation. Equally interesting was the sight of the usually cynical media backing the agitators to the hilt. New terms such as "mandalization of politics" entered public political discourse, generally referring, strangely, to a reprehensible division of Indian society along caste lines – as though caste oppression was a matter belonging to some very distant past. The tone and tenor of the public debate in the media seemed to suggest that but for the political opportunism of V. P. Singh, who wanted to cash in on retrograde sentiments of caste for purely pragmatic electoral purposes, India was well on the way to secular modernity. The debate was illuminating for a whole generation of people who had been brought up in the modern secular values of the Nehruvian era, who also had thought of caste as an injustice of the past.

What became clear in the wake of the Mandal Commission Report, however, was that this large group of OBCs, who constituted close to 60 percent of the population, had a negligible presence in government employment: about 4 percent. Also worth bearing in mind is the fact that even this small representation in employment was restricted to the lower rungs of government jobs. In other words, the overwhelming majority of public services were monopolized by the small crust of upper castes. In one estimate made by sociologist Satish Deshpande, about 20 percent of the population controlled about 95 percent of all jobs. Deshpande has also recently calculated the poverty–caste relationship on the basis of the National Sample Survey Organization consumption data, which confirm the strong relationship between low-caste status and poverty (Deshpande 2002).

What is relevant here, however, is not merely the incidence of poverty among different "backward" caste groups but, more importantly, the fact that even among the relatively better-off and educated sections of Dalits (the Untouchable castes) and OBCs, access to public employment, especially at the higher levels, is severely restricted. In other words, as Ram Naresh Kushwaha, an OBC parliamentarian, had put it in a parliamentary debate in 1978, the upper castes have always had informal reservations operating for them in employment; jobs *were* reserved for them. *Manusmriti* itself, he had claimed, was nothing other than a reservation of certain jobs for a certain category of people.[2]

What was interesting about the agitation, and the highly charged public debate that followed, was that it was entirely conducted, on the part of the opponents of the Mandal Commission, in the most immaculately secular and modern language of "merit" and "efficiency." The question was posed as one of dilution, if not the elimination, of merit at the cost of getting in "unworthy" and "undeserving" people simply because they happened to belong to certain castes. "Would you like to be operated upon by a doctor who had become one through reservations?" "Would you like to fly in an aircraft that was piloted by a reservation pilot?" These were the kinds of questions posed by anti-Mandalites in these discussions. Not once was the question of upper-caste and brahminical privilege ever articulated as a question of caste privilege. Even more interesting was the fact that the more sophisticated among the anti-Mandalites were prepared to accept that there was a question of privilege involved here but that it should be addressed in terms of the secular category of "class": that "economic" rather than caste criteria should be the basis of reservations. The question was really one of poverty, they argued, rather than of caste.

Now, this is an argument that actually erupted in public discourse in the 1990s but has a fairly long and hallowed history. Evidence shows that it was an argument that had been rehearsed over the decades by the modernist upper-caste leadership. Right from the days of the Kaka Kalelkar Commission, set up in the mid-1950s for the purpose of addressing the same questions later taken up by the Mandal Commission, to parliamentary debates and more localized public discussions (at, say, the provincial levels), this was invariably the argument deployed by the opponents of positive discrimination. As Christophe Jaffrelot shows, many members of the Kaka Kalelkar Commission dissented from the commission's recommendations and, what is more, the Gandhian Kaka Kalelkar himself started developing serious doubts even as he submitted his report. Nehru, the immaculate modernist, legitimized this position thus: "If we go in for reservations on communal and caste basis, we swamp the bright and able people and remain second-rate or third-rate" (Jaffrelot 2003: 222–8). On this one question then, the Nehruvian elite and the Hindu Right were always in complete agreement. This agreement, one might venture to say, was fundamental to the post-1947 Nehruvian consensus.

Was Nehru a casteist, then? Were all those who opposed the Mandal Commission in the 1990s, who included respected scholars, also casteist? This is a question being asked today by the Dalitbahujans.[3] The reality is that, by and large, such people were not casteists – at least in the conventional sense of the term. They were opposing the "bringing in" of caste into public discourse on very modernist and secular grounds. They sincerely believed that talking in terms of caste would be a regression into the past that they were so desperately seeking to annihilate. The point that needs to be stressed here is that this time round, caste was the banner of those who had been oppressed by it. The recalcitrance of caste is not a mere repetition of the older story. For in that story, it was the upper castes that held the banner of caste aloft in order to put people "in their place." Now things had decisively changed; it was the upper castes who were in constant and vehement denial of caste. Somewhere in this denial lies hidden the story of Indian modernity, a discussion of which is not, of course, within the scope of this book. For the present, we will simply sketch the broad outlines of that story and underline some of the complexities of present-day caste politics.

Let us return to where we began this chapter. Is there really a "resurgence" of caste? Is it the case that the question of caste has "suddenly" become important? Is the general middle-class perception that caste was dead, until resurrected by V. P. Singh, a correct perception? The answer is both yes and no. Yes, because there was a sense in which caste had been banished from public discourse and, to that extent, its reappearance *is* a new phenomenon. No, because this unspeakability of caste in public discourse was limited to civil society, that is to the domain of the secular modern institutions of society. It had not disappeared from society at large. In another realm, away from the watchful gaze of the modern elite, in the domain of what Partha Chatterjee calls political society, caste was a central category that framed the common ways of seeing and being in the world. The secret story of our modernity is, of course, lodged in the first realm, that of civil society, for it is here that we see the mutated upper-caste modern Indian Self, in perpetual denial of caste (and, to some extent, religion). There is no denying that this modern Self is really and genuinely modern; it wants to excise that shameful thing called caste from society's collective memory. The upper-caste-turned-modern-Self does not ever want to be reminded of this one aspect of its inheritance. It can deal with religion, for that is something that "we all have" – whether we are from the West or from the East. But caste is a blot that has affected the psyche of the mutated modern, the Unconscious, as it were, of the modern moral Self. Yet caste is the hidden principle that gives it access to all kinds of modern privileges precisely because it functions as cultural/symbolic capital.

The Dalit upsurge

To the oppressed castes, especially the lowest among them – the Dalits or the Untouchables, this repression of caste appears to be a conspiracy of the Brahminical castes to deprive them of their voice. It appears to them to displace what is their bitter lived experience to another domain – that of class, for instance. The story that the Dalits want to narrate can be told only with reference to the history of caste oppression. It is there that the secret of their exclusion and cultural mutilation lies. One of the critical elements of the recalcitrance of caste in contemporary Indian politics is, therefore, the search for a past, a cultural legacy, a history and a sense of Self. The oppressive structure of caste functioned, in relation to the Dalits in particular, through their almost complete exclusion from "society" such as it was. Despite a plethora of laws, the situation on the ground has not changed significantly and even at the level of secular modern institutions discrimination continues. This has also led, in the recent past, to a major conflict as many Dalit groups sought to take the struggle to the United Nations. The conflict surfaced around the United Nations Conference on Racism and Related Forms of Discrimination held in Durban, South Africa, in 2001. A large number of Dalit organizations and NGOs took this opportunity to launch a vigorous campaign to raise the question of caste discrimination in that forum. This provoked outraged reaction from the government and other nationalist circles, leading in turn to a vigorous public debate. The argument put forth by the nationalists was primarily that this was an "internal matter" of the nation and could be redressed within the forums provided by the law of the land (Thorat and Umakant 2004: xxiii). This did not cut much ice with the Dalit leadership, which had witnessed the operation of the law and governmental machinery at (bitter) first hand during the five decades since Independence. Others – among them academics and journalists of some standing – also joined the debate with the argument that "caste" after all is not "race" and unlike race, is not a biological matter (Beteille 2004.).

Contemporary theoretical developments have assuredly shown how thin this dividing line is, and how race, too, is a matter of social construction rather than a simple biological phenomenon. Moreover, the fact is that both caste and race share a common feature, along with the Burakumin of Japan: that of being discriminations based on descent (and to that extent, caste is a "related form" of racism). Eventually the Dalit leadership did succeed, in the teeth of major opposition, in raising the issue at Durban, though they remained dissatisfied with the outcome (Thorat and Umakant 2004: xxii–iii).

Here, we need not detail the stories of daily humiliation and degradation that continue to be part of Dalit life, as these are by now fairly well documented and discussed (Valmiki 2003; Moon 2002). Suffice it to note that even today, Dalit settlements in villages – and often even in cities such as Delhi – are spatially segregated. Untouchability and hate-speech with regard to them are rampant. Even today, they are not allowed to draw water from the same well from which upper castes get their drinking water. The brutality of this exclusion/oppression is quite unparalleled. And here, the irony is that in large parts of the country, it is the resurgent backward castes who are the most brutal oppressors of the Dalits. This gives a peculiar twist to the phenomenon of the revolt of the lower castes, to which we shall return below.

For the present, let us simply refer, briefly, to one aspect of their exclusion: from any kind of access to learning – of whatever kind, including elementary skills of reading and writing. This was an age-old practice of the caste system. It was, therefore, only with the arrival of colonialism and the opening up of public spaces and institutions to the Dalits, if in a limited fashion (because of upper-caste opposition), that these became accessible to them (Geetha and Rajadurai 1998; Nigam 2006b). It is, therefore, only in the early twentieth century, strictly speaking, that the Dalits really found their voice – in the sense of being able to record their experience of oppression and talk about it publicly. And it was at this precise moment that the mutated upper-caste modern began to legislate a certain modern universalist language, decrying all attempts to talk of caste oppression as "casteism," a sign of "backward consciousness."

There is therefore a peculiar ambivalence that marks Dalit politics and discourse today. On the one hand, it invests tremendous faith in modernity because it is really with modern institutions inaugurated by colonial rule that possibilities of Dalit emancipation opened up in significant ways; on the other, it exhibits a strong aversion to the dominant, secular-nationalist discourse of modernity in India, which it sees as irrevocably "upper-caste" and as the root of the reinstitution of upper-caste power over modern institutions.

Dalits, OBCs and secularism/communalism

This ambivalence is visible not only in the field of cultural politics but equally in the field of electoral politics. While the dynamic in electoral politics is somewhat different, the explanation for Dalit political formations such as the Bahujan Samaj Party (BSP) charting out a course that radically questions the common sense of the secular modern must be understood in the context of its deep distrust of the old nationalist and secular elite. A case in point is the relationship of the BSP and much of the Dalit intelligentsia with the emerging secular political formations, especially in north India. In the state of Uttar Pradesh (UP), the BSP has repeatedly gone into alliance with the main party of the Hindu Right, the Bharatiya Janata Party. It has formed governments with the BJP, not only in 1993 and 1997, but also in 2002, in the year of the massacre of Muslims in Gujarat. In this period, when the BJP and its partner organizations of the Hindu Right had left no doubt about their intentions, the BSP entered into an alliance and formed a government with the BJP in UP, and its top leaders even campaigned for the BJP in Gujarat during the subsequent elections.

There are two levels of problems involved here. First, the relations between different "lower"-caste groups – non-Brahmin or OBC on the one hand and outcaste (or "Untouchable") on the other. Second, the logic of electoral politics. On the face of it, it only seems logical that in order to break upper-caste hegemony there should be a larger alliance of the OBCs/non-Brahmins and Dalits. This had seemed a promising line of action to many leaders of the late nineteenth to the early twentieth century, such as Jyotiba Phule of Maharashtra and Periyar E. V. R. Ramasamy Naicker of what is today Tamil Nadu. Hence they had advocated the idea of a "non-Brahmin" unity (Periyar) or a unity of the Shudraatishudras (Phule)[4] in order to challenge the hegemony of the Brahminical elite. And up to a point this did have an impact in the first half of the twentieth century, insofar as the Brahminical stranglehold over society in these two regions was seriously challenged. Kanshi Ram, too, the chief architect of the present Dalit upsurge in north India, believed that his party should not simply be a Dalit party but a party of "bahujans" (literally, majority). Hence the name, Bahujan Samaj Party. The Bahujan Samaj, in Kanshi Ram's rendering, was to be forged through a broad alliance of the Dalits, the backwards and the minorities – particularly the Muslims. Kanshi Ram also saw clearly that the Dalits alone, comprising no more than about 20 percent of the electorate in any constituency, could not possibly challenge upper-caste dominance. Hence the aggressive slogan of the period of the rise of the BSP: *Tilak, tarazu aur talwar/ inko maro joote chaar* (the Brahmin, the Bania and the Rajput/thrash them roundly with shoes). That was the astute strategy that managed to make the BSP an important force in its early days.

The problem, however, began after the experience of first electoral alliance of the BSP (representing Dalits) and the Samajwadi Party (representing the OBCs) led by Mulayam Singh Yadav, which formed the government in UP in 1993. Within a short time it became apparent that as soon as the political pact that was forged between the parties moved toward the countryside, sharp conflicts between the two groups began playing themselves out. It was during the village panchayat elections that the conflicts took a serious and often violent form. Many Dalit leaders and intellectuals began to recognize the implications of the fact that in many states the immediate oppressors of Dalits in the villages were not Brahmins, but the dominant backward castes who had consolidated their hold following the post-independence land reforms. And it seemed that they were not willing to change their attitude toward Dalits in everyday matters, even in the face of the political alliance at the state level. In many areas it was these castes that forcibly prevented Dalits from casting their votes.

More importantly, this was the period of the sharp rise of the Hindu Right. Very soon, this threat was to become the most important reference point for all future electoral-political alliances. The parties of the OBCs, represented by Mulayam Singh and Laloo Yadav in the two most important northern states of UP and Bihar, positioned themselves firmly against the BJP and its allies. During the period of the build-up to the demolition of the Babri Masjid, discussed in the next chapter, it was these two leaders who had displayed the most determined opposition to the BJP. During his chief ministership, Mulayam Singh used the entire force of the state machinery to prevent the activists of the Hindu Right from demolishing the structure of the mosque in November 1990. When L. K. Advani's notorious Rath Yatra entered Bihar, en route to Ayodhya, Laloo Yadav displayed exemplary courage in arresting Advani, leading to the eventual downfall of the V. P. Singh government of which Laloo was a part. It was in this context that the anti-communal, secular front came into existence, and the OBC parties naturally acquired a crucial position within it, given their stance.

This is where the problems began, as far as the BSP and the newly assertive Dalits were concerned. To throw in their lot with the secular front unconditionally was to tie their own hands. For the conflict with the OBCs in the countryside was now playing itself out in its most aggressive form. The choice was a difficult one and it was aggravated by another circumstance: the BJP with its upper-caste (Brahmin–Bania–Rajput) support base, with the self-confidence of classes who have traditionally wielded power, showed a preparedness to play second fiddle to the BSP in a joint government. This was something that the OBC parties and Mulayam Singh Yadav just could not do – they were as much novices in the game of political power as were the Dalit groups; they were also unprepared to give up any of their social power in order to facilitate a broader alliance. It is quite possible that if Mulayam had made the magnanimous gesture that the BJP repeatedly made, the BSP might still have opted to remain in the secular alliance. But for Mulayam Singh to do this would have meant alienating his primary support base, the backward-caste peasantry. Advocates of secularist unity did not want to upset the apple cart and therefore fell in line with the position of the backward-caste parties – that is to say, they demanded unconditional support in the struggle against the Hindu Right, even at the cost of repudiating the newly emerging political power of the Dalit movement.

This is where the deep distrust of the secular-nationalist common sense, so ingrained in Dalit politics, comes into play. For the BSP did not have a moment's hesitation in joining forces with the BJP in forming a government and there was a whole array of Dalit intellectuals who developed a fairly powerful argument to justify it. The point here is not simply that the BSP went into a power-sharing alliance with the Hindu Right, for many other parties and groups have done the same in different ways, at different times. Even the Left is not entirely free of that taint, as we saw in the Introduction. In that sense, such pressures have always worked in the sphere of political alliance-making in electoral politics in India. The point here is that the BSP entered into this alliance with a clear argument against the dichotomized mode of politics where the "communalism versus secularism" conflict was presented by advocates of the secular front as something self-evident, as though it subsumed all other conflicts and exhausted all other problems. This manner of privileging the "secular versus communal" conflict presented the secular front as a non-negotiable: you had to enter the front only on the terms already set by the dominant partners in it. There was no possibility of any negotiation here, especially with regard to the backward-caste parties.

On the other hand, the BSP, despite its history of attempting to build an anti-upper-caste–Hindu alliance, and despite the fact that it sees its project as irreconcilable with the Hindutva project, refused to take any proposition as given and non-negotiable. The sole concern that guided it was whether its move would help its own project of Dalit liberation. As mentioned earlier, on this occasion, the BJP displayed considerable sagacity by agreeing to play a subordinate role in the alliance.

Even after the collapse of the BSP–BJP alliance for the third time in August 2003, reports from UP indicate that as far as the Dalit masses of UP are concerned, the experiments are seen by them as having been fruitful in restoring a sense of dignity among them. On the other hand, the upper-caste supporters of the BJP, the Rajputs in particular, feel threatened by the growing insubordination of the lower castes during these successive tenures of the alliance. The experiment, whatever its long-term implications for the secular front, has revealed the immense complexity that marks the new era of "caste politics" in India.

This is not a scenario simply restricted to Uttar Pradesh or northern India. Recent years have seen heightened conflicts between the Dalits and the OBCs, one of the most recent being the incident in Khairlanji village in Maharashtra, where four members of a Dalit family were killed and the women were most probably raped before being killed. This is a village with a population of about 800, 750 of whom are OBCs – a mere twenty being Dalits. Some of the OBC villagers had been raising a dispute concerning the small piece of cultivable land owned by the Bhotmange family (the family killed) alleging that they were denying others right of way. In 2004 the dispute went to the Revenue Court, which ordered that a road be built through the family's land. It was this that eventually led to the gruesome murders and the rape of the daughter, whose body was found badly bruised and naked. This incident sparked off a series of major and often violent protests. Such incidents of oppression and violence by the OBCs against Dalits have now become commonplace.[5]

At this point it is necessary to note that the particular logic of conflict between Dalit and OBC interests, discussed above, does not work in the same way everywhere in the country, even though everyday conflicts are pretty much in evidence in most places. In the context of Tamil Nadu, for instance, the OBC identity is the Dravidian one. The term "Dravidian" refers to the politicized racial identity counterposed to the "Aryan" one in southern India, particularly in what is now the state of Tamil Nadu. In this narrative, *c.* 1500 BCE, fair-skinned Aryan invaders from the north of the subcontinent destroyed a pre-existing Dravidian civilization, imposing a Brahminical caste order on the defeated, in which the Aryans became Brahmins, and Dravidians the "lower"-caste non-Brahmins.[6] The Dalit identity is comparatively new in Tamil Nadu (compared to western or northern India), because the anti-Brahmin movement was successful in positing the Dravidian (OBC) identity as the universal non/anti-Brahmin one, subsuming Dalits within it. Over the 1990s, though, a strong Dalit critique of the Dravidian movement has emerged, with sharply polemical exchanges between Dalits and non-Brahmins (Dravidians) becoming "endemic" in Tamil politics (Pandian 2007: 233–44). Today Dalits are a visible political constituency, and there is growing Dalit assertion against assimilation into Dravidian politics (Lakshmanan 2004).

The electoral logic, too, in Tamil Nadu is somewhat different, because with the state's long history of anti-Brahmin politics, rivalry between its two powerful anti-Brahmin (Dravidian) parties – the Dravida Munnetra Kazhagam (DMK) and the All India Anna Dravida Munnetra Kazhagam (AIADMK) – is the decisive factor in deciding political alliances. Despite their core ideological similarities, alliances of the two parties with the party in power at the center, whether Congress or BJP, are determined by the dynamics of their rivalry in local politics in the state, rather than in terms of OBC–Dalit or secular–communal conflict. For instance in 1999, the AIADMK withdrew support to the Vajpayee-led BJP, leading to the collapse of the government, while the DMK, by no means a communal party, supported the BJP in the vote of confidence which it lost (Subramanian 1999).

Backward castes and the Women's Reservation Bill

In 1996, the 81st Constitutional Amendment Bill, called the Women's Reservation Bill (WRB), was first announced, proposing a reservation of 33 percent of seats in parliament for women. A decade later, at the end of 2006, the fate of this bill remained uncertain, the opposition to it seeming insurmountable. This, despite wide-ranging support for it across the political spectrum, from the BJP on the Right, to the veering-right-of-center Congress, to all the shades of parties on the Left and all women's organizations in the country. The opposition to the measure, termed as patriarchal and anti-women, emanates largely from the parties representing backward castes and Dalits. What is becoming increasingly clear is that the questions thrown up by the timing of the bill and the responses to it reveal "caste" to be the key to understanding what is at stake. It is misleading to frame the story of the WRB solely within the framework of women's rights.

The question of reservations for women in representative institutions has long been debated in India. It had come up in the Constituent Assembly (1946-49), but had been rejected by women representatives as it was felt that the working of democracy in the normal course would ensure the representation of all sections of Indian society. The suggestion was also seen to underestimate the strength of women to compete as equals. Over twenty-five years later, in 1974, the Committee on the Status of Women in India (CSWI) considered the same question and came to more or less the same conclusion.

The latest phase of the debate began with the National Perspective Plan (NPP) 1988-2000, recommending a 30 percent reservation of seats for women in panchayats and zila parishads (village and district councils). Subsequently states such as Karnataka and Gujarat implemented some form of reservation for women in these institutions, known as Panchayati Raj Institutions (PRI). In 1993, the 73rd and 74th Constitution Amendments provided for one-third reservation for women nationwide in these bodies. By the general elections of 1996, women's organizations put forward a joint demand to all political parties for reservations for women in state assemblies and parliament (Mazumdar, V. 1997: 16). The major parties supported the demand although they themselves gave less than 15 percent of their total number of tickets to women, and the 81st Amendment Bill was introduced in 1996. It could not be passed and was referred to a joint select committee. In 1998 the bill (by now the 84th Amendment Bill) was introduced again by the BJP government to strong opposition, and was once again derailed; and so it went on until its latest incarnation in December 2006, when it could not be introduced in parliament for lack of a consensus.

What were the developments between 1974 when women's movement activists in the CSWI rejected reservations for women in parliament, and 1996, when almost the same representatives of the women's movement as well as every non-OBC/Dalit party had come to demand such reservations? In the years that passed, there were two significant developments in Indian politics. By the mid-1980s, as we have seen, backward-caste assertion had begun to transform the nature of the political arena and the composition of the Lok Sabha. Yogendra Yadav points out: "The influx of lower orders into the field of democratic contestation has ... [made] it respectable to talk of caste in the public-political domain. The emergence of social justice as a rubric to talk about caste equity [and] *political representation of castes and communities* ... is a distinct achievement of this period" (Yadav 1999: 2393). Not unexpectedly, upper-caste anxiety at this phenomenon was correspondingly on the rise.

The other development was that women had emerged as a significant force in politics. Women had been at the forefront of the movements against corruption and price rises that preceded the imposition of Emergency. The "second wave" of the women's movement in the 1980s saw the emergence of vocal and visible autonomous women's groups, which placed feminist issues firmly on the public agenda – dowry, rape, violence against women. The term "autonomous" refers to their autonomy from political parties, most of them having emerged out of left-wing parties, frustrated by their inability to engage with questions raised by feminist critique (Gandhi and Shah 1992). Even as the political terrain was transformed by the presence of these groups, it was also becoming evident that women were under-represented on representative bodies. Already in 1988, by the time of the NPP 1988–2000, therefore, there was both an acknowledgment of women's militant participation in politics as well as of their absence in decision-making bodies. Vina Mazumdar, who was Member Secretary of the CSWI, points out how as "daughters of independence" her generation had been critical of special representation, but gradually "we have found our understanding of nation-building changing radically" (Mazumdar, V. 1997: 15). By 1996, then, the "daughters of independence" had come to acknowledge that abstract citizenship was only a cover for privilege, and that difference had to be acknowledged.

Thus two very different (even opposed) sets of concerns – feminist and upper-caste – tie in at this particular conjuncture to produce the sudden general acceptability of women's reservations. While the protagonists make their arguments in terms of gender justice, it may be noticed that the arguments against the bill come from two opposed positions – a less influential voice that stems from opposition to reservations in general, and the powerful voice of the OBC and Dalit parties, who charge that a blanket reservation of seats for "women" is in effect an upper-caste ploy to stem the rising tide of lower castes in politics. In this context, we must take into account the experience of women's reservations in Panchayati Raj Institutions since 1993. Studies in Gujarat and Karnataka have confirmed that the entrenched power of the dominant castes has been strengthened by women's reservations (Nair 1997). It is not surprising, then, that OBC and Dalit leaders are highly suspicious of the WRB. In an interview, Mayawati, the Bahujan Samaj Party leader, while demanding a 50 percent reservation for women in parliament, insisted that, within this, there should be separate reservations for Dalits, backward castes and minorities.[7] Mulayam Singh Yadav of the Samajwadi Party has consistently opposed the bill, saying that in its present form it is anti-minority and anti-Dalit.[8]

The alternative proposed is called the "quotas-within-quotas" position, demanding a reservation for OBC and Muslim women within the 33 percent. The arguments against the WRB, in other words, are not simply patriarchal.

Most interestingly, prominent BJP leader Uma Bharati, herself from a backward caste, argued for quotas-within-quotas, a position opposed to that of her party. Unlike Sushma Swaraj, the upper-caste

BJP woman leader most vocal in support of the bill, Uma Bharati's feminist argument for reservations asserts also that a backward-caste or Dalit woman is doubly oppressed, and so should have a place within the quota. Characteristically, Uma Bharati does not grant a quota for Muslim women, even while conceding that they are among the most oppressed, but she does not reject the idea of reservations for Muslims altogether. Her solution is, instead, to give reservations to Muslim caste groups included in the Mandal OBCs, for example, *julahe, bunkar, ansari.* Thus, in a move that challenges the BJP's nationalist Hindutva perspective, she decisively privileges caste identity.[9] It is this difference of opinion within the party that kept the BJP from pushing through the measure even during the years it was in power.

The real question is: why are "women" acceptable to the ruling elites as a counter-measure to deal with rising backward-caste presence in parliament? Why are women and the women's movement not only *not* perceived as a threat to social order, but even as a force that can restore the control of upper castes and classes? One possible explanation could have to do with the cooptation and domestication of gender issues by the state and NGOs through the 1990s. The emergence of "autonomous" women's groups (autonomous, that is, from political parties) during the 1980s marked a new, and militant, highly visible phase of the women's movement, but by the end of the 1990s, almost all of these groups were running on funding from government and international bodies. That is, these groups, which began as an attempt to create spaces outside the orthodoxies of party women's wings, are now far from autonomous, given their need to get and retain funding.

Further, while the "empowerment of women" is a slogan much in use by government agencies, it has been argued that this kind of government program aims at empowering women only to the extent of harnessing women's contribution to "growth," to attain which there is considerable external pressure on the government. Writing on the increasing circulation of the term "empowerment" in the context of World Bank-directed new economic policies in India in the 1990s, Manoranjan Mohanty argues that empowerment, particularly of women, is understood in international documents not as a goal but a prerequisite for productive investment. Terms such as empowerment, civil society, and democratization, which form part of the new liberalization discourse, therefore, are not a response to the struggles that have marked Indian politics, but have been given a restricted meaning and oriented in order to "serve the present global drive of western capitalism." Since market development is a key feature defining the stage of development of "civil society" in this understanding, those who are weak or unorganized, or who reject the prevailing system, are excluded from "civil society." Thus, he concludes, "the agenda of globalisation promotes democracy for those who can participate in the bargaining process" (Mohanty 1995: 1434-6). The growing statism and NGO-ization of the women's movement are a cause for concern in this sense.

This is a feature of which the movement is very aware. A report (1991) by six women's organizations from Delhi and Bombay, investigating the dismissal of some employees of the Rajasthan government's Women's Development Programme (WDP), came to the conclusion that the WDP, designed with the active cooperation of feminist activists, had been successful in reducing people's distrust of the state by appropriating the legitimacy garnered by the women's movement. The report urged a serious consideration of the implications of this.[10] So a harsh conclusion that we seem to be forced to confront is that as far as the ruling elites are concerned, "women" are something they can deal with.

A more complicated reason for "women" being acceptable while "OBCs" are not, has to do with the way in which identities emerge in politics. Indian politics has shown often enough that class, religious, caste (or any other) identity has tended to prevail over gender identification. In Hindu right-wing mobilization or issues such as the Uniform Civil Code (UCC),[11] or the anti-Mandal upper-caste agitations, "women" have tended to rally as upper/lower-caste or Muslim/Hindu (Dietrich 1994). The women's movement has been as much attacked by Dalit women for being upper-caste as the Dalit movement has been attacked for being patriarchal, and feminists of minority communities have challenged the women's movement for being Hindu by default, in its claim to being secular (Agnes 1994a: 1123; Omvedt 1990: 31). Thus, by the late 1980s, the women's movement had to accept that "women" as the subject of feminist politics, and gender justice as an issue, would have to be inflected through the lens of other identities.

What this means in the context of the WRB is that when confronted with upper-caste concerns that seem to tie in with feminist concerns at this conjuncture, the women's movement must make the moves necessary to undercut the upper-caste project – and quotas-within-quotas seems to offer that possibility.

Within the broad feminist camp, the suggestion of "quotas-within-quotas" has received mixed responses. Most women's groups accept it in principle, but while some groups are prepared for a redrafting of the present bill to include such quotas, others, such as the Left groups, continue to insist that the bill must be passed first, and further quotas can be worked out later.[12]

"Mandal II" and the electoral calculus

We have seen that the first round of implementation of OBC reservations had emerged from the long-drawn-out struggle of the backward castes spanning close to four decades. The implementation of the Mandal Commission recommendations in 1990 was, however, eventually restricted to the arena of employment. Education was left out. In early April 2006, the UPA government announced that it would implement the Mandal Commission recommendations in all central educational institutions (Mandal II, as it has come to be known), including the elite IITs and IIMs (Indian Institutes of Technology and Indian Institutes of Management, respectively). In itself this would be a long overdue and welcome step, were it not for the fact that it was done without the necessary groundwork, with an eye on elections that were due in some states.

As S. S. Gill, who was the secretary of the Mandal Commission, recently emphasized, "27 percent reservations were only a palliative" and only one of the many recommendations made by it. According to him, "the other important recommendations were: the radical alteration in production relations through progressive land reforms; special educational facilities to upgrade the cultural environment of the students, with special emphasis on vocational training; separate coaching facilities for students aspiring to enter technical and professional institutions; creation of adequate facilities for improving the skills of village artisans; subsidised loans for setting up small-scale industries; the setting up of a separate chain of financial and technical bodies to assist OBC entrepreneurs" (Gill 2006).

In the sixteen years since the first implementation of the Mandal recommendations, no government took up any of these measures. The UPA government, too, restricted its intervention to extending reservations to educational institutions, and even in this measure, took the easy way out. Anticipating hostile reactions from various quarters, it announced an increased intake of students by about 50 percent in order to accommodate the quotas without reducing the "general" seats. What should, ideally, have preceded this decision was then done after the fact: a committee to prepare the roadmap for the implementation of these recommendations was set up. This committee suggested a 54 percent expansion to accommodate the quotas and suggested that this plane be executed in a phased manner, over a three-year period.

It needs to be remembered here that over the years, the banner of "reservations" has become a potent symbolic weapon of electoral mobilization used by most mainstream parties. Once the Mandal Commission Report was implemented and there was a veritable clamor for inclusion in reservations by all kinds of groups claiming historical disadvantage, this became a kind of self-fulfilling game. The more substantive issues that needed to be dealt with, if the Mandal recommendations were to be implemented, gave way to this logic of the electoral calculations. The recent move is one such instance where an opportunist gamble was played. The extreme and near hysterical reactions from the privileged upper-caste sections to such demands has prevented any reasonable debate and a dispassionate engagement with the demands of social justice in the public arena. A reassessment of the entire logic of reservations has been made impossible by the prevailing atmosphere. It is possible to argue, after all, that in all circumstances reservations may not be the best form of affirmative action. Indeed, it may be problematic to institute a mechanism that ends up freezing identities through the logic of governmentality.

Expectedly, as battle lines were drawn, upper-caste youth rose in defence of their privileges in the name of merit. The aggression of the upper-caste youth was played out at an everyday level against fellow students from Dalit and OBC backgrounds. There were vicious incidents of targeting and humiliation of Dalit students in premier institutions such as the medical students' hostel at the All India Institute of Medical Sciences in Delhi, often directly aided and abetted by the authorities, who became openly partisan in such games.

Even one year after the announcement of the government's decision, protests continue in different and less spectacular forms, such as localized strikes, sit-ins, and signature campaigns. A case is also pending with the Supreme Court where the legality of the decision has been challenged on the grounds that the economically well-off "creamy layer" among the OBCs – and indeed among the Dalits and tribals, with retrospective effect – be excluded from availing of the benefits of the reservations. Indeed, this argument has now acquired the status of common sense and further questions regarding it are seldom asked. It should be abundantly clear to anybody even remotely familiar with trends in primary education that it is only the so-called "creamy layer" that manages to cross school level. Any idea of reservations would be meaningless if the only sections of a group that can avail of reservations were to be excluded from them.

In the past few years, however, there have been many more people, at least among the intelligentsia, who seem to have applied their minds to thinking through the logic of reservations, as a result of which the public debate this time yielded some interesting new policy alternatives. These proposals built on other ways of thinking about affirmative action, some of which have been in operation in universities such as Jawaharlal Nehru University in Delhi for some decades now. These models do not simply reduce the question of affirmative action to a single dimension, that is, caste. Since the question of OBC reservations is quite different from that of reservations for Dalits and tribals (for which India's Constitution-makers had compelling reasons), such alternative models could have been considered by the government. These models can in principle give weightages for different kinds of historical disadvantage apart from caste (gender, regional backwardness, religious minority identity, and so on), rather than simply reserving seats for specific fixed groups. One such model was put forward by two Delhi-based social scientists, Satish Deshpande and Yogendra Yadav, which advocates such a policy design, based largely on information already available in admission forms in their present form (Deshpande and Yadav 2006).

Mandal II is also problematic in that it plans to go ahead without going into any of the other recommendations of the Mandal Commission mentioned earlier. Not enough thought was given to expanding or improving existing infrastructure or "special educational facilities to upgrade the cultural environment." Educational institutions in most parts of the country have been running at suboptimal levels for decades – except for the elite and highly government-subsidized IITs and IIMs. Most other institutions neither have adequate faculty and facilities, nor the capacity for the kind of expansion that this move requires. A more well-thought-out policy initiative should have considered a proper plan of upgradation of these institutions alongside.

In conclusion, we might note that the recent upsurge of lower-caste struggles is an extremely complex affair that has a dynamic that is specific to the lived experience of the different caste groups, especially Dalits. Among the OBCs, too, there are caste groups who share a status somewhat similar to that of the Dalits – except that they are not "Untouchables" in the ritual sense – who can be mobilized on either side of the divide. Further, OBCs themselves, when mobilized by the BJP as in Gujarat, have played a directly communal role acting as foot-soldiers of Hindutva, unlike when they have emerged as an independent political force, as in UP and Bihar. Much thus depends on the exact nature of political equations in any local situation and the nature of political mobilization.

2 | Politics of Hindutva and the minorities

The 1990s are marked by the triumphant onward march of the Hindutva movement. The first peaking of this politics was the demolition, by a mob, of the 400-year-old Babri Masjid in Ayodhya in 1992. This was a mosque built by the Mughal emperor Babur's commander-in-chief Mir Baki, supposedly after destroying a temple that stood there, on the birthplace of Ram, one of the deities worshiped by Hindus. Both these claims – that there had existed a temple that was destroyed, and that this is Ramjanmabhoomi, the birthplace of the mythical Ram – are historically debatable, and are asserted largely as a matter of faith.

The second peak of the movement is the large-scale massacre of Muslims in the state of Gujarat in 2002, while a BJP government was in power there and a BJP-dominated coalition ruled at the center. Since the beginning of the 1990s there have been numerous small and large incidents of violence against Christians and Muslims, increasingly aggressive rhetoric against minorities, and a transformation of the very terms of political discourse on secularism. In villages and small towns, in many parts of the country, endemic daily terror against the minorities has become the norm.

Key features of Hindutva ideology

Hindutva, which means Hinduness, is a form of Hindu cultural nationalism and is the political philosophy of the Hindu right wing. Its founder, Vinayak Damodar Savarkar, held that Hinduism is not merely one of the religions of India, but is the Indian way of life. It is through this equation of Hindu with Indian that the BJP lays claim to being truly secular as opposed to the "pseudo-secularism" of other political parties in India, which "pander to minorities."

As one BJP leader and MP put it, "... BJP is the party of Indian nationalism, pure and simple ... and since India is overwhelmingly Hindu, under our democratic system this nationalism cannot but have a Hindu complexion" (Malkani 1994:13).

The strength of Hindutva as a political ideology, however, is that it is not restricted to organizations or political parties, and has succeeded in shaping common sense among sections of Hindus who may not necessarily be anti-minority. In fact, it can be argued that in the early decades of the twentieth century, Hindutva merely built on and systematized the prevalent common sense in literate Hindu society regarding "nationhood" and "Islam." This partly explains the sudden shift to the BJP, from the late 1980s, of large numbers of retired army officers and bureaucrats, who might have been secular in their official positions, but whose world-view, apparently, had been consistent with Hindutva.

Assimilationism Are non-Hindus Indian? Yes, but only if they agree to being "Indianized" and recall that "their forefathers were Hindus" (Ghosh, B. 2000: 1). For Savarkar, one could claim genuine belonging to the nation only if one considered India both the fatherland (*pitribhu*) and the holy land (*punyabhu*). The reference is to the supposed alien origins, holy places in foreign lands (the Vatican and Mecca) and consequently, the assumed divided loyalties of Christians and Muslims (Basu et al. 1993). Hindutva thus has an assimilationist program, in which all non-Hindus are to be "brought back" to the Hindu fold. This is not considered as conversion but as "reconversion," the assumption being that everyone in India is naturally Hindu. The Hindu Right is thus sharply opposed to proselytization and conversion (which in Hindutva discourse refers exclusively to conversion out of Hinduism). It is because of Hindutva's claim that Hinduism is the only native religion that Hindu nationalists the world over contest the position that Aryans were invaders or migrants from Europe. For, if that were so, Hinduism too would be foreign and the equation of Indianness with Hinduness would become problematic.

It is in keeping with this assimilationist program that a certain strand of Hindutva, the one closest to its founder Savarkar, is committed to the ending of the caste system, which keeps Dalits and other "lower" castes from identifying themselves as Hindu. In this view, all other religious communities except the Muslim and Christian – Sikhs, Jains, and Buddhists – are sects of Hinduism. M. S. Golwalkar, a Hindutva philosopher and chief architect of the RSS (see below), included even Parsis, India's Zoroastrians, as members of Hindu Rashtra (Hindu Nation) because they are fire-worshiping Aryans (Kumar, P. 1994: 47). This understanding is firmly rejected by the communities Hindutva would assimilate. Thus, when the BJP government in the state of Gujarat passed an amendment (2006) to the Freedom of Religion Act (an ironically named piece of legislation that strictly limits religious conversion) classifying Jains and Buddhists as Hindus for the purposes of the act, there were strong protests from representatives of these communities, which claim minority status. While Hindutvavaadis (adherents of Hindutva politics) claim these communities as part of the Hindu mainstream, Jains and Buddhists hold that, on the contrary, many features of modern Hinduism (for example, vegetarianism) have emerged in response to the reformist challenge posed by these newer religions. Hindus in ancient times both performed animal sacrifice as well as ate meat (and many Hindu communities still do so). Thus, they argue, modern Hinduism could be said to have assimilated features of Jainism rather than the other way round (Patil 2006).

Hindutva also claims tribal people (called Adivasis, meaning "original inhabitants," in large parts of peninsular India), as Hindus. The Constitution lists several communities in the Fifth Schedule as "tribes" for the purposes of affirmative action. The term is used to designate a whole cluster of diverse "non-Indic" or "semi-Indic" communities who are mostly non-Aryan and remained outside the Hindu caste system. They are understood to be the indigenous people of India, who lived on the subcontinent long before the Aryans entered, around 1500 BCE. The more than fifty tribes that constitute the Scheduled Tribes speak a multitude of languages. They are also religiously diverse, with some following animism, while others have adopted Hinduism, Islam, or Christianity. The social customs of most tribals distinguish them from the country's majority Hindu population. The name Adivasi is itself contentious, because it is derived from Sanskrit, not from any of the tribal languages (and is therefore a Hinduized term), although by now it has come to be used in self-definition by many political movements of tribal people in peninsular India. The term Adivasi, however, is not in use in the north east, where a quarter of the population is tribal. The nomenclature and religious identity of these communities are the subject of heated debate among anthropologists and historians (Baviskar 2005).

Hindutva politics has stepped up "reconversion" drives among these communities during the 1990s. Tribal people who have not converted to Christianity or Hinduism (or more rarely to Islam) follow their own ways of life and worship. Many of these ways have been, over time, incorporated into Hinduism, but whether all tribal religious practices are by default Hindu, or can be translated into Hinduism, is the contentious issue raised by the politics of Hindutva.[1]

The unconverted tribals are considered backward and savage by other dominant groups, whether Hindu, Muslim, or Christian. They are also among the most culturally and materially marginalized groups in India. Under these circumstances, the Hindu Right's "reconversion" campaigns through *Ghar Vapsi* (Returning Home to Hinduism) activities among tribal people provide them with opportunities for upward mobility, while being simultaneously a conversion to the politics of Hindutva. They adopt dominant Hindu practices such as vegetarianism, as well as the Hindutva opposition to Muslims and Christians (ibid.). One could say they become Hindu the Hindutva way.

The large-scale participation of Adivasis in organized violence against Christians in Madhya Pradesh and Gujarat in the late 1990s and against Muslims in Gujarat in 2002 has been seen by many scholars as "indoctrination" and a distorted form of class struggle for resources (Punyani 2002). As Amita Baviskar points out, however, in a situation of widespread dispossession of tribal people, we are forced to consider the possibility that there are many routes to tribal power, "including the path of affiliating with Hindu supremacists" (Baviskar 2005: 5109). There is also no doubt that Hindutvavaadi organizations have launched creative initiatives among these communities. For instance, in Uttar Pradesh, Badri Narayan has traced the manner in which the RSS and BJP have searched out Dalit heroes of the past, constructing them as "warring identities against Muslim invaders" and relocating them within the broader project of constructing memories of a "Hindu" identity stretching back for time immemorial (Narayan 2006).

Mobilizing women Deftly weaving images available within Hinduism of Woman as both nurturing mother and the fearsome destroyer of evil, Hindutva ideology has succeeded in giving women visibility and agency in the public realm. Both in the Ayodhya Ramjanmabhoomi movement and in the Gujarat violence, both at leadership levels and in mass participation, women are present everywhere in the movement, articulate and active (Basu, A. 1996; Sarkar, T. 1998; Butalia and Sarkar 1995; Sangari 1999). According to Tanika Sarkar, "Older forms of gender ideology are merged with new offers of self-fashioning and relative political equality in the field of anti-Muslim and anti-secular violence" (Sarkar 1998: 104).

A television image from the days of the violence in Gujarat in 2002 illustrates this to chilling effect: Hindu women laugh and chat together in the winter sun on a rooftop, smiling shyly at television cameras as they make missiles and firebombs with homely materials: old saris, stones, kerosene oil from their kitchens. Much as they might get together to make pickles and *papads* at other times.

Sexuality Anxieties around sexuality are central to Hindutva mobilizing. Images of the virile, aggressive Muslim male, the fast-reproducing Muslim community with four wives to every man, the need for Hindu men to be both disciplined and celibate as well as sexually potent and capable of offering a challenge to the Muslim rival, abound in popular literature produced at various levels (Gupta, C. 2001). The Hindu woman was to be chaste and virtuous while the Hindu male fantasy was to conquer "the Other's" women, a fantasy played out during the Gujarat violence in particular, by mass public rapes of Muslim women (Agnes 2002; Sarkar, T. 2002).

The Hindutva fear of Muslim fecundity must be understood in the context of modern democracy where numbers matter – what if Muslims breed so fast that they overtake the Hindu majority? These fears are constantly played out over census figures. For instance, the 2001 census data were released in September 2004 by the Registrar General of Census in such a way that initial reports suggested that in the period 1991-2001 there had been a 36 percent rise in the Muslim population. Compared with the 20.5 percent rise for Hindus, this was startling. After this news had provoked the predictable paranoid and aggressive pronouncements from the Hindu Right, and as other voices joined the controversy, the Census Registrar suddenly announced that the initially reported figures had been "unadjusted," and that the "adjusted" figures in fact showed a deceleration in the growth rates of Muslims.

As it happens, the 1991 census had excluded the two states of Jammu and Kashmir, and Assam (both of which have substantial Muslim populations), due to the rise in armed insurgency there.[2] The inclusion of these states in 2001 would naturally show a sudden rise in the Muslim population as a whole. The Census Registrar, an appointee of the previous BJP-led government, had clearly manipulated the release of the census data – the mistake is too elementary – the term "growth rate" cannot be used between two non-comparable data sets (Chatterjee, M. 2004; Ray, S. 2004; Joshua 2004; Menon, N. 2004a).

Organizations of the Hindu Right

The politics of Hindutva is represented by a group of political organizations known collectively in their self-definition as the Sangh Parivar (Sangh Family) after their parent organization, the Rashtriya Swayamsevak Sangh (RSS). Not every organization in this formation refers to itself as "Hindu." This flexibility in self-designation is precisely the electoral strength of the BJP, which can appeal to both the "Hindu" vote as well the vote of sections of the Indian elite who are not necessarily anti-minority, but see the BJP as a modern, secular party that will not pander to minority-ism.

a) Founded in 1925, Rashtriya Swayamsevak Sangh (RSS) describes itself as a cultural organization, and is the ideological fountainhead of Hindutva politics. The RSS does not contest elections, but its indirect control, guidance, and pressure decides the policy of the electoral face of Hindutva politics, the BJP. Many top leaders of the BJP are also members of the RSS. The visible work of the RSS focuses on running educational institutions and other such activities that can be described as social work, but these institutions are also used to propagate rabidly anti-minority views among impressionable young children.

RSS claims of being a cultural organization should not blind us to its identity as an organization drawing inspiration from Hitler, with a commitment to eradicating minorities should they refuse to comply with the Hindutva insistence on assimilation. It is a militaristic, hierarchical organization, and its cadres, dressed in khaki shorts, routinely perform Hindu militancy with martial discipline in public places as a show of strength.

b) The political party that is now the public face of this movement and represents it in national-level electoral politics is the Bharatiya Janata Party. In the aftermath of the Emergency, its predecessor, the Bharatiya Jan Sangh, had merged into the Janata Party. After the fall of the Janata Party and its break-up, the BJP spent practically the whole of the 1980s out in the cold. During that period, the party adopted its present name, attempted to stand upon a different platform, and to live down its past as a communal organization.[3] It claimed "Gandhian socialism" as its new ideology and raised issues such as price rises and corruption, which it expected to attract broader sections than a Hindutva platform. This shift, however, did not help it achieve any significant growth over the next five years. The change came in the mid-1980s, when some related developments led to the realization that there was greater potential in reviving its Hindutva platform – namely, the Shah Bano issue and the Ayodhya movement, which we discuss later.

The BJP then successfully deployed Hindutva and emerged after the 1989 elections with an impressive tally of eighty-eight seats in the Lok Sabha (the lower house of the parliament), where it previously had two.

The BJP last formed the central government in the general elections of 1999 in a coalition with a range of parties, most of which did not share the political programme of Hindutva. This development must be seen in the context of the logic of coalition politics as discussed in the Introduction. Through the 1990s, after the demolition of Babri Masjid, the BJP projected a conservative right-of-center image, which could, if need be, moderate its strident anti-minority stance and would be able to build alliances with regional parties that, given their local equations with the Congress or other rival parties, found the BJP to be the best alternative. The BJP-led National Democratic Alliance stayed in power for its full term, being defeated only in the next general elections of 2004 by the Congress-led coalition, United Progressive Alliance.

c) The Vishva Hindu Parishad (VHP), founded in 1964, came into being through the movement to ban cow-slaughter (the cow is sacred to most modern Hindus) and to build a temple at the site of the Babri Masjid. The VHP is a global organization, and its international profile is again one of promoting "Hindu culture," but both the issues on which it came into being are clearly anti-minority, and both have been used to mobilize violent attacks on Muslims.

The explosive potential of the cow-slaughter issue is evident from the lynching by a mob, in 2002 in the state of Haryana, of five men suspected of cow-slaughter. The five men turned out to be Dalits, from castes whose traditional occupation was leatherwork. People of this community get the raw material for their work from the carcasses of dead cattle that have died of natural causes. In a revealing clarification, the local Hindu right-wing organizations (including the VHP) sought to explain the incident as one of "mistaken identity" in which Dalits were mistaken for Muslims[4] – the killing of cow-slaughtering Muslims being part of the agenda of Hindutva politics, while the alienation of Dalits would be counter-productive to the project of a Hindu Nation.

Neither cow-slaughter nor the Ramjanmabhoomi movement can be anything other than highly emotive issues to mobilize "Hindu" sentiment against minorities. The Bajrang Dal,[5] allegedly the VHP's youth wing, founded in 1984, is openly armed with *trishuls* (tridents that can be used to kill, and are often used during communal violence). As with the RSS, however, links to the Bajrang Dal are difficult to establish, given the high levels of secrecy with which they work.

For example, when Graham Staines, a Christian missionary, was burnt to death with his two little sons in their vehicle by a mob in the state of Orissa in 1999, an incident that provoked nationwide outrage, the killers were well known in the locality as Bajrang Dal supporters, but this fact could never be proved.

d) Swadeshi Jagran Manch (SJM), based on the nationalist slogan of *swadeshi* (of one's own land), a term from the era of the Independence struggle referring to a nationalist economy, was founded in 1991 on a platform opposing "economic imperialism." It takes strong positions against the activities of multinational corporations in India, and against international instruments such as GATT and WTO. It also seeks to build a Hindu value-oriented Indian corporate culture. Often it participates, along with the RSS trade union wing, the Bharatiya Mazdoor Sangh, in joint campaigns with Left groups and parties in India against corporate globalization.

SJM and most of the other organizations of the Sangh Combine take strong anti-globalization,[6] nationalist positions, while the BJP and the Shiv Sena, when in power, back "liberalization" and privatization policies. It is therefore common on the Left to accuse the Sangh Combine of hypocrisy on the issue of globalization. The differences between the two positions, however, must be understood as arising from the different compulsions that act on a political tendency in three different situations – when it is a political party, when it is a trade union or other front organization, and when it is in government. Similar differences in attitudes toward globalization can be seen on the part of the Communist Party of India (Marxist) as the government in West Bengal, the party itself, and its trade union. It is not very useful to assume that there is a pure anti-globalization position on the Left and a necessarily compromised one on the Right. We argue that the responses vary from *government* to *party* to *trade union fronts* of the Left and Right, and to collapse the several distinct strands into two homogenized positions is to lose a sense of the textured nature, both of globalization as well as of responses to it. This issue is explored at length elsewhere in this book.

e) Another Hindu right-wing organization is the Shiv Sena, which is not a part of the Sangh parivar but shares a common strand of Muslim hatred. The Shiv Sena is a regional political party, founded in 1966, active mainly in the state of Maharashtra. It has often been in government in the state. The Sena's ideology is based on a certain idea of Hinduness and *bhoomiputra* (sons-of-the-soil), and the two are not always compatible. In the Sena's politics, both these ideas can be serially deployed as and when expediency demands. All too often, the "sons-of-the-soil" slogan has been interpreted by it as "Maharashtra for the Maharashtrians" and has easily turned even against Hindu migrants from other states. This was truer of its earlier politics. Its initial aggressive anti-non-Maharashtrian politics was modulated in the 1990s to build a Hindu base, delineating the Muslim and non-Hindu in general as the enemy of the Hindu nation, rather than the non-Maharashtrian as the enemy of Maharashtrians (Hansen 2001). This aspect of Shiv Sena politics, however, is always just below the surface and can come up any moment. Thus it successfully mobilizes urban unemployed youth and is able to direct their disaffection in campaigns such as its violence on non-Maharashtrians (including Hindus) appearing for recruitment by Indian Railways in Mumbai in 2003.

Below we discuss two key issues around which the BJP, and Hindutva forces in general, mobilized from the late 1980s through the 1990s.

The Uniform Civil Code (UCC) debate

In 1985, Shah Bano became the name around which the BJP was able to revive its Hindutva agenda, and today her name remains a symbol the BJP invokes in order to establish its "true" secular credentials and its commitment to women's rights as opposed to the "pseudo-secular" Congress Party. Shah Bano was a Muslim woman who claimed maintenance from her divorced husband in the Supreme Court, under section 125 of the Criminal Procedure Code (Cr.PC), which applies to all citizens of India. Her husband claimed that under *shari'a* or Muslim personal law, it was not necessary for the husband to pay maintenance beyond three months after the divorce. The judgment held that there was no inconsistency between the *shari'a* and section 125, and granted maintenance to Shah Bano, arousing strong protest from some leaders of the Muslim community, who held this judgment to contravene Muslim personal law. There was equally vocal support for the judgment from large sections of the community, however, including public demonstrations by Muslim women. Ignoring this voice, the Rajiv Gandhi government passed an ordinance to overrule the judgment, later passed as the Muslim Women (Protection of Rights Upon Divorce) Act, removing Muslim women from the purview of section 125 Cr.PC (Kumar, R. 1993).

As we noted in the Introduction, by the early 1980s the Congress had started on a path of instrumentally using communal sentiments for political gains. In the late 1980s to early 1990s, we see a series of capitulations by this government, to the sectarian interests of one community and then the other.

The Shah Bano issue enabled the BJP to press its general argument of "appeasement of minorities," and to renew its demand for a Uniform Civil Code (UCC). But we also need to understand why the Shah Bano judgment provoked such an outcry from sections of Muslims, when in two earlier judgments (1979 and 1980) the Supreme Court had upheld the right of Muslim women to maintenance under section 125 and there had been no reaction.

The debate over the UCC arises from the tension in the Constitution that pits women as individual citizens against religious communities that have the right to their personal laws. Since these personal laws cover matters of marriage, inheritance, and guardianship of children, and since all personal laws discriminate against women, the women's movement had made the demand for a UCC as long ago as 1937, long before Independence. The UCC, however, has rarely surfaced in public discourse as a feminist issue. It has tended invariably to be set up in terms of National Integrity versus Cultural Rights of Community. In other words, the argument for a UCC is made in the name of protecting the integrity of the nation, which is seen to be under threat from a plurality of legal systems, while the UCC is resisted on the grounds of cultural rights of communities.

Thus the BJP can stand unambiguously for a Uniform Civil Code, for underlying its national integrity argument is the explicit assumption that while Hindus have willingly accepted reform, the "other" communities continue to cling to diverse and retrogressive laws, refusing to merge into the national mainstream. Indeed, such an understanding marks not only Hindu right-wing arguments but is part of nationalist judicial common sense more generally. The judgment on Shah Bano, for example, having ruled that the *shari'a* and Section 125 were mutually consistent, went on, contradicting itself, to urge a Uniform Civil Code on the grounds that "it will help the cause of national integration by *removing disparate loyalties* to laws which have conflicting ideologies" (ibid.: 163, emphasis added).

Later judicial pronouncements on Muslim personal law, too – for instance an Allahabad High Court judgment on triple *talaq*[7] (1994) and a Supreme Court judgment in the Sarla Mudgal case (1995) – made this argument explicitly. For example, the 1995 judgment stated: "In the Indian Republic, there was to be only one nation – the Indian nation – and no community could claim to remain a separate entity on the basis of religion" (Agnes 1994b).[8] But as one feminist group put it, the judiciary consistently raised the demand for a UCC only in the context of cases dealing with Muslim personal law, and never in dealing with cases of gender discrimination in Hindu Law (Gangoli 1996: 9).[9]

By the mid-1980s, the growing presence of organized Hindutva politics and a general legitimacy for it was becoming evident. The Shah Bano judgment too was hailed by the media as a victory against Islamic obscurantism. Hence the knee-jerk reaction of the self-styled leadership of the Muslim community to the judgment. But the Shah Bano judgment and, subsequently, the legislation overturning the judgment, mark also, for a different set of reasons, the beginning of the rethinking in the women's movement of the demand for the UCC with its implicit legitimizing of the national integrity argument. It was becoming increasingly clear that "integrity" always came with a majoritarian cast.

Positions within the women's movement, even those that reiterate the need for state legislation, now prefer terms such as "common," "gender-just," or "egalitarian" codes over the term "uniform." This disavowal of uniformity in the 1990s is significant in that it marks the women's movement's recognition of the need to rethink both the nation as a homogeneous entity, and of the legitimacy of the state-led social reform.[10]

The UCC debate is exemplary from the point of view of understanding the way in which Hindutva works in a democratic polity such as India. By emphasizing "equal" and "similar" treatment of all communities, the BJP is able to use some aspects of liberal democratic thinking to suggest that any recognition of difference is necessarily contrary to the principles of secularism. Since "Hindu" has already been equated with "Indian," Hindu practice, by definition, can never be one of many different practices in India. All "difference" to be eliminated is thus, necessarily, difference from the Hindu/Indian norm.

Ayodhya, Babri Masjid and Ramjanmabhoomi

In early 1986, the Faizabad District Court ordered the opening of the locks on the Babri Masjid, permitting Hindu worship of the idol of Ram inside. The controversial issue had been on the back burner for decades, so this move was widely perceived to be an effort by the Congress government to recover lost ground with Hindus after the Muslim Women's Act.

Although Babur's commander, Mir Baki, is supposed to have destroyed a temple to build the Babri Masjid in 1528, the first conflict at the site erupted three centuries later, in 1853, with an attack on the mosque by a sect of Hindu ascetics. As a compromise, the British government permitted Hindus to worship at a small platform close to the mosque, called *Ram chabootra*, believed to mark the birthplace of Ram, which had become an object of worship in the late eighteenth century. Then, in 1949, someone broke into the Babri Masjid and placed an idol of the infant Ram (Ram Lalla) inside, in what was hailed as a miracle by Hindutva activists. Firm action was taken by Nehru, however, and the mosque was locked, ending all worship there. This did not lead to any counter-mobilization and the issue lay dormant until 1984, when it was revived by Hindu organizations at different levels, backed by VHP, building up mass movements to "liberate" the birthplace of Ram. And then in 1986 came the court order permitting Hindus to worship the idol of Ram inside the mosque. This development, however, only gave fresh impetus to the Hindutvavaadi demand for a temple to be built at the site (Jaffrelot 1996).

Christophe Jaffrelot offers us a densely documented and vivid account of this period. In 1990, the VHP relaunched the Ramjanmabhoomi movement, without much support initially from the BJP, which at the time was supporting the V. P. Singh-led National Front government. But when V. P. Singh decided to implement the Mandal Commission Report, the BJP found itself having to move more clearly into the VHP camp. It could not endorse the Mandal Commission reservations without alienating its traditional support among the upper castes, and in any case as a party of Hindu nationalists, it is opposed to highlighting divisions among Hindus. On the other hand, it could also not afford to alienate the OBCs, 52 percent of the Indian population. Its solution was to urge reservations based on economic criteria rather than caste, while it simultaneously launched its campaign to build Hindu solidarity on the emotive Ramjanmabhoomi issue. Within a month, Lal Krishna Advani, President of the BJP, had launched the *Rath Yatra*, traveling ten thousand kilometers in a Toyota vehicle designed to depict an epic chariot, departing from Somnath temple in Gujarat[11] and planning to cross eight states before reaching Ayodhya in October to inaugurate *kar seva* (voluntary work) to begin construction of the temple there. It was an extraordinary mobilizational move, imaginative, visually striking, leading to delirious crowds all along the route. And all along the route, expectedly, there were planned attacks on Muslims – the route of the *yatra* was marked by blood.

Much more blood was to be shed, including the blood of some *kar sevaks* in firing by security forces in Ayodhya, and their deaths ("martyrdom" in Hindutva mobilizing) were to fuel more bloodshed in violence against Muslims along the route of processions bearing their ashes, organized by the VHP. The entire campaign was to culminate two years later in that stunning image that shook the foundations of secular India – cheering men atop the dome of the Babri Masjid, saffron flag fluttering, some hours before the ancient mosque was reduced to rubble with the most primitive of hand-held implements. Violence followed all over the subcontinent, killing thousands (Jaffrelot 1996; Ludden 1996).

The paradoxical aspect for the BJP of this dazzling success was that it could not openly claim the credit for the demolition, as a party in parliament bound to uphold the Constitution. Indeed, the BJP leadership continually asserted that the actual demolition had not been pre-planned, and that it was a spontaneous act in which people's emotions had overtaken them. As a party that had to fight imminent elections, it had to assert its democratic and constitutional character, while the political gains of the demolition would be harnessed by other members of the Sangh parivar.

BJP in power: the National Democratic Alliance

After its inability to build up sufficient alliances to stay in power for more than thirteen days in 1996, the BJP perfected its skill of coalition-building. When it won the highest number of seats in the 1998 general elections, it was in a position to put together the National Democratic Alliance, a twenty-four-party coalition with regional parties, most of which were decidedly anti-communal. These parties were motivated to join the NDA not for ideological reasons but because of the logic of the political configuration in their states – for instance, the Trinamool Congress opposed the Congress and CPI(M) in West Bengal, Telugu Desam the Congress in Andhra Pradesh, and the MDMK and DMK in Tamil Nadu were in rivalry with the other Dravidian party in the state, the AIADMK, whose withdrawal of support to the previous BJP-led government had led to its fall. Thus by the mid-1990s, the logic of regional politics had come to be decisive in government formation at the center. Indeed, the coming into power of the UPA in 2004 can partly be seen as the result of the Congress having successfully learned the BJP strategy of building and maintaining coalitions (McGuire and Copland 2007; Adeney and Saez 2005).

Soon after assuming power, in May 1998 the NDA crossed the "nuclear threshold" and tested the nuclear bomb. In doing so, this government ended the policy of "nuclear ambiguity" that had hitherto been the hallmark of Indian policy, which involved "both affirming and denying" that India had nuclear weapons capability (Bidwai and Vanaik 1999: 69). Within a month Pakistan also tested a nuclear bomb. In less than a year, the first military conflict in thirty years took place in Kargil, now between two nuclearized states, brought to an end under pressure from the USA. South Asia would henceforth be "on a short fuse" (ibid.) and increasingly susceptible to US control.

While the other constituents of the NDA were not adherents of Hindutva politics, nevertheless, their participation continued unabated even as the stakes were gradually and alarmingly raised. The BJP launched a program of rewriting history textbooks produced in the 1970s by historians of worldwide repute, following the explicit agenda of redressing what is claimed to be a distortion of the past. In this redressal, the declared aim was to valorize "Hindu" achievements and to present the "Hindu" community as one that has existed from time immemorial, and one that has always been and continues to be egalitarian. The attempt was to evoke a homogeneous community that basically looks like the nineteenth-century, north Indian, upper-caste version of Hinduism, with all its taboos and beliefs presented as eternal, but with caste inequality carefully excised. The other aspect of this project is the assimilation of all religions other than Islam into the fold of Hinduism, and the representation of Islam and Christianity as alien and inimical to Hindu civilization.

One of the most significant moments of the NDA rule was the state-sponsored massacre of Muslims in Gujarat in February–March 2002. In what amounted to a virtual ethnic cleansing exercise, Muslims were driven out of their homes in villages and massacred in towns. In the language of Hindutva it was a necessary step to remind the Muslims of their true place in India – an essential part of establishing Hindutva and its assimilation/elimination programme. Thus, Gujarat under BJP chief minister Narendra Modi during this period was openly hailed as the "laboratory of Hindutva." This ethnic cleansing was justified by the Hindu Right as a spontaneous reaction to an attack by Muslims on a train at Godhra station in Gujarat, carrying *kar sevaks* coming back from Ayodhya, in which a bogey of the train was set on fire, resulting in several deaths. Later, in 2006, the report of an inquiry committee under Justice U. C. Banerjee confirmed what several other investigations since 2002 had suggested: that the fire had begun from inside the bogey and not from outside, where the "Muslim mob" had supposedly collected.[12] There is no doubt that the pogrom had been planned in advance, and awaited a pretext for setting into motion. And yet, so successfully has the Hindutva campaign interwoven "Godhra" and "Gujarat" in the public mind, that even secularist critique of the Gujarat violence often uses the term "Godhra riots" or "post-Godhra riots," thus legitimizing both the supposed provocation as well as the idea that these were spontaneous riots instead of pre-planned, targeted violence.

Indeed, most "riots" in India are far from spontaneous and involve what Paul Brass has called "institutionalised systems of riot production," which are activated during political mobilization or elections (Brass 2006: 65). Gujarat was no different in this sense, but it is unprecedented in some others. The violence against Muslims and their property was not simply perpetrated by specifically politicized sections of the population; it was conducted at a generalized level. A vast cross-section of the Hindu population, including Dalits and Adivasis, were involved. Not surprisingly, in the elections held immediately after the violence, Narendra Modi, the chief minister who presided over it all, came back to a two-thirds majority in the state assembly with about 50 percent of the votes.

At this crucial juncture, too, the NDA remained silent while the massacre of Muslims in Gujarat was conducted, under the umbrella of the blatantly partisan BJP state government, police, and other state machinery (Vardarajan 2002; Menon, N. 2002). Some of them, such as the Telegu Desam and the Trinamool Congress, did make some oppositional statements in parliament, but they decided to stay with the coalition right through the months of crisis.

A second feature that marks Gujarat as a landmark in communal politics in India is the fact that, unlike other places that go back to some degree of normalcy once the crisis passes, Gujarat's once prosperous and confident Muslim community now lives a ghettoized and insecure existence (Jha 2006).

The last general election (May 2004) that routed the BJP-led NDA alliance has certainly dealt Hindutva a blow, but it would be a mistake to understand it simply as a vote against communalism. As we have seen, the states of India have different dynamics and political configurations, separately reflected in the contests in each state. Thus the final tally does not necessarily reflect a countrywide trend. Further, different considerations come into play during national and

Politics of Hindutva | 53

local elections. It is noteworthy that a mere three months after the general elections of 2004, when the Congress won the Lok Sabha seat from Junagadh in Gujarat, the BJP swept the municipal corporation elections, capturing thirty-five of the fifty-one seats.[13] It would be an oversimplification, therefore, to derive any one lesson from the overall result of the general elections.

Indeed, some sections of the Hindu Right have taken away from the election results the lesson that their defeat proves that the people have rejected, not Hindutva, but its "dilution" by the BJP. This dilution is naturally to be countered by renewed communal mobilization. One recent instance is a series of violent incidents in coastal Karnataka in October 2006. For some years now, Hindutva forces have been very active in the region, and the MP from the area is from the BJP, as are most of the local MLAs. Economic factors, such as competition between Muslim and Hindu traders and disputes between some sections of the fisherfolk and Muslim traders, have been used by Hindutva forces to whip up anti-Muslim sentiments and consolidate their presence. Investigative reports say that the violence is believed by many locals to be planned; that BJP and Bajrang Dal leaders, including some occupying top positions in the present Karnataka government, have played a leading role (Sikand 2006; Taneja 2006). Indeed, the worrying recognition is emerging that Karnataka may be the next Gujarat.

The BJP–RSS link had frayed somewhat since the electoral defeat. The RSS is the more recognizable Hindutva organization, while the BJP has tried in the past, and continues to hope, to be accepted as a moderate right-of-center party. As we have seen, within the world-view of the BJP it is entirely possible to be a party of the Hindus while simultaneously espousing the language of abstract citizenship. Within this framework of abstract citizenship, it is easy to claim that it is "communal" to raise the issue of religious identity at all, and casteist to assert caste identity.[14] The pressures of electoral-democratic politics always push the BJP toward emphasizing the aspect of its politics most appealing to a section of the elite. For the RSS, such niceties are not quite welcome and tensions periodically emerge. Recently, however, the RSS reasserted its hold over the party. When the BJP's highest decision-making forum met in December 2006, an aggressive Hindutva agenda was declared and the party constitution was amended to strengthen RSS control over it. Clearly, this is the route the BJP expects will bring it back to power.

Muslim politics: the secular/communal question

The emergence of Hindutva as a powerful political force in the 1990s has led to a concerted attempt by secular-liberal and left-wing parties and intellectuals to set up a secular versus communal polarity. To an extent, this has been supported by important backward-caste parties such as the Samajwadi Party in Uttar Pradesh and the Rashtriya Janata Dal in Bihar. This is also backed by important sections of Muslim leaders who have been feeling immensely persecuted, especially during this period since the 1990s. Needless to say, such a situation of persecution and targeting of a particular community is bound to generate a sense of inwardness that demands closing of ranks and intolerance of internal dissent. And without doubt this has been the mainstream representation of the Muslim community in contemporary India.

While it is important to understand this strand of politics, it is equally important to understand the new challenges that have emerged from within the community that essentially form a part of the internal struggle for its democratization. These new challenges point to a complex dynamic that we cannot discuss in any detail here. It is important, however, to understand the broad directions these are taking.

First and most significant is the gender dimension of the challenge to the authority of the exclusively male religious leaders who are largely responsible for steering the community into fundamentalist directions in the present. As we saw earlier in this chapter, there was an outcry from the "custodians of the community" over the Supreme Court judgment on Shah Bano, claiming that it was contrary to Muslim personal law. The government's surrender to these forces, by enacting a law overriding the judgment, provided the Hindu Right with a means to put into operation all the arguments against the Muslims in their arsenal. These included arguments about their "backwardness," their "refusal to merge into the national mainstream," their "innate separatism," their refusal to change, and so on.

What was lost to the public gaze was the fact that large and vocal sections of Muslim women and men actively opposed both the government's surrender as well as the attempt by the mullahs to clamp down on issues pertaining to women. The struggle has continued since, and has been fought not just by secular, middle-class women and men but also by women within the community, who have demanded a space within the religious order and its social institutions. Thus, on the one hand, the constitutional validity of the Muslim Women (Protection of Rights on Divorce) Act 1986 was challenged by two Supreme Court lawyers Daniel Latifi and Sona Khan and the court ruled that the divorced woman had the right to maintenance for life, unless she remarries (Khan, S. 2004). On the other hand, probably much more effective struggles have emerged at an everyday level within the community. Indexing such a struggle is the instance of Daud Sharifa of Tamil Nadu, who emerged as a key rallying point for women demanding a women's mosque. According to Sharifa, the fight for a mosque was important because "we want our space to meet, talk, discuss our grievances and pray. We want to have a say in community rulings" (Biswas, S. 2004). This struggle received the support of Badar Sayed, who was also chairperson of the Tamil Nadu Waqf Board.[15] While the official All India Muslim Personal Law Board (AIMPLB) has been forced to sit up and take notice of developments such as these,[16] in 2006 a number of women in Lucknow went ahead and even formed a counter-body, the All India Women's Personal Law Board, claiming that the AIMPLB simply does not take the woman's position into account on matters of marriage and divorce (Awasthi 2007). Throughout this period, related issues kept coming up, such as the controversial Imrana case, leading to further restiveness among Muslim women.[17]

The other challenge to the traditional leadership of the community has come from the lower-caste groups. Although Islam is predicated upon a notion of social equality, the actual practice of Islam in India has exhibited both a classist and a casteist disdain for the lower orders by the elite political (and religious) leadership, the ashrafs. For many of the Hindu lower castes who converted to Islam, the road to social equality was barred by the ashraf elite. Organizations such as the Pasmaanda Muslim Mahaz (PMM

– Backward Muslim Front) or the All-India Backward Muslim Morcha (AIBMM) have emerged in the last decade or so and have challenged the dominant and traditional leadership of the community. The AIBMM was set up 1994 in Bihar by a young Muslim doctor, Ejaz Ali. According to Ali, the traditional Muslim leadership "had been championing merely symbolic issues, rather than taking up real bread and butter issues," questions of jobs and education for the poor and backward Muslims (Sikand 2004a). The AIBMM has focused, since 1994, on the mobilization of Dalit Muslims and OBC Muslims and has now an organizational network all over north India. Ali Anwar, founder of the PMM, a journalist who quit his job to organize backward Muslims, recalls how the very organization of the first public rally by the PMM, in 1998, elicited a hostile reaction from the established classes. He mentions a national seminar organized by some elite Muslims who styled themselves "Muslim Social Scientists," where the PMM was branded dangerous for Muslims. The organizers, according to him, worked directly under the AIMPLB. Similarly, the All India Milli Council organized an "international conference" against what it deemed "divisive" politics among the Muslims.

Apart from the traditional dominance of the ashraf elite, the more immediate fundamental conflict here is over reservations. The recent publication of the Justice Rajinder Sachar Committee Report on the current status of Muslims points to a gross all-round under-representation of Muslims in practically every sector of the economy and employment. Clearly, this under-representation is a consequence of a series of mechanisms of discrimination – visible and invisible – that concern the community as a whole. In this context, one of the important factors animating the movement of backward and Dalit Muslims is the demand for recognition that they constitute sections of the OBC and Dalit populations and are not simply "Muslim." In part this is a reply to the efforts of leaders such as Syed Shahabuddin, one of the most important of the modern elite leaders, to posit the idea of a Muslim community for purposes of reservations. Clearly, Shahabuddin and other leaders believe that a separate recognition of OBC and Dalit Muslims for these purposes would weaken the community, while on the other hand, leaders of the PMM and the AIBMM believe that if Shahabuddin's idea works, the ashraf elite will once again corner all the benefits of affirmative action.

Political assertions such as those discussed above should be seen as attempts to move away from platitudinous invocations of the secular/communal divide. For, while these new assertions among Muslims certainly share a common ground with secular liberal politics, they also attempt to challenge the established community leadership which continuously invokes the threat of the Hindu Right in order to demand closing of ranks. Most of the voices of the kind referred to above, on the other hand, involve a refusal to defer their specific issues any longer in the name of a larger community identity. It is an insistence that the real interests of the community and "essential practices" of Islam can be decided only by a democratized community.

Caste politics and secularism

This aspect has been addressed at length in the previous chapter. If the secular nation functioned at the level of the modern institutions of civil society, excluding the non-modern masses, another crucial, perhaps central exclusion, was that of caste. Consider the provocative statement made by Dalit intellectual Chandra Bhan Prasad: "The British came too late but left too early." Prasad's point is that "secular" India has tolerated caste inequality with equanimity both before and after Independence. It was only the British who made any dent in it through policies such as legally ensuring that "Untouchables" could attend government schools. When upper-castes in Andhra Pradesh seceded from these schools and set up their own, the British government restricted jobs in government to government school graduates (Prasad 2000).

Everything that is critical of "secular" politics need not, in other words, be simply "communal." So completely does the opposition of secular/communal shape theorizing on Indian politics, that the active presence of actors who constitute themselves outside of this polarity often fails to be seen independently of it. As we saw in the last chapter, the alliance of the Dalit party, the BSP, with the BJP in Uttar Pradesh is too easily read as opportunistic support for

Hindutva when it is more centrally about the politics of caste. The BSP needs to secure allies for Dalits against the dominant backward-caste (predominantly Yadav) parties of that state since backward castes rather than Brahmins are the immediate oppressors of Dalits in the villages of northern India. These parties are opposed by the BJP too, with its largely Bania–Brahmin support base; hence the alliance between the two.

We have to recognize that "secularism" has been implicitly regarded as Hindu upper-caste and modernized upper-class all along (Nigam 2006b). This recognition might enable us to see that the energy expended in producing the supposedly unmarked "Indian" citizen hid from us two kinds of counter-currents: one, subaltern voices (Dalits, Adivasis, laboring populations) asserting their identities and needs against the development juggernaut; and two, majoritarian voices, such as those of Hindutva (Menon, N. 1998). And as we have seen earlier, allying with Hindutva has been one route of subaltern empowerment. Many of the political developments of the last decade, in particular, are in fact incomprehensible without a framework that gives visibility to community/caste identity. Indeed, some scholars would argue that caste is as central to communal politics as it is invisible to secular politics. Dilip Menon (2006), for instance, suggests that communal violence is Hindutva's attempt to displace its internal caste violence on to an external Other. This is an argument the lineage of which actually goes back to B. R. Ambedkar himself, who had often argued that Hinduism targeted Muslims and Christians as a way of dealing with their own lower-caste/Dalit people, who wanted to exit from the Hindu social order.

Hindus and Hindutva

Is there a community of Hindus whom the BJP can expect will unfailingly vote for it? Would the RSS win an election if it contested one, even if the voters were all Hindu by birth?

As far as practicing Hindus are concerned, the answer is no. Even among Ram-worshipers, Hindutva politics is not an obvious choice. One of the staunchest opponents of the Ramjanmabhoomi movement was the head priest of the Ram temple at Ayodhya, Mahant Lal Das. He was vocal in his opposition, and paid with his life – he was

Politics of Hindutva | 59

found brutally murdered on November 16, 1993. Within Ayodhya itself, there is organized opposition from local Hindu residents to the building of a temple at the site of the demolished mosque, and it is telling that fifteen years after the demolition of the mosque, and despite six unbroken years of the BJP being in power at the center, no temple has been built there.[18]

Or let us take the story of the Sankat Mochan temple in Benaras that was the site of a bomb blast in 2006. Veer Bhadra Misra, the *mahant* (head priest) of the temple, saw to it that prayers were resumed within hours of the blasts. Thereafter he evicted from the premises all representatives of the Hindu Right, including the Bajrang Dal and BJP leader, Vinay Katiyar. He then joined hands with Abdul Batin Nomani, the Mufti-e-Benaras and the imam of the adjacent Gyanvapi mosque, and together they went around visiting the injured in hospital, organizing joint programs including campaigns and music festivals and the recitation of the Hanuman Chalisa[19] by burqa-clad Muslim women (Subrahmaniam 2006).

Another instance of the non-malleability of Hindu society in relation to Hindutva designs was seen a couple of years ago. The BJP tried to mobilize a "Hindu" wave after its electoral defeat in 2004 around the arrest of the Shankaracharya of Kanchi, a Hindu spiritual leader of south India, in a case involving internal rivalries within his *muth* (religious organization). The issue simply failed to take off, the Shankaracharya's significance being limited to one sect of Brahmins in the south. It is revealing that the BJP miscalculated the importance of this issue to Hindus in general.

It is as political actors, not as believers, that many Hindus are mobilized for the politics of Hindutva. But there is also determined resistance from within the ranks of "Hindus," for varying reasons, to being mobilized in this way – from Dalits voting with their feet as mass conversions to Buddhism continue to be staged publicly; from feminists; from the emerging movements of gay and lesbian people (a banner at one of the protests against the Hindu Right's violent attacks on the film of lesbian love, *Fire*, read defiantly, "Indian and Lesbian");[20] from corporate executives and businesspeople ("India Inc.," as this section has come to be known), fearing insecurity that will affect investments;[21] from the thousands of ordinary Indians of all communities and walks of life who poured into Gujarat to help rehabilitate the Muslims affected by the violence there, disavowing the politics of Hindutva.

The politics of Hindutva is thus neither religious fundamentalist nor anti-modern. Ashis Nandy has long argued that communalism is in fact a product of the logic of modern governance (Nandy 1985). For Nandy, paradoxically, the demolition of the Babri Masjid was "proof that the secularization of India had gone along predictable lines" (Nandy 1994: 10).

When the Babri Masjid was demolished in 1992 the shock in secular ranks was matched by the confidence that this was only a matter of a short sharp battle. Over ten years down the line, with Gujarat behind us, secular India looks back on that shock as well as that optimism with disbelief – why was it taken so off-guard? And why did it appear to be such an easy battle to win? Why, to begin with, had the battle raging beneath the polished surfaces of Nehruvian secularism been invisible?

Locating secularism as it has developed in the Indian context, we suggest a distinction between secularism as a *value* (of non-discrimination, acceptance of difference, mutual respect) and secularism as a *principle of statecraft*. Recognizing the latter's implication in statist and authoritarian discourses, political theory needs to unhinge secularism from the state, to rework it into our everyday practices. That reworking will have to confront the uncertainties of democratic functioning in political society, and not depend on moral and normative certainties to impose secularism from above. We believe it is possible to continue to call ourselves secular in the first sense while mounting a critique of the practice of secularism by the Indian state. Perhaps the greatest gain of the last decade and a half for democracy in India is the recognition that "secularism," sixty years down the line, is and will always be in the process of becoming.

3 | Globalization I: accumulation by dispossession[1]

The advance made by the 18th century shows itself in this, that the law itself becomes now the instrument of the theft of people's land. (Karl Marx, *Capital*, vol. I, pp. 677–8)

Accelerated development

On January 8, 2002, the *Indian Express* published a news story entitled "Experts rule out submergence, MP town relieved." Based entirely on an interview with one person, the managing director of National Hydro Power Corporation (NHPC), the story claimed that "the experts of NHPC" could ensure that the people of Harsud town in Madhya Pradesh and one hundred neighboring villages would not "meet the fate of the two hundred other villages" that would be totally submerged once the Indira Sagar reservoir (the largest dam on the Narmada river) came up. The managing director told the newspaper that a detailed survey had been conducted, on the basis of which it was clear that by building a guide bund around the town, it could be saved. In addition Harsud would have twenty-four-hour drinking water as well as metaled roads linking it to nearby towns and to the railway station, thus giving "a boost to Harsud's business and economic activities."

Two and a half years later, in June 2004, as the waters of the Indira Sagar dam started rising inexorably, armed police and bulldozers arrived in Harsud to forcibly evict the residents from their homes. The 700-year-old town was reduced to rubble. The oustees were made to move to New Harsud, a stony inhospitable site with a few tin sheds for shelter, and with no water supply, not even for drinking, let alone for construction, no toilets, no avenues for employment, and absolutely no way of reconstructing their lives. The petty amounts of cash compensation some of them received (in order to be eligible for which they had to spend their own money to raze to the ground what was left of their homes) were to evaporate very quickly under the pressure of this cruel and sudden dislocation.

Three months later, a rally of thousands of oustees reached the office of the Narmada Hydroelectric Development Corporation (NHDC), a profit-making corporate body in a joint venture with the NHPC and the state government. The chairman of NHDC just happened to be the very same managing director of NHPC who had predicted a glorious future for Harsud in the *Indian Express*. The NHDC has unlimited power over construction, impact assessment, and compensation. In the two and half years since the interview had been published, evidently the NHDC not only did nothing either to protect Harsud or to make New Harsud habitable, but it arbitrarily took the decision to raise the height of the Indira Sagar dam one year ahead of schedule. Thus it violated with impunity the Narmada Water Disputes Tribunal Award (1979), which lays down that all resettlement should be completed *six months prior* to submergence.

The desperate rallyists that September wanted to place before NHDC officials a charter of demands, including the extravagant one for drinking water, but they found that the offices were deserted and the officers had fled.

The tragedy of Harsud is merely one, and certainly not the last, of a myriad such in post-Independence India. The rubble of Harsud and its human debris, swept off to the tin sheds of New Harsud, stand testimony to the utterly unsustainable policy of the Indian state on "development." A policy strongly backed by the Indian elites and deeply implicated corporate English media, its striking feature is its calm callousness toward the powerless. Its commitment to a supposedly abstract goal – development – is revealed as a commitment to very concrete, specific groups who benefit at the expense of the majority of the population. Most alarming of all is its myopia concerning ecological issues.

Such a policy of development was inaugurated at Independence: a policy of encouraging capitalist industrialization through big dams and power projects and large-scale extraction of natural resources, including uranium mining for nuclear energy plants. Since Independence, development projects of the Five-Year Plans have displaced about five hundred thousand people each year, primarily as a consequence of land acquisition by the state. Nor have these mega-projects delivered on their promise, now that many of them are being reassessed, following the bitter controversy and struggle over the Narmada Valley project, discussed below.

For instance, reassessing Bhakra dam, the first "Temple of modern India" as Nehru famously called it, a recent study by a team led by scholar and activist Sripad Dharmadhikary reveals that Bhakra played a relatively small role in India's Green Revolution (Dharmadhikary et al. 2005). Other factors – high-yielding crop varieties, chemical fertilizers, and pesticides – played a much larger role. The irrigation required for this did not come from the inadequate, unreliable, and limited supply of canal water from the dam, which was not conducive to intensive farming with the new seeds. It was groundwater-based irrigation that was crucial. Proponents of the Bhakra dam often argue that the rise in groundwater irrigation has been possible due to groundwater recharge through seepage from Bhakra's canals, but in fact most of the water for tube-wells comes from groundwater mined from the reserves underground. Groundwater mining now constitutes around 50 percent of Punjab and Haryana's irrigation. The increase in tube-well-based water mining has resulted in a drastic fall in groundwater levels. The extensive chemical fertilizer use as well as a cropping pattern dominated by high-yield rice and wheat inaugurated by the Green Revolution have destroyed the soils of Punjab and Haryana. Today's farmers are struggling to pay ever-increasing prices for agricultural inputs and electricity for pumping water, while having to cope with declining agricultural returns. Large numbers of farmers are trapped in debt and the suicide rate among farmers in Punjab and Haryana is fast increasing.[2]

With the accelerated pace of "development," a crisis point has been reached in agriculture as the neoliberal dispensation has forced it to transform and produce increasingly for the global market. It has been pointed out that the rapid shift from rain-fed cereal crops to non-food cash crops that has occurred in the last two decades has led to an ever-increasing need for cash for investments in the new crops. Cash is now required to a much greater degree for seeds as well as fertilizers and pesticides, leading to increased recourse to borrowings (Sridhar 2006; Jodhka 2006; Suri 2006; Mohanakumar and Sharma 2006; Rao and Suri 2006). This has led to a manifold increase in rural indebtedness. In states such as Andhra Pradesh, and to some extent in others too, the added problem seems to be that the moneylenders (who are often the traders who procure their produce for marketing) have also "of late become the source of knowledge and information on cultivation practices" given that most traditional ways are being forced out. The traders/moneylenders also lead them to believe that "they need to use more of these inputs to reap a better harvest" (Rao and Suri 2006: 1547). The scenario of increasing farmers' suicides has been most intense in the southern states such as Andhra Pradesh, Karnataka, Kerala, and the western state of Maharashtra. Punjab, once the model for modern agriculture during what has come to be known as India's "Green Revolution" from the 1960s on, has registered a high intensity of farmers' suicides among the northern states.

Private corporations and Special Economic Zones

Not only have the 1990s been marked by the rapid acceleration of such development; another feature specific to the neoliberal 1990s is the entry of private companies into arenas where, earlier, it was the state that had the sole right. Today, private corporations benefit from government support of various kinds, with the government acquiring lands from peasants and tribals and making them available to these companies at hugely subsidized rates. In the face of protests, the corporations get the full backing of state apparatus such as the police. So, for instance, in January 2006, when the tribals of Kalinganagar in Orissa protested against the acquisition of their lands for a steel plant owned by the Tatas, one of India's largest industrial houses, the state police opened fire, leading to the instant death of sixteen people, four also dying later on the way to hospital.[3] In this case, the district administration had been trying to take over the land for Tata Steel for many months and finally on the morning of 2 January, 2006, the administration led by the collector, the superintendent of police and Tata officials arrived at the site to build a boundary wall along the "earmarked" land. They were accompanied by twelve platoons of armed police. As the tribals got wind of it and began protesting,

Accumulation by dispossession | 65

to cut a long story short, their protests were met with tear gas and, eventually, bullets.

Orissa, being a mineral-rich state, has borne the brunt of murky deals on land and mining, but this is a more general story that continues through the 2000s, now pursued with much greater vigor. The strategy of conducting these operations is revealing. Often it takes the form of plain and simple intervention by the state and its different arms, making the process ostensibly "legal." But often enough the methods and procedures are patently illegal. For example, the Orissa High Court struck down the mining deal between the state-owned IDCOL (Industrial Development Corporation of India Limited) and a private company Jindal Strips Limited, for chromite mining in Tangarpada mines in Dhenkanal district, finding the concessions and tax exemptions granted to the company objectionable under the laws of the land (Das, P. 2004). What is significant is that the case came to court because of a challenge from the Tata Iron and Steel Company (TISCO) and VISA Industries – both of whom had put in competing bids for the same project. It is also important to note that the concessions granted to Jindal were illegal only because the deal had not come under the new policy for Special Economic Zones, put in place by the NDA government in 2000. By 2006, Jindal Limited was "awaiting a nod" for its proposed SEZ in Orissa.[4]

Special Economic Zones (SEZs) are supposed to be duty-free and tax-free enclaves that are to be treated as "foreign territory" for trade operations, duties, and tariffs.[5] As the Environment Protection Group, Orissa, puts it, "These zones are going to be spread across thousands of hectares of common lands, forest areas, coastal areas and even on fertile agricultural lands."[6] These areas are also supposed to be exempt from many laws of the land such as labor and environmental laws. Even though there are formal requirements for environmental clearance before work on SEZs moves into action, there is open violation of such laws as in the case of the infamous Vedanta Alumina Limited's project of bauxite mining in the Niyamgiri Hills, Lanjigarh. In this case the Ministry of Environment and Forests of the central government (by this time led by the Left-supported UPA government), granted it environmental clearance in September 2004, despite the fact that the Niyamgiri Hills are pristine forest lands and a schedule V area as defined by the Indian Constitution, which prohibits transfer of tribal lands to non-tribals (Kohli, K. 2006).

In Uttar Pradesh in 2005, the state government acquired thousands of acres of land, where populated villages and prime agriculture have thrived for generations, and handed it over to the corporate giant Reliance to build a power plant and township.[7] Not only have the farmers been forced to sell at lower than market rates to the state; as of July 2006 they had not received even the full amount of compensation offered. After eight months of non-violent protest, unheeded by the government, they pulled off the boundary fencing set up around their lands by Reliance and decided to plow it. The state's armed police, the UP Provincial Armed Constabulary, was immediately deployed. It dealt brutally with the protestors, causing several injuries and damage to their homes.[8]

So while the SEZ policy was initiated by the right-wing-dominated National Democratic Alliance government, it is being pursued with renewed vigor by the Left-supported United Progressive Alliance government that came to power in May 2004. Indeed, the state of West Bengal, ruled by the Left Front, has recently been in the eye of the storm for its acquisition of 997 aces of farmers' land in Singur for the Tata group to manufacture cars. What happens to the farmers whose lands are taken away is only one part of the question. In the case of Singur, the point is also that there are a large number of sharecroppers who work on the land and have no "claim" – not being landowners. Some officials of the Left Front government have claimed that the landless will be given jobs in the factories – knowing full well that in SEZs, the owners will have complete impunity regarding labor practices. If they throw out the workers within a few months, they will have absolutely no hope of any justice as these areas will be enclaves of high degrees of exploitation of the working class, with no recourse to any labor dispute laws. Singur is, of course, technically not planned as an SEZ but Nandigram in East Midnapore district of West Bengal is. Nandigram was the flashpoint of a recent struggle against land acquisition that led to mass violence and the death of at least fourteen people. The immediate crisis has been controlled but Nandigram simmers, as do large parts of rural West Bengal.[9]

Accumulation by dispossession | 67

While it is true that the advent of foreign capital in India in this period has often meant higher wages in some of the MNCs, there has also been resistance on the part of such managements to any kind of union activity. This came to light dramatically during August 2005 when there was industrial unrest in the Japanese-owned Honda Motorcycles and Scooters India, over the fact that the management resisted the formation of a union in this skilled workforce, trained in Industrial Training Institutes (ITIs). Eventually it decided to get rid of some 2,000 of the workers who had been recruited as trainees, and get in their stead a fresh lot (Reddy 2005: 32). The protests spilled on to the roads of Gurgaon, the township near Delhi where the plant is located. Over a few days, thousands of unarmed militant workers faced down the might of the Indian state – police, lathis,[10] water cannon – deployed in the interests of the Japanese corporation.

Private companies operate in dams of the Narmada Valley Project (NVP) too, as we saw with the Indira Sagar at the beginning of this chapter. At another dam on the Narmada, the Maheshwar dam, the work of construction and power generation was handed over to S. Kumars, a textile magnate. In 1998 there were militant protests by villagers of Jalud, which would be the first village to be submerged by the dam. Several thousand villagers captured the site of the Maheshwar dam, facing severe action from the police, including mass arrests and physical injuries requiring hospitalization. There were conflicting accounts, as usual, in the national press. The report of a team from Delhi organizations in solidarity with the movement (including one of the authors), which went to Jalud, found it to be a "village under siege":

> The boundaries of Jalud were fenced off with barbed wire, marked with boards saying *Pratibandhit Kshetra* (Forbidden Area). There were about a hundred policemen at the entrance of the village. We learnt that police presence is an overwhelming presence in the villagers' daily lives. Their activities are restricted and the fencing has made inaccessible – or very difficult to get to – their grazing grounds, cemetery, temple and vegetable fields. This state of affairs has been in existence for about four months. In short, this village of unarmed

people is being treated as enemy territory, and the villagers live under constant intimidation and insecurity. (Awasthi et al., 1998)

Democracy, protest, and the nation

While the presence of private companies under government protection is one striking feature of the 1990s, another feature is equally marked. The period since the late 1980s has seen growing resistance to such policies by dispossessed groups in different parts of the country. Thus, continued pressure from the movement and international solidarity actions resulted in the withdrawing of funds from the Maheshwar dam by the German government and by US and German corporations. In what water activists hope is the final nail in its coffin, the Environment Ministry in June 2006 directed the Madhya Pradesh government to stop all work on the dam pending a credible and comprehensive rehabilitation plan.

There is an older history to struggles, especially of tribal peoples, against being dispossessed by the state, going back to the colonial period. But there is one crucial difference. All struggles, from the late nineteenth century to 1947, that survive in memory today, do so by being accommodated into the history of anti-imperialist struggle, tucked cosily away into a pleat of Mother India's sari. With the coming of Independence, however, any such assertion is instantly transformed into an anti-national act. The overwhelming legitimacy of the anti-imperialist struggle and of the newborn nation-state was successful in deleting from history over two thousand families displaced by the Bhakra Nangal dam in the 1950s, of which less than half had been resettled even twenty-five years later. Those displaced by the Hirakud dam linger in national memory only because they were the audience for Nehru's stirring words to them: "If you are to suffer, you should suffer in the interests of the country." Two hundred thousand people were displaced by the Rihand dam in 1964. In the absence of any resettlement program, tens of thousands of them ended up on the banks of the reservoir, settling there and cultivating the land exposed when the reservoir receded in the summer. A second time round they were displaced by the Singrauli thermal power plant, then by coal mines, and so on in successive waves of industrialization, including, in a final tragic irony, to make room for compensatory afforestation – displacing people uprooted several times over, in order to placate nature for the damage inflicted so far (Kothari, S. 1996). From the late 1980s onward, however, the dispossessed have shown a marked aversion to going quietly into oblivion. There have been organized and increasingly militant struggles of varying degrees of efficacy. The intensification of both these processes – the penetration by state-backed market forces as well as resistance to such forces – is increasingly testing the claims to democratic functioning of the Indian state.

It would help to frame this story within Sudipta Kaviraj's formulation on "modernity." He argues that modernity is not the name of a single process, but a conjunction of several processes of social change that tend to occur in combination. He identifies these processes as a) the increasing centrality of the modern state, b) social individuation, c) capitalist industrialization, and d) the rise of nationalism and democracy. The sequence in which these processes occur can differ from society to society and in different time periods. Thus, Kaviraj argues that while in the West the processes of capitalist industrialization stabilized themselves *before* the pressures for democracy began, in India the two processes emerged almost simultaneously. In the West, therefore, the initial disciplining of the working class in a regime of capitalist production was achieved well before democratic obstructions could be placed in its path. The Indian state, on the other hand, faces challenges that capitalist industrialization in the West never had to face in its initial stages, having to deal with the compulsions of a democracy while enforcing capitalist transformation (Kaviraj 1995, 1996, 2000).

Dispossession by law: the case of the NVP

The Narmada Valley Project is the single largest river valley project in India, envisaging several thousand dams of different sizes on the river Narmada. One dam of the NVP alone, the Sardar Sarovar, will cost more than the entire amount spent on irrigation since Independence.

The now well-known movement against this ill-conceived project, the Narmada Bachao Andolan (NBA), came into being in 1985 initially in opposition to two of the largest dams, the Indira Sagar which submerged Harsud, and the Sardar Sarovar, the second largest dam of the NVP in terms of area submerged and population displaced. The NBA's opposition to the dams has moved from the question of rehabilitation for the displaced population (about 400,000 people in 245 villages in three states, the majority of whom are tribal, but only half of whom are officially considered to be "project-affected" and eligible for compensation), to a critique of the developmental model as such. Popular mobilization in the Narmada Valley has been strengthened by alliances with movement groups and NGOs in different Indian cities as well as with environmental NGOs in the West. Intense international campaigning led to the World Bank appointing an Independent Review Committee on the Sardar Sarovar Project (Baviskar 1995).

The Morse Committee, as the IRC was known, confirmed the worst fears of the NBA. Its report concluded that "the Sardar Sarovar Projects as they stand are flawed, that resettlement of all those displaced by the Projects is not possible under prevailing circumstances, and that the environmental impacts of the Projects have not been properly considered or adequately addressed."

It pointed out that the central government and the three state governments concerned (Gujarat, Maharashtra, and Madhya Pradesh) were willing to grant right of compensation only to landowners with formal title to their land, thus depriving thousands of tribal families with customary rights to forest land (60 percent of those ousted) of all rights.

As for environmental impact, the committee found that the government had conducted no study on the matter, even though five years had passed since the Rajiv Gandhi government had given conditional clearance to the project, the condition being that such studies be conducted alongside the construction.[11]

The damning evidence of the report, as well as continued pressure from international NGOs, led to the World Bank stopping its funding in 1993. The Japanese government, too, coming under pressure from Friends of the Earth, suspended aid to the project. The Indian government and judiciary, however, step in where the World Bank fears to tread. In a shocking judgment in 2000, in response to a petition filed by the NBA in 1994, the Supreme Court permitted the construction of the Sardar Sarovar to continue. In a majority judgment it refused to consider that there might be any environmental costs: "The dam is neither a nuclear establishment nor a polluting industry ... [I]t will not be correct to presume that the construction of a large dam like Sardar Sarovar will result in ecological disaster ... On the contrary there has been ecological upgradation with the construction of large dams" (Bhushan 2000).

The dissenting minority judgment by Justice Bharucha makes it clear, however, that the court had access to the information that the government's Department of Environment and Forests had refused to give environmental clearance to the NVP because the impact of the two largest dams had not been adequately studied. This decision was overruled by Prime Minister Rajiv Gandhi in 1987, and conditional environmental clearance was given, permitting the project to continue alongside the requisite studies. In other words, the project was allowed to continue before its environmental impact was fully known, and on the assumption that these studies would reveal nothing that might necessitate withdrawal of the clearance given. Even by 2000, at the time of the judgment, such studies did not exist. Construction of the dams, however, proceeded apace.

In addition, according to Justice Bharucha, it was mandatory, under the conditions of clearance, that the full rehabilitation of all displaced people be completed before any water was impounded in the reservoir. These conditions notwithstanding, let alone actual rehabilitation, the government did not even have a master plan for rehabilitation. Justice Bharucha, therefore, in his order, said that construction was to stop immediately and the project was to be subjected to a comprehensive review (Roy, A. 2000).

The majority judgment that swept aside this evidence was, of course, the operative one. It is significant that, celebrating this judgment, the home minister of the BJP-led coalition in government at the time hailed it as an aspect of "developmental nationalism," locating the judiciary's decision on the dam within a grid of three historical events he claimed as the achievements of Hindu nationalism: the Sardar Sarovar, the nuclear explosion in Pokharan in 1998, and the Kargil war with Pakistan in 1999 (Sangvai 1994).

The NBA and scholars working on the issue have repeatedly made the argument that the NVP is misconceived not only because of its enormous human and ecological costs, but because big dam projects do not deliver what they promise. The Indian government invests most of its irrigation outlay in major and medium irrigation projects that irrigate only as much land as do minor irrigation projects – the latter at a quarter of the cost of the former per hectare. As for the claim that the Sardar Sarovar Project (SSP) will provide drinking water to Gujarat's villages, the NBA points out serious fallacies in the arguments of its vocal supporters. This project, it claims, was never intended to provide drinking water. It was as late as 1998 that even feasibility studies for drinking water supply were initiated and there is no provision at all in the budget of the SSP for drinking water. Despite all this, however, the work on the dam has finally been completed as of December 2006 with hardly any rehabilitation being carried out.

Displacement, compensation, and relocation

In 1994, the Supreme Court reiterated the principle of eminent domain – "the power to acquire private property for public use is an attribute of sovereignty and is essential to the existence of a government. The power of eminent domain was recognized on the principle that the sovereign state can always acquire the property of a citizen for public good, without the owner's consent."

It is important to note here that the principle of eminent domain (the right of the state to decide on what is in the common good) is, in principle, a measure that can be and has been used for redistributive measures such as land reforms. Today the principle of eminent domain is deployed largely in order to dispossess communities of common property resources and to transform the commons into private property. Where private property has been acquired, it has been that of small and medium farmers, for which cash compensation is invariably given at less than the prevailing market rates.

Moreover, as critics point out, the law has been constructed on the assumption of the individual dislocated person. There is no understanding of communities as the subjects of dislocation or of ways of life that are destroyed. There is an abyss of incomprehension on the part of the Indian elites toward rural and tribal communities. Ripping these out from lands they have occupied for generations and transplanting them overnight into an alien setting (which is the best they can expect) is understood as rehabilitation and liberation from their backward ways of life.

The more fundamental question, though, is whether cash adequately "compensates" for land. The sudden access to large amounts of cash is something that requires a particular training in market behavior to deal with advantageously. Study after study of dislocated communities, conducted by independent groups, has found that even in the case of settled urban populations (for example when industries offer workers cash packages in voluntary retirement schemes), immediate access to cash leads to its dissipation in things such as medical expenses, marriages, and so on. The particular cultural sensibility required to make the most of cash is even more starkly lacking among most of the communities that get displaced, more than half of which comprise tribal populations, and most of whom have had limited interaction or familiarity with the market.

Thus, "an overwhelming sense of depression and bewilderment" is what was encountered by a democratic rights group, the People's Union for Democratic Rights, that visited the resettlement site of tribal people displaced by an alumina mining company in Orissa, in 2005 (People's Union for Democratic Rights 2005). With inadequate drinking water, since most of the hand pumps installed were not in working order, having lost their lands and means of livelihood, their access to forest, forest produce, and land for grazing cattle, they were at a loss. The cash they had been given seemed to have been blown away, either in legitimate expenses or, in many cases, in alcoholism. With no prospect of jobs in the company for the majority of them, they were faced suddenly with the end of the road. They had nowhere else to go.

As for the mythical land-for-land provision (which, as we have seen, in any case excludes the vast majority with only customary rights to land), there simply is not enough land to resettle the enormous numbers who have been dislocated and those who continue inexorably to swell their ranks. The Madhya Pradesh government has already declared in the Supreme Court that it cannot provide land to the hundreds of thousands already displaced by the Bargi dam in 1990 and about to be displaced by the dams on the Narmada.

The Supreme Court in its judgment on the Sardar Sarovar in 2000 held that displacement per se does not constitute violation of fundamental rights, since at the rehabilitation sites "there will be better facilities than in the tribal hamlets." Moreover, it is all to the good that tribals will be "gradually assimilated in the mainstream of society," or, as officials of the Central Water Commission put it at a seminar on the Sardar Sarovar, displacement from land is crucial for releasing labor for industry and other "useful jobs."

And indeed, we can be sure that the vast majority of those ripped out from forests and the land will end up as debris in urban slums, periodically flushed out from the city, only to come trickling back again – to build its roads and flyovers, to scurry across its underbelly performing the myriad tasks that keep the city alive, and to remind us that at every single stage of the long and dark history of development, alternatives were always available. They were simply not chosen.

Courts and environment

At this point we must consider the role of courts, especially the Supreme Court, in determining environment-related issues, a role that has become an extremely problematic one. The Public Interest Litigation (PIL) era was inaugurated in the 1980s, a period which, as we argued in the Introduction, saw the effect of the accumulated democratic aspirations of the post-Emergency era. PIL was intended to ensure legal rights to people who "because of poverty, helplessness or disability or socially or economically disadvantaged position" were unable to reach the court themselves. This made it possible for citizens to approach the Supreme Court on grounds of violations of fundamental rights on behalf of others, in the public interest, and not only when they were themselves the aggrieved party. In the 1980s, therefore, PIL initiatives resulted in important judgments protecting human rights, for example the 1982 Asiad workers' judgment on a PIL filed on behalf of construction workers, holding that non-payment of minimum wages was a form of bonded labor punishable as such by law.

Accumulation by dispossession | 75

Gradually, though, by the 1990s, the situation had changed dramatically, as the logic of corporate globalization took hold of the Indian elites. From now on, we find that PIL petitions, challenging large infrastructure projects and urban "beautification" projects on the basis of environmental and rehabilitation issues, are met by the Supreme Court speaking in the voice of the developmentalist rational state, valorizing the voice of "experts" and ignoring the pressures of democracy altogether. In order to achieve this end, different judicial strategies have been used at different times.

While dismissing petitions on environmental grounds against the Tehri Hydropower Project and the Konkan railway in the 1990s, and the NVP in 2000, the Supreme Court apparently exercised judicial restraint. It claimed to be limiting its own powers by holding that it was not the court's business to determine whether the executive had taken the right decision, but only to consider whether it had taken the decision after a consideration of all relevant aspects (Upadhyay 2000).

In other cases where the government, under democratic pressure, withdraws or postpones an unpopular measure such as slum demolitions, the courts have not hesitated to rap it on the knuckles for failure to protect the environment. In 1999, a court-appointed committee had recommended the demolition of *jhuggis* (slums) in a Delhi locality because of the "unhygienic" conditions produced. The government did not move on this order because of its inability to find an alternative site for relocating the people who lived there. In 2006, the court hauled up various government authorities for contempt of court, and demolitions were carried out forthwith. The inhabitants of Nangla Maachi joined the statistics on inconsequential lives cleansed from the city beautiful.

Then again, in 1992, when the rights of the National Thermal Power Corporation to set up a super thermal plant were disputed by Adivasis claiming customary rights to the land NTPC had acquired, the Supreme Court allowed NTPC's claim, citing the need for industrial development in the national interest (ibid.).

Despite their apparently different arguments – whether exercising judicial restraint or undertaking judicial activism – these judgments are remarkably consistent in one respect: all of them essentially protect, by omission or commission, the interests of propertied classes and powerful groups.

The city beautiful: producing the global city

It is instructive to examine the breathtaking urban transformations of the past decade – often conducted behind the shield of the judiciary, taking place in the name of "environment," "health and hygiene." In 1996, the Supreme Court earned the sobriquet of "The Green Bench" in the English media, when in response to a PIL (with follow-up orders in 2000 and 2001), it ordered the closure and relocation of "hazardous industries" and "non-conforming industrial units" in Delhi, leading to large-scale dislocation and the sudden unemployment of around two million people employed in about 98,000 industrial units.[12] The order came after an eleven-year-long court battle, at no point during which were the workers employed in these units ever made party to the case. Nor were the employers held liable for compensation to workers or payment of back wages. Over fifty thousand workers have since left the city and gone back to their villages in neighboring cities, which they left in the first place because they had no means of livelihood there. Those who stay back are then drawn into the even more exploitative area of daily casual work. It is important to remember that the case represented one of the earliest attempts by a "rights-bearing citizenry" to cleanse the city of its laboring poor. The specific case in question was filed by an environmentalist lawyer, M. C. Mehta, and tied up with another where the court took *suo moto* cognizance of a report in a daily newspaper regarding the pollution of the Yamuna river. It is not that there were no conflicts between the middle-class citizens and the subaltern populations of the city living on the fringes of legality in the past; what is distinctive about the new situation is that the claim is now being made and pressed in the language of rights. As political theorist Partha Chatterjee has suggested, the distinctive feature of subaltern existence in the city is that it has never been possible to sustain it in the name of right; it was a duty that the government owed to the populations it governed to provide the minimum basic requirements for a decent life, failing which the moral claims of the subaltern population continued to provide some kind of a horizon

Accumulation by dispossession | 77

for policy-making. This position was generally accepted common sense till about the mid-1990s. Soon all this was to change, as claims over urban space became increasingly contentious.

Equally important, however, was the new consciousness of "environment" and health concerns that were then mobilized to create the image of "world cities" which would have world-class infrastructure – roads, flyovers, smooth traffic, malls, and multiplex entertainment places. These do not, of course, always fit in with a concern for a clean environment – in fact, most often they do not. What marks these transformations is the reterritorialization of the third world city, a "dislocation from their national location and insertion into the grid of the global economy" (Nigam 2004: 73).

It cannot also be entirely a coincidence that of the 168 "polluting" industries closed down in the first round in Delhi, many large factories were "sunset" industries, the owners of which were looking for an opportunity to divert their capital to less risky and more lucrative ventures. They had been held back by labor laws that would have required them to pay out large amounts to workers in back wages, compensation, and so on. In addition, they occupied lands given to them at a subsidy by the government; from which, after the court order, they stood to make huge profits, by selling at market rates. The Supreme Court orders came at the right time as far as these were concerned.

Is pollution not an issue then? Of course it is, but it does not appear that the government and the courts were serious about fighting it. By ordering the relocation of polluting industries, they revealed a classic "not in my back yard" attitude. Simply relocating industries to Himachal Pradesh and Uttar Pradesh, which is what the court orders accomplished, meant relocating pollution from the back yard of Delhi's elite to wherever human life could be assumed to be cheaper. It also does not seem to have concerned the court that the pollution choking the city would also have been affecting the workers employed in the concerned units. Surely, if the intention is to fight pollution it must be tackled at source, which requires social auditing of industrial enterprises. In existing units it requires the setting up of pollution control measures that are open to public scrutiny and, in the long run, the involvement of the citizenry in deciding crucial questions of choice of technologies, and environmental impact assessments of units before they come up. None of these questions was addressed in the court orders.

Through the 1990s such attacks on the subaltern, laboring populations increased, with demolitions of *jhuggi jhonpris* (shanties and slums) taking place all across Delhi. *Jhuggi* dwellers were shunted out into distant suburbs from where it was a near-impossible task to commute to their places of work – both in terms of money and time. In some cases they were provided with some land, on which they had to construct houses at their own cost, but the virtual impossibility of commuting to work daily under forbidding transport conditions made it increasingly difficult for them to stay there.

The courts have, expectedly, played a vanguard role in this new assertion of rights of the citizen over the moral claim of governmental rationality. Responding to a PIL in 2000, the Supreme Court ordered the Delhi government to remove slums and unauthorized colonies from "public land." Denying that the government had any responsibility to find the estimated three hundred thousand people alternative accommodation, the judgment said: "[T]he promise of free land at taxpayers' cost in place of a *jhuggi* ... is a proposal which attracts land grabbers. Rewarding an encroacher on public land with a free alternate site is like giving a reward to a pickpocket." Further, "when a large number of inhabitants live in unauthorised colonies with no proper means of dealing with domestic effluents, or in slums with no care for hygiene, the problem becomes more complex."[13]

With these two statements, the survival needs of the poor are conflated with the activities of the land mafia ("land grabbers") and the poor identified as responsible, and therefore to be punished, for living in unhygienic conditions.

In another chilling response in 2006, dismissing a PIL against the demolition of slum clusters that supposedly pollute the Yamuna river in Delhi, during the course of which lawyer Prashant Bhushan claimed the right to shelter as a fundamental right, the Supreme Court (Justices Ruma Pal and Markanday Katju) observed: "Nobody forced you to come to Delhi. Is there a right to live in Delhi only? Stay where you can. If encroachments are to be allowed on public land, there will be anarchy."[14]

Accumulation by dispossession | 79

It is another matter that the courts see no danger to the Yamuna or possible anarchy arising from other encroachments on public land. Built right on the aquifer of the Yamuna river, the huge complex of the Akshardham temple got environmental clearance from the BJP-led NDA in central government at the time, in the teeth of opposition from environmentalist groups. Similarly, the Delhi master plan was modified in 2004 to accommodate an information technology park lying just south of the demolished slums, which had already been under construction for a year – in other words, a de facto regularization of an illegal encroachment (Bhan 2006).

The fact is that the planned and authorized parts of the city need the unplanned presence of thousands of migrant laborers. As Amita Baviskar (2003: 91) says:

> Thus the building of planned Delhi was mirrored in the simultaneous mushrooming of unplanned Delhi. In the interstices of the Master Plan's zones, the liminal spaces along railway tracks and barren lands acquired by the Delhi Development Authority, grew the shanty towns built by construction workers, petty vendors and artisans, and a whole host of workers whose ugly existence had been ignored in the plans. The development of slums was, then, not a violation of the Plan; it was an essential accompaniment to it, the Siamese twin.

Simply in order to continue living in these conditions, slum dwellers have to enter into a series of transactions that occupy the gray zones of porous legality – periodic bribes, illegal tapping of electricity lines, and so on. They are perpetual "encroachers," their existence criminalized by the very fact of survival (Ramanathan 1996, 2006).

Delhi's experience must be contextualized within the overall narrative of urban planning in India. A study of over three decades in the existence of Navi Mumbai, the satellite city supposed to have taken care of the increasing congestion of Mumbai, points out that Indian cities have evolved with a dualistic structure that invariably excludes the poor from adequate access to basic civic amenities. The author, Annapurna Shaw, argues that this mode of planning entailed the opening up of new areas, such as Navi Mumbai, before the old were properly serviced. Moreover, the land policy of the state has meant state acquisition of the lands of small agriculturalists and farmers living on the edge of the city, while it is the urban middle and upper middle classes who enjoy the new housing and infrastructure built on it. It has been pointed out by several scholars that the massive scale of urbanization-induced displacement is not recognized as an issue because the alienation of people from their productive land for city development and industrialization is apparently the result of voluntary sales (even though at lower than market rates). However, these sales are often due to pressure from the building mafia (Shaw 2004).[15] Indeed, this process of people being alienated from their productive lands through the urbanization of fringe areas of growing cities is to be seen all over the country (Sharma 2003).

Note that courts' responses to PILs on slum dwellers in the 1980s (in a few cases, even up to the early 1990s) differ sharply from the way in which they respond once the logic of corporate globalization has become common sense. In an earlier judgment on a PIL brought on behalf of slum dwellers in Mumbai (Olga Tellis Case 1986) the court had held that the arbitrary eviction of pavement dwellers without providing alternative accommodation was the abrogation of their fundamental right to life guaranteed in the Constitution. In a PIL on demolition of slums in Bangalore (Karnataka Kolageri N. S. Sangathana Case 1992), which argued that the government has an obligation to evolve affordable housing for all, the court passed an order directing the authorities to look into the grievance, giving both parties an opportunity of negotiating in a conciliatory manner. The precedent set by these judgments is ignored in the new climate of opinion, in which "environment" is invoked only in the context of the leisure and lifestyles of the urban middle classes.

So we see that this process happened earlier with Mumbai in the 1980s in a somewhat different form. It continues in other parts of the country today. In Kolkata 77,000 slum dwellers were evicted in 2004 and in Mumbai large-scale slum demolitions took place in 2005 soon after Prime Minister Manmohan Singh pledged a budget of $30 billion to give Mumbai a "facelift" that would, he promised, turn Mumbai into Shanghai. In Hyderabad, the state government leases land at highly subsidized rates to business houses, international airports, shopping complexes, corporate hospitals, and railway tracks. Over 10,000 houses belonging to the poor were demolished in the late 1990s to beautify the city that prides itself on being the new globalized "Cyberabad." When Bill Clinton visited the city at the invitation of the chief minister of the state, Chandrababu Naidu, all the poor settlements – called "encroachments" in the new language – along the route to be taken by Clinton's convoy were removed. Thousands of vendors were dislocated, and around 5,000 beggars rounded up, including disabled ones, and sent to temporary homes.[16]

The trajectory of a city such as Bangalore is somewhat different, as Janaki Nair's important study of the city (2005) shows, insofar as it has rapidly grown from a relatively small town to a metropolis. With its breathtaking transformations in barely a decade and a half, it has acquired the name of "India's Silicon Valley" and by 1998, it came to be "included within an elite group of ten cities energized by a surge of high-tech innovation," by *Newsweek* magazine (Heitzman 2004: 1). By 2001, it had over two thousand information technology (IT) companies functioning in the city and its spatial configuration was changing rapidly in consequence (ibid.; Nair 2005). Massive corporate as well as state government investment in the city, in areas ranging from new IT companies to mega-projects, have transformed the face of the city (Benjamin 2000). The city is being cleansed of the old industries and in their place appear the IT industries with huge sprawling complexes. These complexes have been built like huge campuses with in-house malls, mini-golf courses, swimming pools, gyms, and air-conditioned workspaces (Liang 2005).

Clearing the city space in keeping with this first world desire has meant forced dislocation of slum populations in Bangalore too (Nair 2005: 191–2). Another index of the change in Bangalore could be seen in what Nair refers to as the "erosion of plebeian rights to the [Cubbon] park" alongside the banning of public political rallies in it (ibid.: 214–15).

As urban planner and architect K. T. Ravindran (2007) puts it, Indian cities, in the vision of city planners in the 2000s, seem to be "on a new binge of building... thoughtless structures that only aid the automobile as a sign of progress towards a 'World Class City,'" while everywhere, this model is being increasingly seen as unviable. Ravindran is here referring to the frenzied construction of new flyovers, freeways, and spaghetti junctions that drive the visions of a global city. As opposed to this, he spells out the idea of a "Compact City" that is environmentally sustainable, centers on self-sufficient localities that need minimum long-distance travel on a day-to-day basis, and focuses on building up public transport at the cost of private vehicles. This vision is beginning to be talked about among some planners and architects – and has indeed found resonance in some government circles. Whether it will be taken heed of before it is too late, of course, remains to be seen.

4 | Globalization II: new economies of desire

In the previous chapter we saw the new global order identified with the logic of the free market being put in place by the long arm of state institutions – elected governments, an activist judiciary, the police, and the bureaucracy. Ironically, it seems that it is precisely what escapes the state, primarily through the market and new media forms, that provides – at least in contemporary India – a shelter from the violence of corporate globalization. What we refer to here as the new economies of desire include the explosion of a series of new aspirations, some of which we will explore in this chapter: new forms of the economic everyday; sexualities struggling against the state and against colonial law banning "unnatural" sex; new explorations of language in the Hindi public domain, seeking to break free of the nationalist, state-imposed language policing of yesteryear; the celebration of the city and of capitalism by sections of the most oppressed, especially the Dalits.

Much of this transformation has to do with the dismantling of the state-led import-substituting industrialization model in the last two decades, especially since 1991. Characteristically, the stories of this period follow two diametrically opposed narrative modes: one celebratory of the new liberation ("India Unbound," as the title of one book puts it),[1] and the other the mournful, resentful one of loss espoused by various shades of the Left and Right. What is lost in the shrillness of the rhetoric that marks positions on both sides of the political and intellectual divide is the texture of the transformations of everyday life in contemporary India, not all of which can be subsumed within a narrative of doom.

Consider for example the following stark but fairly accurate description of a fragment of life in urban India in the mid-1980s where the author describes attempts to make a long-distance call as involving a wait for "half the day at a crowded telephone exchange for the chance to make an exorbitantly costly, barely audible phone-call" (Greenspan 2004: 4). Those were the days when C. M. Stephen, the communications minister of Prime Minister Indira Gandhi's cabinet, could simply fly into a rage when questioned about the inadequacies of the telephone system in parliament and reply that telephones were "a luxury, not a right" and "anybody who was not satisfied with the telephone system could return his phone" (ibid.)

The story of what were known as "dead" telephones is just one part of the bigger, more excruciating tale, for even in the mid-1990s most middle-class people in cities such as Delhi, Chennai, Mumbai, or Kolkata did not possess telephone connections. The wait for a telephone connection could take years after registering with the state-owned telephone departments. Even something as ordinary as a two-wheeled vehicle, for instance, could involve a long, long wait. As a recent newspaper feature on the fifty-fifth anniversary of India's Independence put it, "to possess a scooter you had to wait months, maybe years" or alternatively, "you had to approach a chief minister for an 'out of turn' allotment." "Perhaps," the report goes on to say, "you could have asked an NRI cousin to apply under a dollar-payment scheme."[2] Such was the case with almost anything from liquefied petroleum gas (LPG) gas connections for domestic fuel, to the availability of kerosene oil, which most households had to use in the absence of the former. Shortages and long queues were part of urban life right up to the mid-1990s.

To take just a few instances listed by the same news feature, in 1991 there were 5.07 million phone lines, while the waiting list ran into 2 million and an out-of-turn allotment required "a certification of a life-threatening disease in the house and a convenient cousin in the communications ministry." The waiting list for LPG connections in 1997 was an unbelievable 1.42 crores and even by April 2000, there were said to be 63 lakh (1 lakh = 100 thousand) people waiting for a connection. Today any of these things can be bought straight off the shelf, and in fact for many urban dwellers without a fixed residential address, the mobile phone has come as a cheap and less cumbersome alternative to a landline. Already by 2001, the number of telephone landlines had gone up to 32.44 million and cellular phones to 51.3 million – registering a sixteenfold increase from a decade earlier. In fact, it has been estimated that by 2003, with the entry of the private sector in telecommunications, "intense competition ... led to some of the most spectacular price cuts in the world, with the Reliance group offering mobile telecom rates ... that are among the cheapest anywhere on the planet" (ibid.: 7). In other words, it is within the space of the last ten to fifteen years that everyday urban life in India has undergone a major transformation. With the easy availability of many of these goods, which have in some sense become essential to urban life, the imaginative horizons of the ordinary urban Indian have expanded and changed beyond recognition. A part of this story, however, goes back to the earlier days of liberalization: to the initial steps in the 1980s.

Unshackling the imagination

The 1980s was the decade of what Peter Manuel (2001) has called "the cassette revolution." It began with the spread of audio cassettes but soon the video revolution caught up. In terms of media forms, this moment of the cassette revolution could be said to be a defining moment insofar as it represents that precise moment when the technologies of cultural production break out of corporate and governmental control. Though the initial entry and circulation of cassettes and cassette players can be traced back to the late 1970s, it was not until 1984–85 that the "real cassette boom" began. For it was around this time that the shift from records to cassettes actually began, according to Anil Chopra, editor of *Playback*. As he put it, it was because "(T)he cost of raw materials [the molded shell of the cassette, the bubs, the rollers] has become dirt cheap – available all over the country" that between 1982 and 1985, record dealers too switched to cassettes "and the *pan-walas* [betel-leaf sellers] started selling them" (ibid.: 62). Through this period such cheap music cassettes could be seen selling on pavements everywhere.

The 1980s is also remembered by economists as the decade of a major break from what economist Raj Krishna had described as the "Hindu rate of growth" of the Indian economy – hovering between 2 and 3 percent annually. The decade saw a dramatic change in industrial growth and, within it, of the consumer durables sector, which has a lot to do with the loosening of imports as well as tie-ups and collaborations of Indian companies with foreign partners. Televisions, audio and video cassette players and recorders, washing machines, automobiles, and such other items of middle-class consumption led the growth of the economy during the decade, this sector itself registering over 14 percent annual gowth. Many left-wing critics of this growth never failed to point out that this was a self-defeating strategy, predicated as it was on a certain pent-up demand among middle-class consumers, which was bound to reach saturation soon. The experience of the subsequent decades was to prove these left-wing critics to be completely off the mark, at least in this respect. What they presumably missed was the fact that among the many bad things that may have come with rampant consumerism, it was the unshackling of imagination and the production of a new economy of desire that would push the growth of the future. What the left-wing critics missed – and continue to miss – is the fact that the new economy was not simply about consumption; it was equally about desire, pleasure, and production at a dispersed and molecular level.

In this context, it is interesting that while, by the mid-1980s, cassettes accounted for about 95 percent of the recorded music market, the share of Hindi film music in the total production dropped despite phenomenal expansion of the market, from 90 percent to less than 40 (ibid.: 63). The effective restructuring of the music market that this indicates gives us some clue to what exactly was happening. The new music production was now addressed to regional and local markets of different languages (so-called "dialects") that have no separate literate traditions but strong oral cultures and a sense of identity. The music produced by the small new cassette-based producers now included folk music, devotional music, and various kinds of locally produced "fusion" and "remix," the last mentioned being a way of bypassing copyright by getting new artistes to sing old popular numbers. The smaller producers themselves were of small means and often produced with very low budgets – new and young artistes performing for free also thus finding arenas of self-expression. So, as Manuel puts it, "the average non-elite Indian is now, as never

New economies of desire | 87

before, offered the voices of his own community as mass-mediated alternatives to His Master's Voice" (ibid.: 64).

It is important to underline what is happening here. At one level, the monopoly of large gramophone companies is breaking and a new pirate economy is rapidly depleting it. This has, of course, been the industry's – and indeed Manuel's – major concern.[3] Manuel notes three pervasive forms that piracy took in its wake. These are bootlegging, that is "marketing of an unauthorized recording" of live performances. The second was dubbing of particular songs requested by individual customers. The third and most prevalent form is the "unauthorized mass duplication and sale of copies" of recordings that already exist (ibid.: 79–81).

For consumers not steeped in the corporate logic of profit, however, there is nothing "immoral" or "unethical" in any of these forms listed by Manuel – they are but different ways of sharing the pleasure of cultural consumption. A new market, new consumers, new producers, and new artistes are making their appearance in this sphere called "the economy." And all of them, we might suggest, have always lived and operated in a shared economy that enters into conflict with corporate industry and the state the moment they enter this realm of the economy (involving profits, taxes, incentives). It is also important to remember that these developments actually become possible because of the new technologies of cheap production and reproduction. Often the mode of production can be as simple as recording programs off the air and circulating them, as the episode below shows.

In May 1988, *India Today*, the popular English news magazine, reported that the "circulation of Hindi movie cassettes has come down by half" because "everyone asks for Pakistani tapes" (that is, tapes of serials telecast by Pakistan TV). Owners running video libraries in Delhi reported high demand for these serials, while those from Bombay claimed that these were "as popular as a new Bachchan film." The phenomenon was not restricted, of course, to the metropolises, for according to the report the demand for these serials was high even in smaller cities such as Lucknow, Jodhpur, Srinagar, and all over Punjab. Punjab, in fact, was said to have "started the craze by video-taping the programs off the air."[4] The unshackling of the imagination was thus also evident in the phenomenon of Indian audiences actively viewing and circulating programs from the television of the "enemy state" – a taboo from the point of view of the state and nationalist elites. Owners of video libraries found these more profitable for another reason: the producers of these programs, unlike those of Hindi films, could not hound them for royalties, being in faraway Pakistan!

What cassette technology made possible was greatly enhanced by the advent of digital technologies and compact disks. Combined with the Internet, they fueled the process of what we might call consumer-production. This transformation of the supposedly passive "consumer" into an active producer could be said to be one of the most significant cultural events of the last two decades. The Internet, of course, is quite different from the other technologies insofar as it relies predominantly on literacy, but even there the logic of dispersal of production through websites, blogs, list-serves, and so on, enable radically different imaginations to proliferate than those purveyed through state and corporate power.

From the mid- to late 1990s there is a veritable explosion of the media. An important component and marker of this new explosion is the entry of cable/satellite television. Making its first appearance in 1991 in some elite areas of Mumbai and Delhi, during the first Gulf War, the various satellite television channels relayed through local cable networks soon spread across the length and breadth of the country.

As Anna Greenspan puts it, "In no time, countless entrepreneurs sensed the opportunity and began an anarchic race to wire their local communities" and even though private non-state broadcasting from within India was illegal, "scores of smalltime cable operators – or cable wallahs – found ways to bypass this obstacle, producing videos in India ... and sending them to other destinations in Asia such as Hong Kong and Singapore, where they could be transmitted by satellite." Greenspan refers to an article in *The Economist* magazine which observed that "the land of the 'license raj' somehow forgot to regulate cable." She also cites a somewhat dramatic observation from Kanwal Rekhi – a top Silicon Valley entrepreneur – to the effect that "the entire process [of setting up cable TV] went under the radar. The government wasn't even watching. By the time they became aware, there were 50 to 60 million subscribers already" (Greenspan 2004: 5).

The point, of course, is that the sudden new transformations produced effects that were entirely unintended and continuously slipped out of the control of the state – even, it should be underlined, the reforming neoliberal state. The state did not see deregulation as desirable across the board. Deregulation for the top end of society was, as we have seen in the previous chapter, accompanied by the continuous fear of unregulated and chaotic production and consumption at the lower end.[5]

Hindi and the media explosion

One significant transformation of the cultural terrain of north India, facilitated by the revolution in the media, has been the breaking free of over a century of attempts to control and police Hindi – the language that nationalists wanted to institute as the national language.

To return to the story on Pakistani serials mentioned above, it is interesting to note an interview with a Doordarshan (state television) official, asked for his opinion on their popularity. Apart from the production quality ("these are perfect TV dramas, well written, with short crisp dialogues and natural acting"), the official specifically mentioned language: the Urdu used by these serials, he said, was "modern," not Persianized, and "the drama was relaxed, urbane, never high-pitched." Doordarshan's own language first started breaking free of the constraints of the state-imposed, Sanskritized and highly synthetic Hindi of its news programmes only after mass-entertainment television serials started in the late 1980s.

It seemed that globalization was indeed responsible for what nationalists of all hues – from the Left to the Right – feared most of all: "cultural pollution." Official Hindi, the sanctity of which had been protected within the heavily guarded precincts of state-controlled institutions, was in imminent danger of losing its purity. Their fears proved to be correct. In the initial stages, Western news channels such as Star, CNN, or BBC and music and entertainment channels such as MTV and V, dominated the scene, but very soon there was an explosion of various regional television channels such as Eenadu (ETV) of Andhra Pradesh and Asianet of Kerala, or Zee television. These channels rapidly took over the entire domain of entertainment in the Indian languages. As these channels moved into twenty-four-hour entertainment and news telecasts, they had to innovate. This was so for at least two reasons. In the first place, it was the sheer volume of content that they had to generate and the rapidity with which the new experiences had to be communicated. Second, many of these channels were now beaming to global audiences – to the diasporic communities in West Asia or other parts of the world.

In the so-called "Hindi region" of northern India, these combined pressures led to the emergence of a strange hybrid of what has been referred to as "Hinglish": Hindi with a liberal mix of English. It is worth remembering that the history of Hindi for over a hundred years has been about keeping it "pure" – excising from it all traces of its co-emergence (and co-habitation) with Urdu from a former common universe. It was one of the axes around which anti-colonial mobilization articulated a nationalist identity that would be woven around the triangle of "Hindi–Hindu–Hindustan," Hindi clearly projected as the language of the Hindus. Hindi thus went through a long process of cleansing where words of Persian and Arabic descent were removed from its vocabulary. Hindi's love affair with Urdu, however, could never be effectively policed and as has been noted by many scholars, it survived in all its splendor in the Hindi (Bombay) film industry. As the shackles over its movement broke, remarks Sudhish Pachauri (2000), a leading intellectual, Hindi became "promiscuous," flaunting its open relationship with its old flame Urdu as well as its new relationship with English.[6]

Navbharat Times, one of the newspapers to have initiated Hinglish in the print medium, recently congratulated itself on its own achievement in a feature appropriately entitled "Language Vahi Jo Public ko Bhaye" ("Language Is Whatever the People Want" – with the words "Language" and "Public" written in Roman script). The feature remarked that "today, in the times of globalization, the young generation is adopting new life-styles and ideas and so the language that society speaks is no longer what it used to be … global trends are becoming a part of daily life and a close relationship between Hindi and English is developing." It goes on to say, "newspapers cannot keep away from this language as they speak directly to the public."[7] One of the reasons for the emergence of the new hybrid may have been the limited linguistic resources of the new upwardly mobile professional, and there might be legitimate reasons to view it with concern. The anxiety it caused among the state and old nationalist elites, however, had more to do with loss of control to the masses.

Desire, sex, and the city

It is interesting that right from the early days of the video cassette revolution, pornographic films became one of the early items of consumption. Prior to this period, it was the morning shows of cinema halls in Delhi and other cities that were reserved for viewing of soft-porn films – usually English films with "sexy" Hindi titles but also often regional films, mainly from the south (Kerala or Tamil Nadu). The audiences for such films usually comprised the male, unorganized sector working-class population in cities. With the advent of the video, at least two major changes took place. Small, informal video parlors sprung up even in relatively far-flung small towns and these would charge some very small amount and often show the latest pornographic films made in the West. Viewers here too were mainly male, but the reach of these parlors far exceeded what was ever possible in formal cinema halls. The second major change was that private collective viewing now became possible and, in some of these, exclusively women viewers participated (Nigam 2006b). This was relatively easy, as both the recorder-cum-player as well as cassettes could be had on rent at very cheap rates.

The real explosion was visible in the cities. As Abhay Dubey notes, the first sex survey on sexual attitudes of educated, urban men was conducted by the soft-porn English magazine *Debonair*, in 1991. This was immediately followed up by a sex survey among women of a similar background, initiated by another glossy magazine called *Savvy*. In the meantime, primarily due to the scare caused by the outbreak of AIDS, relatively open discussions on sex and sexual attitudes became possible and necessary. The sex surveys carried out by *Debonair* and *Savvy* were followed by a series of such surveys (Dubey 2005:

120). Even though these surveys concentrated on relatively "formal" aspects of the sex lives of the respondents and did not really explore new questions of desire, according to Dubey, nonetheless, they were the first indications of the fact that urban Indian men and women were getting ready to talk about sexual matters. Dubey identifies five different and new kinds of spaces that became available during the 1990s, which made possible the veritable explosion of sexual desire. First was the greater spread of the automobile through the late 1980s and 1990s, which constituted a specific kind of mobile but private space of intimacy and bodily contact. The second space was provided by the cellular phone, which along with the third space, that of the audio-visual media and the Internet, made direct communication and expression much easier. The fourth space that opened up was through the mushrooming pubs, discotheques, and multiplexes – all of which become arenas of consumption and unleashing of desire. The fifth space that he identifies is the overarching one of the market and the "consumer revolution" (ibid.: 121). All these factors coupled with the fact that cities such as Delhi have migrant populations, brought about a certain air of freedom from traditional behavior.

Dubey also points out that this period has seen the emergence of a whole range of dating advertisements in mainstream newspapers such as the *Delhi Times* section of the *Times of India*, where the contact addresses are invariably virtual – email addresses. This makes it possible for seekers of friendship and sexual pleasure, of all ages, communities, and all kinds of families, to play out their fantasies (ibid.: 132). Closely allied to these could be said to be the newly sprouted friendship clubs, where new relationships can be struck up. All these avenues, according to him, "pulsate with the desire and possibilities of sexual adventure" and represent the new face of urban India.

The interesting thing is that as it became possible to talk openly about sex and sexuality, it also became possible to question dominant heterosexual attitudes as the norm. Dubey describes Delhi as the "capital of male homosexuals," where after seven o'clock in the evenings, public parks – Nehru Park, Central Park in Connaught Place, and the Jahanpanah Forest of Chiragh Dilli – become the theater of their desires (ibid.: 124).

Feminist rethinking on sexuality

The "second wave" of Indian feminism in the 1980s crested with making visible sexuality in the public arena, in the form of heterosexual violence on women, susceptible to legal remedies of different kinds. Through the 1990s, though, and into the early years of the new century, sexuality began to appear in feminist politics and scholarship in a variety of forms, still concerned with sexual violence, certainly, but increasingly recast as desire going beyond the bounds of heteronormativity.[8] As the opening up of the media in the 1990s made sexuality visible in public spaces, both elite and non-elite, sexually explicit and suggestive images from the West flowed in through private cable television channels, effecting a certain degree of banalization of the hitherto unspeakable. Consequently, a new entrant into the campaign against "obscenity" in the 1990s was the Hindu right wing. Obscenity had been a key issue for Indian feminism of the 1970s and 1980s, involving the targeting of "obscene" films, posters, and advertisements, including actions such as picketing of films and the physical pulling down of offensive hoardings and posters. While feminist interventions of this kind continued, though at a lower ebb, in the 1990s, a different feminist voice began to emerge, challenging both right-wing and feminist demands for censorship.

Primarily, the concern of this new voice is about the troubling continuity in the pro-censorship positions of the Hindu right wing and secular feminists. The former attacks "obscenity" and promiscuous "Western" culture as a threat to traditional "Indian" values, while the feminist argument is as critical of traditional Indian values as it is of sexist representations of women. Nevertheless, if the feminist project is one of "recuperating and theorising desire and pleasure," as Ratna Kapur puts it, then despite ideological divergences, pro-censorship feminists unwittingly participate in the Hindu right-wing policing of sexuality (Kapur 1999: 353). It would make more sense, argues Shohini Ghosh, for feminists to demand "space for greater sexual expression on the part of women. There has to be a conscious attempt to struggle to create space for consensual erotica in which women are willing and active agents" (Ghosh, S. 1999: 255).

The second is the issue of the state. It is argued by many feminists that powers of censorship inevitably empower a state that feminists do not otherwise trust to remain within democratic limits. While the explosion of media in the 1990s led some feminists to lament the retreat of the state which left the media open to corporate owners, for others, this lament is "absurd," for "the history of state-owned media is one of gaps and absences. All India Radio, Films Division and Doordarshan have consistently erased dissent and marginalised any speech or representation that has run counter to immediate state interests" (ibid.: 235).

Increasingly it is being argued that the only defensible feminist position is to ensure the proliferation of feminist discourses about sexual pleasure and desire, while recognizing both that what is "feminist" will itself be the subject of internal contestation, and that there will always be other discourses of sexuality that are not feminist in any sense.

It is not surprising for feminists, then, to recognize that the reconstitution of sexuality as "desire" has not been only a *feminist* project though the 1990s. Scholars of Hindi films have noted the convergence of the "heroine" and "vamp" figures in the 1990s, with the new sexually confident heroine in revealing clothes, who nevertheless retreats behind traditional norms of chastity once Romance has triumphed (Mazumdar, R. 1996, 2002). The popular media, visual and print, both in English and other Indian languages, are full of accounts and images of the sexual revolution that India has supposedly undergone in the last decade of the twentieth century, lifestyle stories about hetero- and homoerotic desire, non-marital live-in relationships, single women and their sexual choices, and so on. Much of this reporting is sensationalist and voyeuristic, not always approving of these trends, and quite often sexist and homophobic. "Never has it been so legitimate (or so compelling) for women to be sexy," writes Shilpa Phadke. But equally crucially, "women are expected to demonstrate their respectability ... [they] have to be both sexually desirable and sexually virtuous" (Phadke 2005: 68).

Thus, simultaneously with proliferating discourses of sexual desire, pleasure, and agency, leading to dramatic changes in public behavior, there have been moves at different levels since the 1990s to control activity identified as "sexual" and "illegitimate." Increasingly, heads of educational institutions have been issuing restrictive dress codes to prevent female students from wearing "revealing clothes." Hindu right-wing groups routinely attack heterosexual couples on Valentine's Day, an occasion that is increasing in popularity even in small towns in India. There are police raids on cyber cafés for pornography-surfing, and drives by police as well as private vigilante groups to "clean up" public parks by arbitrarily rounding up heterosexual couples. Homosexual men and *hijras*[9] are routinely harassed under section 377, a legal provision that criminalizes "sexual acts against the order of nature." Such actions, however, are accompanied by prompt protests from feminist, gay, and human rights activists and those involved in AIDS prevention work.

There is increasingly, then, in feminist politics in India, an appreciation of the uncontainable fluidity of sexuality and desire, and of the complexity of representational practices.

Dalit celebration of consumption

December 23, 2005: a party – a get-together, not a political party – is organized to celebrate capitalism. Capitalism in general, but especially what the organizers called Dalit capitalism. The party is held in a modest apartment in the eastern part of Delhi, on the east bank of the river Yamuna. The organizer and host of the party is a young and charismatic Dalit intellectual and journalist, Chandra Bhan Prasad, who has emerged, within the space of the past few years, as almost a cult figure, known for his extremely provocative and unconventional political positions. The two-page invitation letter for the party begins by recognizing that the idea might appear quite "socially incorrect" as "Dalits and Capital are a contradiction in terms." This is certainly how the Left views it. Even left-wing intellectuals sympathetic to the Dalit cause see the two as antithetical entities. The invitation letter proceeds: "Like a remorseless despot, history mauled and molded us into the grave world of the untouched, unheard and unspoken ... Frozen into the time frame of history ... we now desire to defrost ourselves, and dissolve into the emancipatory world of Capitalism ..." It is interesting to note the intertextuality of the imagery of "dissolving into the emancipatory world of Capitalism" and of "defrosting ourselves" here. For it recalls, in a not-so-hidden way, the well-known passage in the *Communist Manifesto*, where Marx and Engels celebrate the advent of capitalism as the new revolutionary force which builds a world in its own image: "all that is solid melts into air; all that is holy is profaned." A former leftist himself, Prasad is familiar with Marxian texts and draws quite often from them in elaborating his argument (Prasad 2004: 11).[10] Thus the invitation letter continues: "Options are not many. Feudalism ought to be defeated, socialism stands self-defeated; Capitalism, which triggers industrialization and urbanization, remains the hope." Feudalism here stands for everything pre-/non-modern, especially the institution of caste and the "Hindu religion" that sustains it. This is a point again that appears very often in his writings. The letter goes on to say, however, "Indian Capitalism, like Islam, Christianity and Marxism, has got overwhelmingly Indianized." In Prasad's language Indianization means simply one thing: all these great ideologies have become incorporated into or reframed by caste and the manifold ways in which caste hierarchy continues to live in modern Indian society. Capitalism too has become Brahminical in India. Hence his radical solution: "A few Dalits as billionaires, a few hundred as multimillionaires and a few thousand as millionaires would democratize and de-Indianize Capitalism. A few dozen Dalits as market speculators, a few Dalit-owned corporations traded on stock-exchanges, a few Dalits with private Jets, and a few of them with Golf caps, would make democratic Capitalism loveable."[11]

So the brave new world of capitalism's consumption utopia is at hand. The dream-world of the commodity with all its spectacular forms beckons.

Of course, the element of rhetorical excess, deliberately meant to shock, should not be missed here. After all, the party was being held in honor of a gentleman called Dr K. P. Singh – who is hardly the embodiment of the features Prasad describes. Dr K. P. Singh is described in that same invitation letter as somebody born in Aligarh district, who took his Master's degree from Jawaharlal Nehru University in Delhi and a doctorate from the University of Wisconsin and who now teaches at the George Washington University, Seattle. Clearly Singh is an intellectual rather than a capitalist. But

K. P. Singh is one of the important theorists of this new agenda of Dalit capitalism, and the chief organizer of the Dalit International Conference in Vancouver in 2003. This conference was held in the wake of the landmark Bhopal Conference, discussed below, which conferred a much wider legitimacy on Prasad's agenda and gave it an international dimension.

"Dalit capitalism"

So, what *is* the agenda of Dalit capitalism? In a way the genesis of this idea is linked with the emergence of Chandra Bhan Prasad as one of the most significant critical voices within the Dalit movement.

As India entered the phase of neoliberal reforms in 1991, and started dismantling public sector enterprises, the Dalits immediately started losing out. This was largely because, as a consequence of the heroic fight put up by Dr B. R. Ambedkar during the nationalist struggle, in order to ensure what he called "safeguards" for Dalits, a policy of reservations of jobs for Dalits in government institutions had been put in place. With the state in retreat and rapid dismantling of the public sector underway, the first response of the Dalit intelligentsia was to join the left-wing campaign "against globalization." Most Dalit intellectuals shared in some sort of a left-wing, Marxist understanding of the world, even though they are deeply suspicious of the existing communist parties, which they see as blind to the problems of caste oppression. The initial years of the neoliberal regime were thus spent by Dalit intellectuals in mobilizing for "defending the public sector" and "opposing globalization." This was clearly a lost battle from the very beginning, as it is patently clear that nowhere in the world has it been possible to keep up such an extent of governmental intervention in the economy under the new conditions.

This was the context in which Prasad began articulating a different position – and a different vision. His logic was twofold. First, if it is true that Dalits cannot really defend their gains by rolling back the attack on the public sector, then rather than waste their time and energy in doing so, they must stake a similar claim in the private sector. Why must the private capitalist/corporate sector be exempt from its responsibility as equal opportunity employers? Here he turned to the experience of the United States and its diversity program, where even private corporations have to take affirmative action with regard to people of color. As he puts it: "Another pet-theme of Dalit movements is opposing globalization and indulging in US-bashing. To me, globalization is a global phenomenon. Instead of wasting resources, time and talent in trying to stop the unstoppable, Dalits should seek their share in it" (ibid.: xix). From this arose the demand for what is now called "reservations in the private sector" the moral force of which is now largely accepted across the political spectrum. It was in the course of raising this demand, and the massive resistance put up to it by the Indian corporate sector, that the critique of "Indian capitalism" began to be elaborated by Prasad and a now growing community of intellectuals sharing this position. And here comes the second aspect of Prasad's argument. It was not enough for Dalits to be always the proletarians in industries owned by others. They must themselves become owners of property. They must have a share in industry, trade and commerce. "Democratization of capital" was how he put it in one of his newspaper columns (ibid.: 104–6).

It is in pursuit of these aims that Prasad posits, much to the chagrin of many, the United States as the exemplar. There is an air of the utopian in his representation of contemporary American society and he certainly overlooks the long decades of struggle against racism that have made the recognition of diversity a value. The expression "democratization of capital" is borrowed by him from a paper on one of the US government websites (ibid.: 105). His columns therefore continually draw comparisons between the Indian media establishment and the USA, between the Indian and the US academy, between Indian and US corporations. To the dismay of his left-wing sympathizers he deliberately celebrates corporations such as IBM and Microsoft, and welcomes the advent of foreign capital in India. And yet it would be wrong to read this as simple evidence of his perversity. The argument is simple. For Dalits, it is easier to negotiate with foreign capitalists, free as they are from the ideology of caste, which no Indian is capable of being. Prasad sets American corporations and American civil society against their Indian counterparts and underlines the uncomfortable fact that the starkest forms of exclusion and discrimination continue in India – except within the sphere of state institutions where, largely due to Ambedkar's role in constitution-making, some guarantees and safeguards exist. So when he asks: "Could IBM have achieved its preeminent standing in the IT sector by compromising on 'merit' and competitiveness?" he is actually addressing the Indian industrialists who have been opposing the idea of reservations in the private sector by arguing that caste-based reservations compromise on "merit."

Intellectuals such as Anand Teltumbde, among many others, would still argue that globalization is an unmitigated disaster, especially for the Dalits and the poorest, and hence to be resisted in every possible way (Teltumbde n.d.). Others, such as Kancha Ilaiah, initially responded in much the same way. Marking his disagreements with scholars such as Gail Omvedt and V. T. Rajshekhar (editor of the periodical *Dalit Voice*), who emphasize the advantages of globalization for Dalits, Ilaiah had underlined how Dalit potters, toddy tappers, and shrimp cultivators were being displaced from their jobs, leading to slogans such as "down with toothpaste, up with neem-stick" (twigs of the neem tree are traditionally used for cleaning teeth), and "down with Coca Cola, up with coconut water" (Ilaiah 1997). Very soon, however, things started changing and arguments such as that made by Prasad started gaining wider acceptance. Gradually, intellectuals such as Ilaiah, too, started modulating their position. Ilaiah still believes that at the economic level globalization would be disastrous for the Dalits, but now holds that "cultural globalization" is something to be welcomed. "The recent globalization process has re-opened channels of cultural integration of the productive mass culture with the global culture," he argues. Whereas "for a Brahmin scholar, for example, western culture came through the negation of his own inward-looking culture," for Dalit-Bahujans who learn English and adopt Western culture, the abandoning of their "own culture" presents no problem. "When Ambedkar went to New York for education, he did not have to make promises to his parents or relatives, of preserving his food culture like Gandhi did," he adds (Ilaiah 2003). Such shifts in position should be seen as a manifestation of a larger set of processes and rethinking within the movement at large, though Prasad remains, in a crucial sense, its harbinger and its most forthright advocate.

Bhopal Conference

This new vision eventually found its fulfillment in the Bhopal Conference, held in January 2002 (in the city of Bhopal, the capital of the state of Madhya Pradesh). Hosted by the Congress government under the chief ministership of Digvijay Singh, this huge conference was held inside the Vidhan Sabha (state legislative assembly) building and brought together a wide cross-section of Dalit intellectuals and activists. Thus was born one of the most significant programmatic interventions within the Dalit movement in its post-Ambedkar phase. As the *Bhopal Document* – the concept paper of the conference – put it, the effort sought to liberate Dalit imagination from the grip of the "job-reservation" framework that had dominated the movement so far. It explicitly stated that the movement now seeks land redistribution and the democratization of capital.[12] This meant, in practical terms, not simply a demand for "reservations in the private sector" but more importantly, a need to give a push to Dalit businesses. As Prasad himself put it in the course of his speech to the conference, the almost total exclusion of Dalits from various spaces such as the media and the academy underlined the need for the Dalits to have their own newspaper, for example. And this was impossible given the scale of investment and advertisement revenues required, unless the community had its own entrepreneurs.

The fact that the Bhopal Conference was attended by intellectuals and activists from almost all political currents in the Dalit movement and was endorsed by them, gave the new vision and the program spelt out in the *Bhopal Declaration* unprecedented legitimacy. This position in its different variations is now fast becoming the common-sense view among a cross-section of leaders, spokespersons, and intellectuals. One might for instance consider the fact that, in October 2005, leaders of the All India Confederation of SC/ST Organizations and the Dalit Freedom Network, in the persons of Udit Raj, a fiery mass leader in northern India, Joseph De Souza, Indira Athawale, and Kancha Ilaiah himself, deposed before a US Congressional Committee on International Relations (Subcommittee on Global Human Rights), regarding the question of reservations in the private corporate sector.

The news of the depositions came in for sharp criticism from historian and analyst Ramchandra Guha, to which Udit Raj responded in print. The burden of Guha's criticism was that this was an unpatriotic act and that the matter could be taken up in political forums within the country. Raj's rejoinder emphasized that it was never because of the goodwill of the nation or the nationalists that the Dalits received any concessions. They had got a separate electorate thanks to the British Prime Minister Ramsay MacDonald in 1932 (which had to be replaced by reservations due to Gandhi's obduracy). "After millennia" of Hindu upper-caste rule, it was British rule that gave Dalits reservations in politics and government services. In another piece written around the same time, Raj went on to argue, almost in the same language as Prasad's, that thanks to the diversity program followed in the United States, there are now "75 Black CEOs on major US companies" where there was none not very long ago (Raj 2005b). He then goes on: "In the US Billionaire Club, a few Blacks have found a place. Oprah Winfrey became America's first black female billionaire, according to Forbes magazine ... TV programmes show increasing participation of Blacks in sports, music, films etc." Raj rounds off his rejoinder to Guha by asserting that "if anyone is unpatriotic, it is the casteists and the business houses who are resisting reservations, and not the leaders who testified before the US House Committee." Echoing Ilaiah's argument, he added: "People like Guha welcome economic globalization but not cultural globalization, which is essential to having a liberal approach towards Dalit problems" (Raj 2005a).

It will be clear on a close reading of these positions, however, that the dividing line between the "economic" and the "cultural" is actually very thin. For these Dalit intellectuals, what *cultural* globalization is intended to do is to open the way for the entry of Dalits into different sectors of the *economy* and thus lead to the creation of a Dalit bourgeoisie. It is, at one level, a way of staking a claim in capital and other productive resources of the economy; at another level, however, it is a way of moving beyond the "normal" terms in which the Dalit experience is represented.

The only terms in which the upper-caste elite, even of the radical/liberal, secular kind, can deal with the Dalit experience is in terms of pain, oppression, poverty, and violence on the one hand

and anger and resistance, on the other. In sharp contrast to this, we may note the distinctive idiom of carnivalesque celebration and excess developed by the Dalit community's own representatives and by a party such as the BSP. Such a style is indigestible to caste Hindu liberals or radicals. A case in point is the celebration of BSP leader Mayawati's birthday party in 2003 and the way it was covered and commented upon by the media. Mayawati, who was then the chief minister of Uttar Pradesh, also happens to have been the first ever Dalit woman chief minister in India.

"For the oppressed, covered in diamonds – govt plays host at Mayawati birthday bash" ran the headline in a front-page story of a leading English daily in India a couple of years ago (Vajpeyi 2003). It continued: "Uttar Pradesh chief minister Mayawati today celebrated her 48th birthday in style at a grand function on the La Martiniere grounds here ... The Lucknow bash began with Mayawati, dressed in a pink salwar suit, cutting the cake and distributing colour TVs – sponsored by Bharat Petroleum – to women heads of 47 Ambedkar villages." The report did not forget to add that *"she wore a diamond necklace, diamond-studded earrings and bracelets that had diamond coating over gold"* (ibid.). This is just one sample of a large number of such reports that one could find in the media.

The actual logic of this style is, of course, too complicated to explain in any detail here.[13] Suffice it to note that this style is rooted in the rejection of certain kinds of expected modes of doing politics that privilege renunciation and austerity, best symbolized in Gandhian politics. It enunciates a politics of desire and excess that becomes continuous with and finds its apogee in the celebration of capitalism as such.

In conclusion, we may note that there is a certain line of continuity that runs through the emergence of the consumer-producer, the entrepreneur of the kind discussed earlier, the economies that seek to move away from the limited imagination of wage slavery and the new celebrators of Dalit capitalism. The difference, if any, is probably in the fact that the advocates of the latter theorize it in a self-conscious way, while the others, coming from another universe, simply move into this new economy with relatively greater ease.

5 | Old Left, New Left

The "historic blunder"

In May 1996, as the results of the general elections started coming in and it became clear that no party had a majority, something quite unexpected happened. Veteran CPI(M) leader Jyoti Basu, chief minister of West Bengal at that time for an unbroken spell of nineteen years, was called upon by the hastily put together United Front (UF) to head the new government as prime minister. Former Prime Minister V. P. Singh and even some Congress leaders are said to have contacted him directly to take on this responsibility. This development underlined a sea-change in Indian politics as much as it did a change in the way the Left was perceived by the mainstream.

The immediate background of this development was the fact that the right-wing BJP had now emerged as the single largest party and was likely to be called by the president to form a government. Panic gripped the minorities and the secular-liberal forces in the country at the very prospect of a BJP-led government assuming power at the center. After all, less than four years ago this party and its "fraternal organizations" of the Sangh Parivar had, in an act of mass violence, demolished the Babri Masjid in a blatant breach of commitment made before the Supreme Court.[1]

Basu himself was inclined to accept prime ministership despite his age and indifferent health, but the party Polit Bureau and Central Committee rejected the offer. After the first meeting, V. P. Singh and others made yet another plea to the party leadership to reconsider the possibility. Yet again the party refused, by a majority decision, to participate in a government in which it neither had a majority, nor would be strong enough to determine its policies.[2]

This was an unprecedented situation for the Left. Never before, anywhere in the world, had there been such a widespread consensus on inviting a communist leader to take charge of a government.

Basu was actually being called upon to play the Caesarist leader of the UF – balancing between warring factions and social groups that constituted it.[3] Basu was a highly respected leader across the board whose stature rose far above that of a party leader. Additionally, he had been leading a coalition government with many smaller parties in West Bengal, where his party could have formed a government by itself and did not really need their support. In a country where all other coalition experiments had failed, riven with unseemly bickerings, this was an attractive experiment for some architects of the United Front, such as V. P. Singh. It is also of some importance that Basu was an outsider to the politics of the UF; this gave him the additional edge of being non-partisan and hence acceptable to all factions.

The situation was equally unprecedented for the country. While the Hindu Right waited in the wings, imparting a certain urgency to the situation, there was something else that this conjuncture of 1996 announced: the arrival of powerful backward-caste parties as claimants of governmental power at the all-India level.[4] A whole new grammar of politics that had been forged in preceding years was now overwhelming the old Nehruvian, secular-modernist language with which the Left had been familiar and comfortable, and this had simply added to its bewilderment.

In a manner of speaking the Left, especially the CPI(M), completely missed the significance of 1996. It had been presented with an opportunity to set the political agenda for the future as well as an opportunity to acquaint itself with the new forces and the new language that they spoke. The party's leadership seemed completely unaware of the deep transformations that had taken place, fixed, as their gaze still was, entirely on economic and class questions in the old sense. It was almost entirely preoccupied with what it saw as "resisting the onslaught of liberalization" – a fight that it was rapidly losing with every passing day, thanks to its being tied up within the logic of the state and a vision that could only see capitalist development as progress. It was not as though the party wanted to defend and transform the existing state by creating countervailing powers; rather, it was keen to stay out of all practical political interventions and keep for itself a "pure space" from where it could critique the neoliberal economic reforms. The desire for this "pure space," at a time when it was already well on the way to its "historic compromise" with neoliberalism, was probably the most dramatic expression of the schizophrenia that had gripped it in the 1990s.

At the end of 1996, Jyoti Basu reflected on this entire episode in an interview given to M. J. Akbar, editor of *Asian Age*; he dubbed the party's decision a "historic blunder," unleashing a fresh storm in the party. He amplified this theme in his biography, arguing that "in politics there are moments when you have to rise to the occasion and you've got to cater to the need of the hour and the pleas of the people, our infallible judge" (Banerjee, Surabhi 1997).

The metamorphosis

Within less than ten years of the "historic blunder," the policies pursued by the CPI(M)-led Left Front (LF) government in West Bengal were to become virtually indistinguishable from those of other parties committed to the neoliberal agenda. In recent times, the LF government has turned out to be more zealous than many others in dispossessing farmers of their land, and making it available for capital. Even its earlier achievements in the agrarian sphere are now being rapidly reversed, and if one were to go by the reported statements of the West Bengal state secretary for land reforms, the acquisition of around 120,000 acres of land in the past five years has been accompanied by an increase of 2.5 million landless peasants in the state (Banerjee, P. 2006: 4719).

Indexing this metamorphosis are the recent episodes of peasant unrest in the state. The end of 2006 and the beginning of 2007 saw the CPI(M) faced with massive opposition to its acquisition of land for an industrial project for the Tata industrial house in Singur.[5] The struggle of the peasants in Singur was supported by a wide array of forces ranging from various far-left groups (broadly known as Naxalites), to the Trinamool Congress[6] and its right-wing ally the BJP. Medha Patkar of the National Alliance of People's Movements, who has come to symbolize the struggle against mega-development projects, large sections of the intelligentsia, and students in the state, as well as movement groups and intellectuals from other parts of the country, joined in, extending their solidarity with the movement. Even as

Singur was still hanging fire, reports started coming in of a major struggle that erupted in early January 2007 in Nandigram, in East Midnapore district, where the peasants have been in open revolt against a reported move of the government to acquire 14,500 acres of land for a Special Economic Zone (SEZ). As news of a government order regarding the imminent acquisition of land reached the village, angry villagers set up roadblocks, set fire to the local CPI(M) office, and clashed with the police in a series of incidents (Khanna 2007). In what is widely believed to be a premeditated counter-attack, the CPI(M) mobilized its cadre from neighboring areas and unleashed a violent reprisal, leading to over seven people being killed (Jana 2007). This area was on the boil for months and has led to successive rounds of violence and bloodshed, especially on March 14, 2007, when at least fourteen people are said to have been killed as the state police and the local CPI(M) machinery moved in to "reclaim" Nandigram and restore party and government control.[7]

So overwhelming was the response of the non-party Left intelligentsia to the Singur and Nandigram events that when noted Marxist historian and long-time fellow traveler, Sumit Sarkar, wrote an article criticizing the stance of the West Bengal government, Chief Minister Buddhadeb Bhattacharya felt compelled to reply. It is significant that Bhattacharya justified his party's position entirely on the basis of faith in the rationality of History. Thus he claims that "the process of economic development evolves from agriculture to industry" and if we do not move ahead (in accordance with this logic) "there would be the end of history" (Sarkar, S. 2007; Bhattacharya, B. 2007).

In an equally interesting development, in Kerala, where the CPI(M) is currently (early 2007), in power, it stands sharply divided over an Asian Development Bank (ADB) loan to the state government. The loan is part of a composite package for the Kerala Sustainable Development Project that is meant to "strengthen urban infrastructure" under the five municipal corporations of the state. The US $316.1 million loan comes, as is the case with ADB and World Bank loans, with conditionalities. One of its conditions would end free public water supply from street taps on which millions of people survive. The reformist section of the CPI(M), which negotiated the loan, defends the decision on the grounds that local bodies and not individual consumers would pay the cost. This is a disingenuous argument because it conceals the fact that the proposal only shifts the burden indirectly to tax-payers (Rajeev 2006; Biswas, N. 2007). Matters within the state CPI(M) on this and a series of other related issues came to such a pass that the two factions – the orthodox old guard and the "younger" reformist sections – have descended to street battles. This is at one level also a factional power struggle, and the old-guard chief minister who opposed the loan was asked either to fall in line or leave.[8] As matters came to a head on this issue, the powerful West Bengal unit of the party made it clear that it backed the reformist section and put pressure on Chief Minister V. S. Achuthanandan to back down, largely because the West Bengal government had already gone in for ADB loans since 1998 (Roy, B. 2007). In the meanwhile, however, over a hundred organizations came together under the banner of "People's Forum Against ADB" to fight against the loan and the CPI(M) may end up in a difficult position defending itself.

The irony of the situation is that on the one hand there is the increasingly marginalized doctrinaire old guard which still has little to say about real-life problems; on the other is the increasingly dominant reformist group that wants to deal with the present in unconventional ways but has recourse only to one language – the language of capital. In other states where the CPI(M) and the Left have but a marginal presence, their local units continue to participate in popular struggles, but in West Bengal and Kerala, the logic of all these moves is justified by the reformist leadership in the name of "realism." Thus, Buddhadeb Bhattacharya, who is also a politbureau member of the party, justified his deals with various corporations by claiming: "Marxism is a science ... not a dogma. [It] will have to keep pace with changing times" (Nigam 2006a).

The reformist leadership of the Kerala CPI(M) has been involved for some time now in what was hailed in various left-wing circles across the world as a novel experiment in decentralized planning. Known as the People's Plan Campaign, this was part of a longer-term effort to initiate decentralized, village-level planning in the state, undertaken in the 1990s. It involved mapping of resources available at the village level and proceeding upward toward a state-level plan

(Isaac and Franke 2002). The factional struggles between the old guard and the younger reformist leadership started taking more concrete shape around this project. It does seem in retrospect, though, that the reformist section was already preparing for a kind of controlled decentralization that would suit the kind of decentralization that institutions such as the World Bank and ADB were beginning to experiment with in the context of the retreat of the state from certain sectors. Eventually it was that very leadership, represented in the government by the finance minister T. M. Thomas Isaac, and the local administration minister, Paloli Mohammed Kutty, that negotiated the ADB loan.

It is important, however, while registering this drastic metamorphosis of the CPI(M), to keep in mind the fact that not all issues have been fully resolved within the party. It leads, therefore, a profoundly schizophrenic existence, as it is also susceptible at some level to public opinion and to the pressure of mass struggles in different parts of the country where it is not in power. So widely recognized is this schizophrenia that a Hindi columnist recently described it as CPI(M)'s "dialectical marketism" (Kaul 2007).

Greater role in national politics

The episode of the "historic blunder" underlined a certain political relevance that the CPI(M) and the mainstream Left in general had acquired.[9] As the Congress unraveled and the other regional parties as well as the BJP gained at its expense, an entirely new situation emerged where coalitions became the norm – and might remain so for a long time to come. In that context, the relative weight of the mainstream Left has suddenly greatly increased. The irony, of course, is that this greater political role came to it in the period when, according to its own internal documents, it had reached stagnation – if not a crisis.[10] Yet, from another point of view, it was only fitting that the CPI(M) should be available for this new role precisely when its transition from a party of struggle to a party of governance had made it more comfortable with the mainstream and with the language of the state.

It is important, however, to remember that the CPI(M), and the mainstream Left in general, have played an important role in the past and at least some of their legitimacy today comes from that past. The CPI(M) has played an especially important role in terms of organizing and leading militant mass struggles of the industrial working class and the peasantry, which were crucial in placing important questions like land reforms on the agenda of the postcolonial Indian state. The mainstream Left has also played a pioneering role in the devolution of powers at the local level through institutions of local self-governance such as panchayats in the rural areas in Kerala and West Bengal. This part of what was a crucial Gandhian agenda was practically betrayed by all political parties, given the dominance of local landed interests in them at the state levels. It was only in West Bengal and Kerala that this was realized to a significant extent. In Kerala, the mainstream Left's contribution to the "Kerala Model" of development has also been significant. The "Kerala Model" was basically the outcome of a whole range of practices and histories that led to a situation where the state's performance in relation to most social indicators has been very good, combined though it is with very low levels of economic and industrial development and high unemployment. Thus Kerala's performance with regard to literacy, life expectancy, infant mortality birth rates, and such indicators are far ahead of both the national averages for India as well as of other low-income countries, and are comparable with those of first world countries. This impressive performance with regard to social indicators is understood by CPI(M) theoreticians too, as a consequence of a conjunction of factors: a literacy tradition that goes back to early colonial times, the Kerala renaissance of the 1930s and 1940s, land reforms, and social security measures such as pensions for agricultural workers undertaken as a consequence of the impact of Left movement and governments in the state (Isaac and Tharakan 1995: 7, 8).

In West Bengal, however, the panchayats eventually degenerated into instruments of party control over the affairs of the village, with the nexus between the party, the local administration, and the police establishing complete control. The West Bengal experience, where the CPI(M) has ruled for an unbroken spell of three decades, holds the key to an understanding of the logic of the metamorphosis of the party.

Five

West Bengal: from controlled militancy to neoliberalism

The CPI(M)-led Left Front (LF) has been ruling the state of West Bengal for three decades now and has survived major changes in the world at large. In particular, it saw the end of the era of import-substituting industrialization and self-reliance led by the public sector, and the victory of neoliberalism. It is in this period that the Soviet Union collapsed, along with its empire of "actually existing socialism," leaving the Left practically rudderless. For unlike the European or Western communist parties, the parliamentary Left in India seriously believed in the "socialism" of the Soviet Union. The CPI(M) was slightly better off than the other parliamentary communist party, the CPI, in that it had taken pains to establish itself as a communist party independent of both the USSR and China – a relatively rare commodity in the world in those days. Nonetheless, when the USSR collapsed, the CPI(M) too passed through a serious identity crisis. Since all its arguments were drawn from the arsenal of Soviet-style socialism, all that it had to say in terms of domestic economic policies, too, suddenly began to sound hollow. Yet the LF continues in power; more importantly, it continues to be re-elected despite all odds. The recent elections of May 2006 saw it register an impressive victory in the face of a series of direct interventions by the Election Commission, following longstanding allegations of "rigging" by the LF's opponents.

The situation is quite complex and it is important to understand the ways in which the LF, particularly the CPI(M), has reinvented itself in the current scenario if one is to understand its continuing power in a period of general Left decline. At the same time this reinvention might well be the key to its future undoing, even in terms of popular support in the state. In a crucial sense, it is this experience of running the government that structures the CPI(M)'s present politics at the national level. In its earlier stints in power in 1967 and 1969, as the dominant partner in the two short-lived United Front (UF) governments in the state, the CPI(M) had seen its role as one of unleashing popular militancy for the seizure of surplus *benami*[11] land in the countryside and working-class struggles in cities. It did not believe that anything substantial could be achieved within the constraints of the Indian Constitution.

One of the consequences of those struggles was that though they registered impressive immediate victories, they also led to large-scale flight of capital from the state to other regions, leading to rapid de-industrialization of the state. For a state reeling under high unemployment levels, this had far-reaching effects. In the agrarian sphere, most of the land seized during those struggles was taken away once the government fell and president's rule was imposed by the central government, followed by the installation of a Congress regime after large-scale rigging of elections in 1972. That regime ended with the end of the Congress rule in 1977 and the defeat of the Emergency.

The 1977 elections saw the Left Front come to power through a spectacular victory, and it has been in power ever since. What the CPI(M) learned from past experience was that it had to deliver; that it must reign in militant struggles and focus on industrialization and creation of employment. It also realized that militant land struggles of the earlier kind did not enable peasants to retain the seized land beyond the tenure of the government, and it would therefore have to devise different strategies that were legally and constitutionally sustainable. This led to the well-known "Operation Barga" in the early 1980s – the massive exercise of registering sharecroppers so that they could no longer be dispossessed at will. At this time, many in the state CPI(M) did not really believe that they would be allowed to run the government even for one full term, given past history and the low levels of tolerance of the ruling classes. But this time round, the ruling classes too had learned their lesson; they would not topple the government but test them on their very ability to govern. Very soon it became clear that the CPI(M) had to be prepared to govern for a long time and would have to devise strategies that would enable it to show some concrete achievements.

Thus began the CPI(M)'s long journey toward building capitalism and managing a bourgeois economy in the state. Jyoti Basu, who headed the government as chief minister, has always been considered the pragmatist who does not care much about doctrinal niceties and had already made his mark during the UF governments' tenure, as an astute parliamentarian and administrator. Under his leadership, the party began reining in trade union militancy and creating a new work ethic, with varying degrees of success. It was not easy, however, in the first place, to convince industrialists that the communists would really keep their word and provide them with a perfect investment climate – that is, keep their own unions under check. Equally important, every proposal to set up a new industry had to be cleared by the central government and, except for the brief period of 1977–79, when the friendly Janata Party government was in power, the ruling party at the center, namely the Congress, was hostile to it. In fact some of the LF's proposals, such as the one to set up a petrochemical complex in Haldia, were held up for ten years because the center did not clear it (Basu, J. 2002).

There was another obstacle to industrialization. This had to do with what was called the freight equalization policy that equalized the domestic freight rates for iron and steel. This policy had been introduced in 1956 and its revocation "had been one of the longest standing demands from all West Bengal governments whether led by the Congress party or the Left parties" (Pederson 2001: 657) as it robbed the state of its locational advantage of proximity to mineral-rich areas (Basu, J. 2002). For fourteen years the LF had tried various strategies for the industrialization of the state and achieved only marginal success.

The onset of the neoliberal reforms in 1990s radically changed the situation. No longer did states have to wait for the center's clearances and licenses in order to set up industries; they simply had to negotiate directly with any industrialist willing to invest in the state. The freight equalization policy was also revoked in January 1992. Thus, for the CPI(M) in West Bengal, liberalization came as an unexpected savior. The story thereafter is well known. The state leadership got into the act and very rapidly moved toward inviting private capital – both domestic and foreign – to rescue it from stagnation (Pederson 2001: 659; Datta 2005: 459).

Undoubtedly, there were powerful sections and important leaders within the party who were opposed to this strategy, but the state leadership could show that it had continued popular support, that it was continually being returned to power in different levels of elections in the state. West Bengal was the bastion of the party and even those opposed to the state leadership's policies could ill afford to lose it. The fact that the liberalization of the Indian economy began at the very moment of the collapse of "actually existing socialism" also took away the sting from the arguments of the critics within the party: the West Bengal leadership could point to the fate of the command economies of the Soviet world and argue that even China and Vietnam were now having to invite private capital for development.

Over the past decade and a half the LF has gone a long way down this path and with the beginning of the 2000s, under the new chief minister, Buddhadeb Bhattacharya, it stands among the front ranks of those arguing for industrialization at any cost. West Bengal under the LF is as prepared as any other "bourgeois" state government to remove hawkers and settlements of the poor from Kolkata and other cities, or to take over peasants' land for handing over to private corporations.

In a strange way, then, over the last three decades of its rule, the CPI(M) has become indispensable to the bourgeoisie and to West Bengal. Its massive land reforms and rural devolution of power through panchayats have secured for it a base that is likely to remain for some time – though the possibility of its rapid dissipation in the face of the SEZ policy now seems real. This helps it provide social peace and political stability in a way no other state has. On the other hand, in the urban areas, there has been a significant transformation of the way the CPI(M) is perceived. Over time, the LF under the CPI(M) has come to be seen by the bourgeoisie as indispensable because it alone can provide industrial peace. The most significant barometer of this shift in the perceptions of the corporate sector is the change in the attitude of media empires like the *Ananda Bazar Patrika* and the *Telegraph* group – sworn enemies of the Left in the past, now its ardent supporters. Over and above all this is the upwardly mobile middle class of professionals, which has always lamented the decline of the state under the impact of Left politics but sees in Buddhadev Bhattacharya a new messiah.

Equally, West Bengal has become indispensable to the CPI(M), for it is this state that provides the party with most of its members of parliament, giving it the clout that it has lately begun to enjoy at the center. This is the context in which the CPI(M) has developed deep stakes in the neoliberal dispensation.

Five

Emergence of a New Left

From the 1970s onward there have been smaller left-wing groups and parties, especially in western India, which have resisted taking conventional Marxist paths and which anticipate in many ways what we call the New Left. What we refer to as the "New Left" in this chapter is not a separate, organized formation with a distinct ideology or platform. Rather, we use this term as a shorthand for the new left-wing articulations that are taking shape as part of what Marx called the "real movement" – it has no banners, no blueprints, no charismatic populist or demagogic leaders but arises out of the long and sustained struggles in different sectors of Indian society. Gail Omvedt (1993) has already referred to some of these heterodox Marxist groups of western India as an emergent New Left and we broaden the category in the present context to include others which have emerged from within the mainstream Left and the Far Left. Among the groups and movements that Omvedt discusses, we would also consider the Dalit Panther movement (early 1970s), for instance, to be among the precursors of the New Left, given that its explicit inspiration was Marxism/Maoism on the one hand and the Black Panther movement in the USA on the other, which it attempted to blend with Ambedkarism. Also within this category is Sharad Patil and his Satyashodhak Communist Party. Patil, a former leader of the CPI(M) and a *maratha-kunbi* by caste, came out with a two-volume historical reinterpretation of ancient India, titled *Dasa-Sudra Slavery*, in which he argued for a combination of Marxism with the thought of Phule and Amedkar (ibid.: 67).

Another influential group was the "Magowa"[12] group that maintained an openness to "new left thinking" and feminism alongside Maoism, which produced some of the important feminist figures of the autonomous women's movement (ibid.: 76–80). In Hyderabad, the emergence of the Progressive Organization of Women (POW) from within the Naxalite movement at a time when the mainstream communist parties dismissed feminism as a bourgeois trend, was another such tendency.

In the late 1980s and 1990s, however, as parliamentary communist parties gradually became part of the neoliberal machine, there began to emerge the substantial presence of a distinctive politics which seeks to redefine the contours of the Left. In the remaining part of this chapter we explore some of these tendencies.

- The first of these, a range of non-party movements, had been in existence in a significant way from the 1980s and it was from them that some of the most important critiques of the World Bank, the IMF, and the development paradigm emerged in the early 1990s. In this tendency we include critical voices initially articulated within the mainstream Left, but which have broken away.
- The second tendency emerges in the form of the Maoist-inspired "Naxalbari" revolt of 1967 (deriving its name from the Naxalbari area of West Bengal where it began). It steadily grew through the 1990s and emerged to fill up a space vacated by militant oppositional left-wing struggles of earlier decades. There are several Naxalite groups which have attempted, if in limited ways, to grapple with issues that the mainstream Old Left has failed to confront.
- The third trend is the Maoist movement as such, which is more specifically a development of the 2000s. In one sense, Maoists come under the larger Naxalite tendency in India but the recently formed CPI (Maoist) distinguishes itself from other groups by its exclusive reliance on armed struggle.
- A fourth trend is a range of what can be called citizens' initiatives around issues of feminism, caste, communalism, environment, mass displacement, and more recently SEZs and sexuality.
- Finally there are funded non-governmental organizations, also dealing with the issues that engage citizens' initiatives, but because of their dependence on funding agencies, negotiating a fraught relationship with citizens' initiatives which in their self-definition, are more "political."

Non-party movements and heterodox voices

The 1980s was the decade of the emergence of a wide range of movements that have, over the years, changed the terms of political discourse in India by bringing to the fore questions that challenge the very paradigm of development discussed in Chapter 3. Though some movements go back to the early 1970s, like the celebrated Chipko, which began with hill women of the Garhwal hills hugging trees to prevent their felling by contractors, the 1980s registered a qualitatively different situation. Rajni Kothari saw this as the rise of the "non-party political process," which in his view underlined a major crisis of legitimacy of the formal political process (Kothari, R. 1984: 219). We have discussed the Narmada Bachao Andolan at length in Chapter 3, which in many ways marks a turning point in the critique of development and the relationship of local communities to natural resources.[13]

The question of democratic and decentralized development necessarily raised questions about access to and ownership of natural resources by communities that had traditionally had easy access to them. But what began with dissatisfaction over formal institutionalized politics, and the consequent search for more "people-oriented" kinds of political structures and institutions, eventually moved toward a realization that it was not just the authoritarian-bureaucratic nature of development that was problematic. There grew a recognition of the more fundamental problem with the very ideology of development, centrally tied as it was to the idea of the nation-state's sovereignty over its domain. Thus, as another important theorist and activist of the non-party movements, Sanjay Sangvai, puts it, "confronting the state also takes the form of challenging the 'eminent domain' of the state" (Sangvai 2003: 8).

Another current that we place in this tendency is the heterodox Kerala Shastra Sahitya Parishad (KSSP) – the popular science movement affiliated with the CPI(M). This movement was itself quite remarkable and its popularity and influence have been unparalleled in the history of mainstream communist parties anywhere in India. Under the leadership of one of its chief architects, M. P. Parameswaran, the KSSP, along with important figures such as poet Sugatha Kumari, initiated what might have been the first public debate on environmental issues. In 1978–79, when the CPI(M)-led Left Democratic Front was in power in the state, the government initiated a move to dam the Kuntapuzha river, which would have submerged an entire rainforest, the Silent Valley, known for its rare biodiversity. In the course of the debate the KSSP leadership and

Parameswaran were accused of being "imperialist agents," intent on sabotaging the state's development.[14] The environmental awareness generated in this debate came into play along with the idea of decentralization of power and planning in the 1990s in Kerala. Parameswaran himself tried to follow up these experiments with an attempt at theorizing a vision of "ecological Marxism" which he quite unabashedly describes as being synonymous with "Gandhian socialism." Parameswaran was finally expelled from the party in 2004 and could be said to have joined the ranks of those working toward a different kind of leftist vision.

Similarly, the emergence of the Chhattisgarh Mine Shramik Sangh (CMSS) and its subsequent avatar, the Chhattisgarh Mukti Morcha (CMM) in the late 1970s, represented a new kind of social movement unionism. Though its leader Shankar Guha Niyogi is generally presented as a "Naxalite" by both detractors and supporters, his intervention in the field of working-class politics was far more unconventional.[15] He initially joined the CPI-affiliated All India Trade Union Congress and later formed his independent CMSS, which incorporated social reform questions within its activities. From campaigns against liquor to opening educational institutions (primary schools, a training and production workshop for unemployed youth) and hospitals, to fighting against pollution and for the preservation of forests, this was truly a new kind of politics at work (Sail 1998: 19). Also important was the transformation of the leftwing, working-class-based organization (Chattisgarh Mines Shramik Sangh) into a movement articulating the regional aspirations of the Chattisgarhi people. This transformation also reflects a move away from the high ideology of the Marxist Left, displaying greater accommodation toward a more popular and local sentiment.

Shanhar Guha Niyogi was assassinated in the early 1990s by the liquor and land mafia in the area but the movement continues – though it has undergone a split subsequently. It continues to inspire new ways of thinking about the left-wing project.

A significant development in the 1990s has been the striving toward an autonomous workers' movement. There have earlier been efforts, such as the celebrated workers' takeover of the ailing Kamani Tubes, but during the 1990s, voices within important politically allied trade union centers such as the AITUC and the Congress-affiliated INTUC federations have also called for autonomy from parent political parties (Candland n.d.; Mani 1995). More important politically, however, is formation of the New Trade Union Initiative (NTUI), which incorporates a large number of independent unions as well as those politically linked to one or the other of the Naxalite groups. One of the major components of the NTUI is the National Centre for Labour (NCL), an organization of mainly informal-sector workers, formed in 1995, which includes organizations of fish workers, forest workers, and construction workers.

Naxalbari and the Far Left

The history of the Far Left in India goes back to the 1967 revolt in the Naxalbari area of West Bengal by a section of the CPI(M), inspired largely by the romance of the Maoist peasant revolution in China and the anti-authoritarian and anti-bureaucratic appeal of the Cultural Revolution.[16] On the face of it the revolt was a demand for a return to a more orthodox and dogmatic Marxism; yet there were elements in the revolt right from the very beginning that gave an indication of the other possibilities contained in the movement.

The main bulk of the Naxalite rebels comprised youth who had not spent much time in the party and who were therefore not fully normalized into the bureaucratic practices of democratic centralism. Nor was this section of the youth really immersed in the doctrinaire rigidities of Stalinism that had become the structuring feature of the party over the years. Its idealism had not yet been tempered in the bureaucratic ways and cautious pragmatism of the older generation. This factor really constitutes both the strength and the central weakness of the movement. It is primarily because of this that, despite having broken away from the CPI(M) on certain common issues, the majority was not ready to rush headlong into forming yet another party. Many of them believed that while their critique of the CPI(M)'s positions was clear enough, their own stand on crucial issues such as the relationship to democracy and democratic institutions was still far from settled; nor was there any common understanding among them about the character of the Indian ruling classes and state or other such issues. Many of the rebels, therefore, resisted surrendering their autonomy to any arbitrary authority, though many did momentarily fall in line when the formation of the third communist party – the Communist Party of India (Marxist-Leninist) (CPI[ML]) – was announced in May 1969 by some of the venerable leaders of the Naxalbari revolt. This subordination to "revolutionary authority" however, was quite short-lived. Soon the different groups went their different ways.

This first phase of the movement came to an end with the fall of the second UF government and the regime of brutal terror mentioned earlier, installed by the Congress government that succeeded it after a violently rigged election (Banerjee, S. 1984; Dasgupta 1974; Ray 1988).

The second phase of the movement could be said to have begun just when political analysts and observers, including the CPI(M) leadership, had assumed that it was long over (Karat 1985). With the advent of the 1980s, the different groups that had gone into underground existence came out into the open and many of them regrouped into larger formations. There were attempts at forging a larger unity of the Naxalite groups, though very few of them succeeded. What is clear in retrospect is that once the impatient idea of making the 1970s the decade of liberation proved to be illusory, the movement got down to hard and often unspectacular work in the countryside.[17]

Interestingly, as the movement began to find its way on the ground, it also began to shift into fairly unconventional areas, addressing issues that would take the mainstream communist parties decades to reluctantly recognize. In insisting on basing the agrarian revolution on the poorest sections of agricultural laborers and poor peasantry, the Naxalite movement made a fundamental break from the established practice of mainstream communist parties. Even though the CPI(M) theoretically recognized the need to base the agrarian struggle on the poorest sections, the peasant movement and organization it had inherited from the united CPI was heavily biased in favor of the rich and middle peasants. Most of their leaders were from these sections, as was their social base.

At the lowest end of the social order, the deep caste and class divisions in the Indian countryside overlap to a very large degree. The poorest are also largely Dalits and the very backward OBCs (MBCs or Most Backward Castes). Given the sway of notions of ritual purity and pollution, it is often virtually impossible to build a larger unity of the peasantry comprising the rich and middle (upper-caste) peasantry and poor (largely Dalit) landless laborers – even to get them to sit together in a meeting is not possible in most places. Basing a movement on Dalits and MBCs, then, requires that the party should be prepared to forgo the support of the numerically stronger and more powerful peasantry, a sacrifice the mainstream communist parties could not risk, except to some extent in Kerala.

This is really where the Naxalite movement could make an important, if limited, breakthrough. The very formation of one of its major factions, the CPI(ML) Liberation in the Sahar block of Bhojpur region (the main stronghold of the party), goes back to the early 1970s, when the struggling Dalits of the area sought the party out and joined them (Dubey, A. K. 1991: 180–1).

Such moves to base the movement on the poorest sections, however, were not always successful. As Paramjit Singh Judge notes, in Punjab the movement remained a Jat-Sikh-dominated one – that is to say, confined to the middle peasantry (cited in Sethi 2005: 21). A study of a south Bihar village reveals that while Dalits formed the major base of an important organization, the Mazdoor Kisan Sangharsh Samiti (MKSS), affiliated to a major Naxalite faction in the region, its rival and the most extreme of the Naxalite groups, namely the Maoist Communist Centre (MCC), drew its leadership and support base from the powerful Yadav backward castes (Singh, S. 2005: 3170, 71).[18] The recalcitrance of caste in Indian society and the way it manages to structure even radical politics is only beginning to be understood and requires further study.[19]

Since it remained, by and large, a movement without a party, the Naxalite movement was largely geared in this phase to the specific local needs of the region where the particular group in question worked. Further, since the bulk of its cadre was not quite steeped in orthodox communist traditions, there was always enough room within these groups to creatively link their work with the needs of the local situation. While there were pressures to find the right kind of all-India "line," the limitations posed by this search were also recognized. Thus the Liberation group stated in 1988, in an official document: "our persistent effort to direct every struggle against the landlords and towards land seizure often turned into a futile search for big landlords and large-scale concentration of land" (cited in Omvedt 1993: 107).

Such tensions between doctrinal demands and the accommodation of heterodox tendencies could thus be found to exist more easily among the Naxalite party formations, even if, eventually, orthodoxies struck back. Thus, in Kerala, the first stirrings of an emergent New Left were intimated by the formation of a cultural organization, the Janakiya Samskarika Vedi (JSV), in 1977, affiliated to one of the biggest Naxalite groups in the state. An analyst, K. Sreejith, suggests that there was disquiet within the party leadership over the independent profile being acquired by the JSV. There seem to have been some serious "ideological differences" over the fact that some of them "according to their own admission" came to the movement from an "existentialist and anarchist past" (Sreejith 2005: 5336). It seems, however, that many of them carried their "existentialist and anarchist" tendencies with them into the present. As one of the leaders of the JSV put it: "the second phase of the Naxalite movement in Kerala was anything but politics ... [the activists'] thoughts were determined by existentialism and modern literature ... spiritual discontent led them to the streets" (cited in ibid.: 5337). Eventually, the conflict between the party and the cultural front led to the disintegration of the JSV: "those like Civic Chandran, the last secretary of the Vedi [JSV], broke away citing irreconcilable differences with Marxism, to take up social activism of a different kind. The era of social movements had begun in Kerala" (ibid.: 5336).

Maoism – the third phase of Naxalism

In the last few years, Naxalism is back in the news. The second phase from the post-Emergency period onward was one of intense churning and regrouping, a period of reflection on, and redefinition of, their relationship to democracy and democratic institutions. The current phase has been marked by the reassertion of the path of armed struggle and complete rejection of parliamentary participation. This is not an entirely new development; rather this phase represents the culmination of a long period of guerrilla operations that have been carried out separately by three important groups in different parts of the country. When the different groups started redefining their relationship toward democracy and democratic institutions in the late 1970s and early 1980s, one of the factions in the southern state of Andhra Pradesh, led by Kondapalli Sitaramaiah, formed the "CPI(ML) People's War,"[20] which came to be popularly known as the People's War Group (PWG). Through the 1980s, the PWG built legal mass organizations of students, writers, peasants, and other sections but soon moved into almost exclusively underground military operations and built up what turned out to be the most feared and awesome machinery of a guerrilla army. K. Balagopal (2006), who has been a critical fellow traveler of the movement, suggests that it was in the 1990s that the PWG moved away from mass struggles and became exclusively preoccupied with armed struggle.

It is in this period, especially in the 1990s, that the PWG expanded its guerrilla operations in a whole belt extending from Andhra Pradesh to northern Karnataka, eastern Maharashtra, and neighboring parts of Madhya Pradesh and Orissa. It also established relations with some important non-party organizations such as Chhattisgarh Mukti Morcha and Bharat Jan Andolan, set up by B. D. Sharma, a former civil servant who began working with the tribals of that region after he gave up his job.

The PWG managed to draw these movements into its close circle of allies and expanded its influence quite rapidly, despite the fact that it gradually became reduced to a terror machine, often indulging in wanton killings and extortion to finance its activities. It seems that this expansion of its influence became possible largely because it was precisely in the 1990s that the democratic space for raising questions of poverty and exploitation virtually disappeared. This is one of the relatively understudied ironies of the 1990s which have otherwise been described – correctly in our view – as a period of democratic upsurge. But it is precisely in this period that the virtual erasure of issues of the working class or peasantry from the media and public discourse went hand-in-hand with a massive neoliberal ideological attack on trade unions and organizations of the peasantry. The cynicism and ruthlessness with which the non-violent struggles of the displaced people of the Narmada Valley – to take only the most well-known example – were treated by the power bloc (which includes the media and the judiciary, deeply implicated as they are in this new nexus put in place by the neoliberal dispensation), produced the general scenario within which the PWG seemed to many of the poorest to offer an attractive option.

The second crucial aspect of this situation was the complete abdication by the entire mainstream Left of the space of mass struggles and its confinement to the parliamentary arena. While the main preoccupations of the mainstream Left in this period were with defending the public sector and attacking privatization and foreign direct investment – all largely to do with macroeconomic issues – the real issues that were beginning to emerge on the ground were those that related to accelerated dispossession in the countryside. In northern Karnataka, for example, the major issue that gave the PWG popular support was the defense of tribals who were sought to be thrown out of the dense forests that were their habitat, in order to create the Kudremukh National Park. This dispossession also meant denying the tribals their traditional access to minor forest produce and eliminating a whole way of life that lives in symbiosis with the forest. Elsewhere, in parts of Andhra Pradesh, the PWG confronted the imminent displacement of peasants from their land that the government had acquired for private corporations.

In the second half of the 1990s, the PWG and two other groups that relied exclusively on armed struggle, namely the CPI(ML) Party Unity and the Maoist Communist Centre (MCC), both of which functioned in central and south Bihar, came together to form a legal front called the All India People's Resistance Forum (AIPRF). The AIPRF functioned as a legal coordination center as well as a forum for joint activity in the middle-class constituency and effectively laid the ground for the eventual merger of the three groups. The Party Unity and PWG merged in 1998 and functioned with the latter name till 2004, when it merged with the MCC and adopted the name CPI (Maoist). The taking on of the nomenclature of "Maoist" succeeded in laying claim to a shared project with the powerful Maoist insurgency in Nepal, which had by then made Maoism a household name in the region. Further, the merger of three groups that functioned in different parts of the country, coming together under the banner of "Maoism," conjured up for the Indian state a fearsome vision of the "Red Corridor" – a corridor that, it believes, extends from Karnataka, Maharashtra, and Chhattisgarh, connecting through Andhra Pradesh, Orissa, and the contiguous regions of Bihar and Jharkhand, right up to Nepal. The success of this merger and of the semiotics of its naming is apparent from the fact that Maoism is once again seen as a power to reckon with by its enemies, including the government and the media.

Citizens' initiatives and NGOs

Another kind of social and political action that has emerged in the past couple of decades is what we might call citizens' initiatives. These non-funded and non-party forums came into being out of a sense of the inefficacy of mainstream political parties and their lack of concern regarding vital issues of democracy, freedom, and civil rights. Unlike the movements we discussed earlier, which have emerged from popular struggles, "citizens' initiatives" have been more involved in a watchdog kind of activity and are not generally characterized by mass support. While some are small, self-sufficient groups of long standing, others are broad coalitions formed around specific issues, that bring together parties and trade unions of the Far Left, Gandhian, Dalit, and feminist groups, some of which may be funded NGOs, as well as non-affiliated individuals. The distinguishing feature of such coalitions is that all the constituents are subject to the "common minimum program" set collectively by the forum, and separate party/organizational agenda are not meant to influence the activity of the forum. The tension that this sets up between differing imperatives is usually also the reason for the short-lived nature of such forums, which tend to dissipate after a period of intense and often very effective interventions.

Since the late 1980s, non-party movements and citizens' initiatives have grown and functioned in a complicated relationship with NGOs. The apprehension of being driven by funder agendas, becoming depoliticized and being coopted by funding has kept most movements and citizens' initiatives consciously "non-funded." At the same time many NGOs often provide movements with vital support in terms of infrastructure, campaigns, and educational materials. Thus, while the people's movements fight their battles in faraway rural or forest areas, with little access to the media, it is these NGOs that set up and house the various metropolitan "support groups" whose task it is to approach friendly and influential people in the media, bureaucracy, and academia to advocate the cause of the movement concerned. Such NGOs have often also provided critical research inputs on technical details, environmental impact, and other information required to conduct a credible campaign.

A model illustrative of this symbiosis is the non-funded Ekta Parishad (EP) of Madhya Pradesh, which works with peasants and tribals on issues of land and forest resources. The EP managed to work out a delicate balance with some of its activists working on lien from NGOs. This is a model that has been tried by other grassroots-level organizations and movements as well as by citizens' initiatives, in which the platforms continue to function as non-funded and non-party forums, but with critical and vital support from funded NGOs.

The tension, though, is never far from the surface. While in principle the NGOs are in a secondary position in relation to the movement, often they begin to appear as the voice of the movements, thus representing them. For many NGOs this has been the basis of their receiving continued funding.

Among the first citizens' initiatives that came into existence were those around *civil liberties and democratic rights*. Acquiring particular salience in the immediate aftermath of the Emergency, a number of such organizations came into being throughout the country. For instance, the People's Union for Civil Liberties and Democratic Rights (PUCLDR), set up during the Emergency, later split into the Delhi-based People's Union for Democratic Rights (PUDR), with a more leftist perspective on "rights" including economic rights, while the People's Union for Civil Liberties (PUCL) decided to focus on "civil liberties" more narrowly. There was a string of other such formations in the country. In many states such as Andhra Pradesh (the Andhra Pradesh Civil Liberties Committee – APCLC) and West Bengal (Association for the Protection of Democratic Right – APDR), the main initiative for the formation of such civil liberties and democratic rights organizations came from activists linked to the Far Left groups.[21]

Such groups have continued to play an active role in the years since, painstakingly documenting and exposing cases of violations of civil liberties and democratic rights. In recent years they have also been actively campaigning against capital punishment. While the initial impulse for their formation was the violation by the state of citizens' rights to freedom of expression, they have over the last two and a half decades expanded their activities to address violations of freedoms by non-state actors in the context of caste, gender, and sectarian/communal violence. Some of them have also taken up questions of the worst cases of exploitation of labor, which effectively nullify rights and liberties sanctioned by the Constitution to all citizens.

A recent significant battle fought by one such citizens' group – Committee for Fair Trial for S. A. R. Geelani – demonstrates how effective such interventions can be. Syed Abdul Rehman Geelani, a lecturer of Arabic in a Delhi college, was one of the "prime accused" in the attack on parliament on December 13, 2001. Following as it did on 9/11, the incident got inserted into the stridently nationalist discourse that drew nourishment from both the Hindu-Right-dominated NDA government and the rhetoric of George Bush's "war on terrorism." A group of teachers and students of Delhi University kept up a consistent struggle to ensure a fair trial for S. A. R. Geelani in the bleak days of 2002, when one of the worst state-sponsored carnages of post-Independence Indian history was in progress in Gujarat, and Geelani was not only sentenced to death by a POTA (Prevention of Terrorist Activities Act) court but also subjected to a blatant media trial pronouncing him guilty even before the court verdict. Eventually a national-level committee was formed, drawing in respected academics such as Rajni Kothari and writer Arundhati Roy, while lawyers such as Nandita Haksar and others undertook to fight the case on Geelani's behalf. Their patient and unrelenting work was successful in exposing what turned out to be a blatant frame-up. Geelani was acquitted and released. The Geelani case revealed the extent to which democracy can be subverted by the discourse on "national security." It also demonstrated, however, that spaces for democratic intervention are not entirely closed off.

The December 13th attack on parliament has other, darker ramifications, some of which will be discussed in the next chapter.

Another set of citizens' initiatives that came up in the 1990s involves a whole range of *anti-communal* groups in different parts of the country. One of the earliest of these was a forum called the Nagarik Ekta Manch, formed in 1984 in the aftermath of the massacre of Sikhs in Delhi, discussed in the Introduction. This was an initiative where people from different backgrounds and vocations came together to work in the relief camps – collecting and distributing relief materials, helping people file claims, and so on. At about the same time, another group, the Sampradayikta Virodhi Andolan (SVA), was formed in Delhi, focusing primarily on public campaigns, attempting simultaneously to find a different language in which to conduct such campaigns. A wide debate was sparked in secular circles by one of the slogans evolved by the SVA to counter the Hindu right-wing campaign on Ramjanmabhoomi, discussed in Chapter 2. This slogan, in a radical departure from secular strategy, appealed to the religious Hindu – *kan-kan mein vyaape hain Ram/Mat bhadkao danga leke unka naam* (Ram is in every atom/let not His name be used to incite violence).

These could be said to have been precursors to a series of new initiatives in different towns and cities of India that came into being in the 1990s, especially in the wake of the demolition of the Babri Masjid and the communal violence that followed. Perhaps the most significant part of the citizens' actions of the 1990s was that they took up the struggle that was all but abandoned by political parties – whether ruling or opposition, Right or Left. Through this period groups have worked throughout India, engaging in a range of activities – street demonstrations and sit-ins to engage the public in debate and discussion, designing and implementing educational programs, monitoring the media, pursuing cases in court, providing legal and other assistance to the victims of communal violence, and making every effort to see that the guilty officials and political leaders would not escape punishment. Again, in the aftermath of the Gujarat carnage of 2002, during the long months of continued violence, innumerable individuals and newly formed groups from all over India went to Gujarat, helping in running relief camps, coordinating collections and distribution of relief materials, running schools for children of the victims – and, of course, providing the legal support to fight the cases. These efforts might well comprise one of the most glorious chapters of citizens' interventions in post-Independence India.

Urbanism could be said to be one of the fledgling movements in contemporary India. Prior to the 1990s issues of the urban poor (pavement dwellers, hawkers and vendors, rickshaw pullers) were raised by Left political parties, individuals and groups in Mumbai and Kolkata, largely as questions of poverty and the "state's responsibility" to the poor. The old Nehruvian state was also much more responsive to this call of responsibility. It was in the 1990s, with India's rapid global integration, that urban space really began to emerge as an arena of struggle. Alongside the contests over space arose newer concerns regarding urban congestion, pollution and consequent concerns about health. The state's response – prodded by a section of environmentalists and the judiciary – was to revive the old modernist fantasy of the ordered and zoned city. It was around these issues that struggles started seriously erupting in the late 1990s.

In Delhi, Mumbai, Kolkata, and Bangalore, citizens' initiatives brought together questions of environment and workers' rights and linked them up with the larger question of urban planning. Some groups conducted mass campaigns through their constituent political groupings, but the most significant impact they had was in making urban planning a matter of public debate, drawing architects and planners with alternative visions into the debate. The question of a public transport system, road planning, and such other questions came into the ambit of the debate for the first time. In some cities alternative data were generated on the availability and consumption of water, electricity, and other amenities in settlements of the laboring poor as well as the affluent.

Sexuality is another issue that came to the fore in the 1990s. Though different kinds of sexual practices have existed for centuries in India, by the end of this decade there is a self-conscious and public, *political* assertion of what we term counter-heteronormativity

– that is, a range of activities that implicitly or explicitly challenge heteronormativity and the institution of monogamous patriarchal marriage. Such assertions are seen around the demand for the repeal of section 377 of the Indian Penal Code, which penalizes "sexual acts against the order of nature," and various kinds of political action around issues related to the lives and civil liberties of *hijras* (a traditional community of male-to-female transgendered people), *kothis* (a traditional identity assumed by men who perform femininity with male lovers but may also be married to women and have children), gay, lesbian, bisexual, transsexual people, and sex workers.

From the late 1980s, growing awareness about the AIDS epidemic made it increasingly legitimate to talk of sex outside the realms of law, demography, and medicine – and not only as violence against women or in terms of "population control." For example, a highly political, left-wing, non-funded group supporting the rights of homosexuals, which filed a petition against section 377 in 1992, calls itself AIDS Bhedbhav Virodhi Andolan (Movement Against AIDS-based Discrimination), "AIDS" in effect acting as a code for homosexuality. Sex workers' unions such as Durbar Mahila Samanwaya Committee in Kolkata and Sampada Grameen Mahila Parishad (SANGRAM) in Sangli, Maharashtra, both started as funded peer-education programmes distributing condoms as part of an HIV control project. They now simultaneously function like trade unions, protecting their members in various ways, organizing street demonstrations, initiating legal action against police violence, and standing up to local criminals (Misra et al. 2005).

While non-party women's groups had long had discussions on sexuality, including lesbian sexuality and links with international women's groups, AIDS awareness finally helped produce a critical mass of such an understanding in the public realm in India. It provided the opening and the monetary resources for public articulation of issues around sexuality, for workshops and meetings often providing startling new perspectives, bringing together people from all over the country and international participants, and for mobilization of such politics at a country-wide level (Narrain and Bhan 2005; Rege 1997).

Here we see once again the tension between non-funded and funded politics. While AIDS activism as it arose in the United States and other Western countries was an intrinsic part of gay political activism, in India the official discourse of HIV/AIDS control and the funding generated by it is extremely state-centric, and is about new ways of regulating and controlling sexuality and the population as a whole. Its effects, however, are uncontrollable, and spill over into forms of radicalization it could not have predicted nor desired. At the same time AIDS discourse itself, as well as funding imperatives, can also tame radicalism and the focus on AIDS can be narrowly health-related and de-politicized. Sexual identities like *kothi* tend to get reified by NGOs, the continued funding of which depends on the numbers they have "outreach" with, and competition for funding can splinter solidarity.

It is therefore crucial to distinguish between a political practice that is self-consciously counter-hegemonic and the increasingly acceptable discourse about homosexuality produced by NGOs receiving funding for AIDS-related work, which is restricted to AIDS prevention.

And yet, it often happens that counter-hegemonic voices are able to tip the scales within a constellation produced by a range of ideas and circumstances external to themselves. Thus, by 1998, when Deepa Mehta's film *Fire*, depicting a sexual affair between sisters-in-law in a traditional Hindu household, was attacked violently by the Hindu Right, there was a sufficiently self-aware community for the attack to act as a catalyst for public demonstrations in defense of freedom of expression and against homophobia, on the streets of Mumbai and Delhi and some other cities, of a size and visibility unknown before in India (John and Niranjana 1999; Kapur 2000; Patel 2002; Bachman 2002; Ghosh 2003). These demonstrations brought together opponents of the Hindu Right, defenders of freedom of expression, human rights activists, and gay and lesbian activists.

It is significant that counter-heteronormative movements in India should have turned to the women's movement as a natural ally. In the 1980s the initial response of the established leadership of the women's movement was entirely homophobic, and even today the alliance is not an unproblematic one, but internal contestations have been intense. An important landmark is the Conference of Autonomous Women's Movements in Tirupati in 1994, at which an open and often acrimonious discussion on lesbianism took place, with the greatest hostility coming from leftist groups, decrying lesbianism as an elitist deviation from real political issues. A statement on sexuality acknowledging same-sex desire was finally issued at the conference. Since then the conversations have continued, with lesbian women and allies within the women's movement pressing for greater visibility. Openly homophobic arguments are almost never made (publicly) any more within the women's movement. Rather, the objections from the numerically powerful Left-party-linked women's organizations are along the lines that sexuality is less urgent than bigger issues facing the women's movement.

The response of Left parties' women's organizations also varies from region to region of the country. Thus, while in Delhi they have so far successfully kept out banners with the word "lesbian" from March 8 rallies, in Pune (Maharashtra), with a long history of radical caste politics, the contentious issue is not sexuality, but caste. There, the "lesbian" identity is more acceptable than what is seen as the "divisive and retrogressive" identity of caste.

Nevertheless, today it is clear that challenges to heteronormativity are an unshakeable part of the agenda of feminist politics in India, however internally contested it may be.

We have already discussed, in Chapter 1, in the context of the Women's Reservation Bill, some of the implications of the NGO-ization and institutionalization of *feminist politics*. The very character of what is called the "women's movement" has been affected by this development. Although non-funded grassroots political organizations of women, women's wings of political parties, and small autonomous non-funded women's groups continue to be active, many important legal initiatives have been unilaterally undertaken by individual NGOs, often consisting of only one or two feminists and a paid support staff with no political orientation. For instance, the landmark Vishakha judgment of the Supreme Court in 1997, which laid down guidelines for all employers to protect women from sexual harassment at the workplace, came in response to a petition by some NGOs and individuals following the rape of Bhanwari Devi, an employee of a government program in her village. Unlike in the past, when such legal interventions would be preceded by extensive discussions among feminist organizations countrywide, there were no such prior consultations in this instance. The Vishakha judgment has been generally welcomed by the women's movement, but in practice it is revealing problems that might have been foreseen in wider discussions. Similarly, a draft bill to amend the law on sexual violence, which has been submitted to the Law Commission of India, is generating enormous controversy within the movement because of its provision for gender neutrality in the definition of rape. This bill too was drafted by three individuals, and international funders are acknowledged in the document. The NGO-ization of the women's movement in the 1990s thus has the potential to break up the movement into separate groups, each with its own funder-driven agenda (Menon 2004b).

The contemporary *anti-nuclear and peace movement*[22] in India has its roots in the movements against nuclear energy that began in the 1980s in different parts of the country through groups such as Anumukti and Committee for a Sane Nuclear Policy (COSNUP). Such citizens' initiatives were undertaken to highlight issues such as the dangers of radiation to communities located in uranium mining sites, the undemocratic and opaque nature of functioning of India's nuclear establishment, and, as always, the injustice of displacing populations from their homes and occupations in order to set up nuclear energy plants. More importantly, these groups developed a critique of nuclear energy as such, asserting, along with a growing chorus of voices globally, that it was "neither clean nor safe nor cheap."

One of the names that conjures up the most violent aspects of India's "peaceful" nuclear energy program is Jaduguda, where extensive radiation pollution has been documented. The population of Jaduguda comprises very poor tribal people, whose exploitation and neglect is of little interest to the grand narrative of national development.[23] The devastation of Jaduguda is soon to be replicated in the hills of Meghalaya, where the state-owned Uranium Mining Corporation of India has recently received permission to start mining operations. The local population is strongly opposed to the move, backed by their representative body, the Khasi Hills Autonomous District Council. It is, of course, a battle they are unlikely to win.[24]

The stakes were raised immeasurably by India's nuclear blasts in May 1998. Large-scale protests immediately took place all over India, under the banners of various citizens' initiatives forums set up at the time, often encountering violent opposition in the streets from activists of the Hindu Right, then in power at the center. This anti-nuclear-bomb movement built upon the patient prior work of the small anti-nuclear-energy groups, and came to form the present peace movement, drawing into its fold large numbers of independent leftists, pacifists, and people from other movements. This led to the formation in November 2000 of the large all-India Coalition for Nuclear Disarmament and Peace (CNDP), which has also been active in the mobilization against US aggression on Afghanistan and Iraq. The question of nuclear energy has, however, receded in importance with the growing dominance over the movement of the nationalist, pro-industrialization Left.

A recent alarming development on the nuclear energy front is the proposal to build a giant nuclear power station in Haripur in West Bengal. This is a central government project, but is supported by the Left Front government of the state. The ecological and social consequences of building a nuclear plant in the densely populated Gangetic delta region are fearsome to contemplate. The CPI(M)'s enthusiastic support for it has been characterized by anti-nuclear campaigner Praful Bidwai as "mired in naïve, outdated and techno-romantic 'Atoms for Peace' thinking of the 1950s" (Bidwai 2007).

Conclusion

Increasingly, a synergy is developing between a number of these initiatives and movements, with emerging struggles on the ground. Different currents of political action discussed here, around issues such as environment, displacement and SEZs, feminism, sexuality, and the Dalit struggles for dignity, are coming into conversation with each other. This has been greatly aided in recent years with the World Social Forum process, especially in the run-up to the WSF 2004 held in Mumbai, preceded by the Asia Social Forum 2003, in

Hyderabad. This process also opened up greater spaces of dialogue and interaction between these movements and the institutional Left. Disparate groups came together in a spirit of "reflective thinking and debate," helping establish larger connections among movements. New struggles that have emerged almost completely outside the domain of media representation, especially against land acquisitions, have brought the entire question of industrialization and the development paradigm to the center of a ferocious debate between the Old Left imagination and an emerging alternative one. Somewhere in this region lies the striving for a new politics that we refer to as the New Left.

6 | When was the nation?

It should have become evident, by this point in the story, that the "idea of India"[1] has been a deeply contested one from the moment of its emergence in the nineteenth century. This perspective will emerge more starkly as we discuss some of the most outstanding political conflicts in India today, in the early twenty-first century. Sudipta Kaviraj has pointed out how "European models of nation formation," in which cultural unification preceded the coming into being of the nation-state, were understood by Indian nationalist leadership of all shades to be paradigmatic and universal.[2] Consequently, the nationalist myth, whether secular-Nehruvian or Hindutvavaadi, involved the idea of an already existing Indian nation formed over thousands of years, waiting to be emancipated from British rule. In this understanding the Indian nation had been for millennia "an accomplished and irreversible fact" and any voices that questioned this were of necessity "anti-national" (Kaviraj 1994: 330).

There are, however, regions and peoples residing in the territory that came to be called "India," which have histories autonomous of the Indian nation-state, and which had independently negotiated relationships with the British colonial government. One of the significant achievements of the nation-building elite of what subsequently became India was the incorporation into the Indian nation of these peoples and regions, at varying degrees of willingness. The hegemonic drive of the anti-imperialist struggle as well as the coercive power of the Indian state after independence was deployed to enforce the idea of India as a homogeneous nation with a shared culture. Its very diversity was supposedly its strength, the popular nationalist motto being "Unity in Diversity." The idea that all the multiple identities and aspirations in the landmass called India are ultimately merely rivulets flowing into the mainstream of the

Indian nation, however, was never an unchallenged one. The project of nation-building, therefore, sixty years down the line, continues to be a fraught exercise.

In this chapter we will discuss two striking illustrations of this argument: the north-eastern region of India and the state of Kashmir in the north. It would be misleading to assume, however, that these two well-known "trouble spots" on the borders of India are unique instances of the crisis of the nation-state. Before we move on to Kashmir and the north east, then, let us consider some other instances that illustrate the perpetual anxiety generated by the need to preserve a nation – assumed to be simultaneously eternal and perpetually under threat of disintegration.

First, the issue of linguistic reorganization of states, a longstanding commitment of the Congress leadership prior to Independence. It was recognized that the British government's rationale for forming provinces was purely that of a colonial power. The Motilal Nehru Committee Report (1928) therefore held that the "linguistic unity of the area" should govern redistribution of provinces. After Independence, however, the Linguistic Provinces Commission, set up in 1947, rejected the idea, warning that the assertion of linguistic identities could jeopardize the unity of the Indian nation (Arora 1956). The nationalist leadership as a whole was opposed to such states, Krishna Menon, for example, warning that "We will Balkanise India if we further dismember the State instead of creating larger units" (Noorani 2002). The popular mood, however, forced a rethink. The movement for Telugu-speaking Andhra Pradesh which began with Gandhian fasts in 1951 turned to mass violence in 1952, and the state of Andhra Pradesh was formed in 1953. Other movements for language-based states developed, mobilizing all the passion and emotiveness associated with nationalist sentiments. The fear of the nationalist leadership at the center, that linguistic provinces would have a "sub-national bias" that could strain a nation "still in its infancy" (Navlakha 1996: 81) was apparently well founded. Nevertheless the mass base on which these sentiments drew had the backing of regional leaders, and finally the States Reorganization Act of 1956 created language-based states. Since then there have been other new identity-based states created under pressure from mass movements, the latest being Uttaranchal (from UP), Chhattisgarh (from MP) and Jharkhand (from Bihar) in 2000.

Innumerable and continuing disputes over water-sharing between states, which go beyond bickering between state governments and often take a popular form, are another indicator that the idea of India cannot be assumed but must be subject to a "daily plebiscite" (Renan 1996: 53). One instance of this is the Cauvery water dispute between Tamil Nadu and Karnataka, resulting in rioting and violence against Tamilians in Karnataka (1991), and the Karnataka government refusing to abide by the Supreme Court directive in 2002 to release water to Tamil Nadu (Menon, P. 2002). Another dispute, ongoing at the end of 2006, is between Kerala and Tamil Nadu over the Mullaperiyar dam on the Periyar river arising from an agreement between the British government of Madras Presidency (now Tamil Nadu) and the Princely State of Travancore[3] (now part of Kerala). Significantly, the opposition of the Kerala government to Tamil Nadu's rights to Periyar waters is sometimes expressed in the language of independent nation-states – that the colonial government had arm-twisted Travancore into an agreement that was disadvantageous to it, and that Kerala today should consider its own interests first (Special Correspondent 2006a: 1).

The state of Tamil Nadu and its politics offers another fascinating example of the complex relationship to India that most of its constituents have. The anti-Brahmin Dravidian movement that is the overwhelming political force in the state was flamboyantly secessionist up to the 1960s, when the threat of being banned under Nehru's legislation of 1963 made many of the parties modulate their demand. Over the decades, however, the politics of the state has continued to assert Tamil cultural nationalism and to organize militantly against the imposition of Hindi. The politics of a pan-Tamil identity plays out in continuing links with Sri Lanka's Liberation Tigers of Tamil Eelam (LTTE). In 2002, the general secretary of the party, Marumalarchi Dravida Munnetra Kazhagam (MDMK), Vaiko, was arrested under the Prevention of Terrorism Act for a speech the Tamil Nadu government held to be "calculated ... to stimulate secessionist sentiments in Tamils and to enhance the LTTE's support base in Tamil Nadu" (Venkatesan 2004).[4] It is reported that secessionist Tamil nationalist groups with links to LTTE are "mushrooming" in Tamil Nadu, with the aim of an independent Tamil homeland including the Tamil-speaking parts of the southern states of India as well as of Sri Lanka (Iype 2000). Paradoxically, at the same time, Tamil Nadu in many ways by the 1990s seems to have entered the national mainstream. As we saw in the first chapter, the Dravida Munnetra Kazhagam (DMK) and the All India Anna Dravida Munnetra Kazhagam (AIADMK) are now decisive at the center in the era of coalition governments, and as parties representing OBCs in a post-Mandal age, see themselves as participating in a nationwide community of assertive backward castes.[5]

Thus there are several simultaneous levels at which "non-," "sub-," and "cross-" national identities manifest themselves. However, the two most dramatic flashpoints continually interrogating the nation, continue to be the north east and Kashmir.

The "north east"

The term "north east" refers, in independent India, to the eastern Himalaya and Brahmaputra valley of the India–Myanmar border, comprising the seven states of Arunachal Pradesh, Assam, Manipur, Meghalaya, Mizoram, Nagaland, and Tripura, these ethnicity-based states being formed at various points between 1963 and 1987.

There is increasingly a sense among scholars of this region that the term, "north east," is an "illusive construct" (Misra 2000: 1) and falsely homogenizes "a bustling terrain sprouting, proclaiming, underscoring a million heterogeneities" (Hazarika 2000: 34). The term is unavoidable at one level – this roughly triangular piece of land is linked to the rest of India only by a narrow corridor 20 kilometers wide at its slimmest point, referred to as the Chicken's Neck. Other commonalities are also acknowledged, such as that several of these states were once part of the undivided state of Assam, and that they share problems such as communication bottlenecks, drug-trafficking, illegal immigration, and insurgency. Nevertheless, it is misleading to assume a common north-east perspective, because the states have distinct histories and cultural traditions, different relationships with the British colonial government as well as different levels of interaction with mainland India.

When was the nation? | 139

More importantly, we recognize the implication of recent scholarly work that the region cannot be understood solely as the "north east" of India. It is, after all, also the "north west" of South East Asia. Ninety-eight percent of the borders of north-east India are international borders. This region is part of a tropical rainforest that stretches from the foothills of the Himalayas to the tip of the Malaysian peninsula and the mouth of the Mekong river, spanning seven nation-states. In terms of peoples, it is marked by ethnic affinities that cut across national borders and movements of populations across the region irrespective of nation-states, dictated by traditional forms of livelihood and ecological factors. Like other such border regions, this one, too, exemplifies the tensions produced by the idea of bounded nation-states. From the viewpoint of nation-states, cross-border affinities can only be "anti-national" and unregulated movement across borders can only be "illegal immigration." As Walter Fernandes puts it, "the north east" could be understood as a gateway to closer ties with South East Asia and China, but the Indian state "seems to be obsessed with security and treats this diversity as a threat and the region only as a buffer zone against China" (Fernandes 2004: 4610).

At the same time, the logic of the nation-state is overwhelming. In a context of extreme economic and cultural alienation of indigenous or local populations, the "foreigner" issue is also on top of the agenda of many ethnic movements in the north east. In 1983 nearly two thousand immigrant Bengali Muslims were massacred in Nellie (Assam) by Tiwa tribals, both killers and killed being extremely poor and desperate people. The issues raised by the Nellie massacre remain unresolved until today, with roots going back a very long way – starting with colonial conquest; the establishment of individual rights to private property; the consequent dispossession of indigenous people whose control over resources had been governed by the rules of pre-capitalist social formations; large-scale immigration from the rest of the country and from neighboring countries, especially Bangladesh; and the continuation of a colonial attitude toward the north east by the Indian nation-state (Hazarika 2000: 25–48; Baruah 1999: ix–xx).

Insurgency and state repression

The most significant axis of conflict in the region for decades has been that between the Indian state and political movements demanding differing degrees of autonomy, including complete independence. The creation of different ethnicity-based states over the years could be said to have met some of the regional aspirations, but this could not compensate for deep imbalances in economic development and the centralized exploitation of natural resources for a national-level elite. The Assamese elite, for instance, has always resented the meager returns from the center for its oil and gas reserves (Assam contributes about a quarter of the country's total oil production), both in terms of revenue and development of ancillary industries, which are largely located outside the state (Hazarika 1995). The emerging middle-class elite of Assam thus led a movement that addressed economic issues but which embraced also the whole question of identity, culture, and language.

But most movements here are armed struggles for independence from India, which is regarded as an occupying power that moved in after the British left. For example, in 1947 the Kingdom of Manipur had been constituted as an independent constitutional monarchy with a democratically elected assembly, but the king was arrested under instructions from the Indian government and the state forced into a merger with India in 1949. Similarly, the Naga National Council (NNC) as early as 1929 had met the Simon Commission (set up to examine the feasibility of self-government for India), to petition against Indian rule over Nagas once the British pulled out. When a Naga delegation met Mahatma Gandhi in 1947, he supported the Naga right to independence. He said: "I believe you all belong to one country, to India. But if you say that you won't, no one can force you ... I will go to Naga Hills and say that you will shoot me before you shoot a single Naga" (Baruah 2005a). By that time, Gandhi's distrust of the emerging nation-state was already irrelevant to mainstream politics. Under the Hydari Agreement signed between the NNC and the British administration, Nagaland was granted protected status for ten years, after which the Nagas would decide whether they should stay in the Indian Union or not. However, after the British withdrew, independent India proclaimed the Naga territory part of the new republic.

Thus it is important to note that insurgent groups such as ULFA of Assam and NSCN-IM of Nagaland[6] insist that they are not "secessionist" movements, asserting rather that Assam and Nagaland were never part of India. Both of them consider themselves to be independence struggles for self-determination against the occupying army of a colonial force.[7]

One of the crucial measures that enables the Indian state to keep the incendiary situation in the north east under control is the Armed Forces Special Powers Act (AFSPA), passed in 1958. Under this legislation, all security forces are given unrestricted power to carry out their operations, once an area is declared "disturbed." The AFSPA gives the armed forces wide powers to shoot, arrest, and search. It was first applied to the states of Assam and Manipur, and amended in 1972 to extend to all the states in the region, continuing in force until today. The enforcement of the AFSPA during almost five decades in Assam and Manipur, and over three in the rest of the region, has resulted in the widespread practice of arbitrary detention, torture, rape, and looting by security personnel. In effect the entire population of the north east is viewed as "the enemy" in a civil war. This legislation is justified by the Government of India on the grounds that the region is an integral part of the Indian Union, which cannot be permitted to secede. The AFSPA is "an act of legitimizing the involvement of the military in the domestic space," and ironically, represents the Indian 9/11 – it was passed on September 11, 1958 (Akoijam and Tarunkumar 2005: 7).

We will now take a quick look at three of the states in the region, to indicate the complexity of their histories and their relationship to the Indian nation.

Nagaland The oldest armed ethnic movement in India is the Naga struggle, which for almost six decades now has been confronting the might of the Indian state with its demand for a sovereign Nagaland. The Naga National Council announced a "Declaration of Independence" in 1951 and successfully boycotted the 1952 elections. Armed struggle has continued since then. In 1975, by the Shillong Accord, the Naga leadership agreed to renounce violence and work within the Indian Constitution. This was perceived as a betrayal by many, and the National Socialist Council of Nagaland was formed in 1980 to carry on the struggle for independence, splitting in 1988 into two factions. The Isaac-Muivah faction (NSCN-IM) is now the chief militant organization of the Nagas, still has vast influence in Nagaland and Manipur, and is capable of inflicting heavy losses on Indian security forces. It virtually runs a parallel government in some of the remote areas despite the fact that like many other insurgent organizations, it has been proscribed almost since its formation, and has functioned "underground," the ban being lifted only in 2002.

The question of the self-determination of Nagas is a complex one despite a general agreement that there is a "Naga way of life" distinct from that of the Indian mainstream. The Nagas are a conglomerate of close to forty sub-tribes, and the two factions of the NSCN (the other faction being the NSCN-Khaplang) have support bases within specific tribes (Phukon 2006: 158). These are ground realities that will have to be confronted during any peace process. Nevertheless, the very survival of the Naga struggle over this long period has a logic of its own that has produced "a cohesiveness and a sense of unity which very few nationalities of the sub-continent can lay claim to" (Misra 2000: 16). At the end of 2006, the top leadership of NSCN-IM had arrived in New Delhi (from Amsterdam) for the fourth round of talks with the Indian government since 2003. Immediately upon arrival, the general secretary declared that Nagalim would not be part of India (Jha and Bhattacharya 2006, Bhattacharya, R. 2006). The name Nagalim implies not only independence from India but the creation of Greater Nagaland, bringing under Naga control all parts of the north east where Nagas live. The latter is a contentious issue for other ethnic groups in the region, as we will see later in this chapter.

Assam The "Assam Movement" began in 1979 on the "foreigners" issue with the updating of electoral rolls that declared almost 50,000 voters to be "illegal" immigrants. Led by the middle class, it had a wide popular base both rural and urban, and sustained large-scale civil disobedience for several years, including a successful call to boycott the polls of 1983. The Indian state's response was severe repression, and hundreds of Assamese lost their lives to state violence (Misra 2000: 132–3). In 1985 the Assam Accord was signed between the Indian government and the movement, a broad settlement with clauses the wording of which is revealing. There were to be constitutional safeguards to "protect, preserve and promote the cultural, social, linguistic identity and heritage of the Assamese people"; the Indian government committed itself to "the all round economic development of Assam" and promised to establish advanced institutions of learning in science and technology (Baruah 1999: 115–16). The fact that such clauses, which should be the foundation of a healthy federal constitution, had to be negotiated at the end of a protracted struggle, tells us something about the nature of Indian federalism.

On the question of "foreigners," the agreement was that they would be classified into a number of categories based on when they entered India, and either be given citizenship rights, temporarily disenfranchised, or immediately deported. These measures, however, can be implemented only arbitrarily because of the problems with determining year of entry, in the absence of legal documentation even for most bona fide citizens of India. Because of the logic of Partition it is assumed that Hindu immigrants from Bangladesh have a right to live in India, and so the driving out of "foreigners" works in a sweeping anti-Muslim manner, because of the near-impossibility for Bengali-speaking Muslims to establish West Bengali rather than Bangladeshi origins. (Supposed Bangladeshis are periodically "flushed out" from the slums of Delhi in brutal police drives.) The legitimation of the issue has served many political parties very well, especially the BJP. Indeed, the Asom Gana Parishad (AGP), formed after the accord of 1985, which won the state assembly elections held thereafter, has had poll alliances in Assam with the BJP and has been one of the allies of the National Democratic Alliance. In 2006, the secretary of the AGP was one of the five persons who successfully challenged an order of the UPA government, the Foreigners (Tribunals for Assam) Order, in the Supreme Court. The order had placed the onus of proving a person "foreigner" on the complainant. The striking down of this order by the Supreme Court means that the situation reverts to the 1964 Foreigners Tribunal Order, by which the person accused of being a "foreigner" has to prove s/he is not one. As we discussed above, such proof is almost impossible to produce for the majority of even the legal citizens of India, and in effect legitimizes a form of ethnic cleansing.

Over the years, the AGP has lost much of its shine, its government performing poorly and becoming associated with the lavish lifestyles of its leadership, and with charges of corruption and nepotism. The promises made by the central government to Assam were also not kept, and the Assam Accord remained on paper. Assamese aspirations took a more militant turn with the coming to the fore of United Liberation Front of Assam (ULFA), which had been formed at the beginning of the Assam movement, in 1979. It is an armed struggle for an independent sovereign Assam, Swadhin Asom. ULFA gradually distanced itself from the immigration issue, and began to make its appeal to Asombasi – that is, to all people "living in Assam," rather than to "natives of Assam." It puts forward the idea of a federal Assam where different "nationalities" would possess maximum autonomy bordering on self-rule (Misra 2000; Baruah 1999). ULFA claims to represent "not only the Assamese nation but also the entire independent minded struggling peoples, irrespective of different race-tribe-caste-religion and nationality of Assam."[8] ULFA is understood by some to have made a radical shift by the 1990s, from its position in the early 1980s, becoming influenced by Maoism, and attempting to give a leftist direction to Assamese nationalism (Gupta, A. 1990; Mishra 1991).

A new aspect of ULFA's ideology emerged, however, when in July 1992, in a publication addressed to "East Bengal migrants," ULFA identified not only the Indian state, but "Indians" as the real enemy: "East Bengal migrants are to be considered Assamese ... They ... work hard for the betterment of Assam, sacrificing themselves for the future of the State. They are our real well wishers, our friends, better than the Indians earning at the cost of the Assamese people."[9] These views were reiterated in the ULFA journal *Freedom* in December 2006 (Kashyap 2006). This campaign against "Indians" has resulted in a number of targeted killings of poor migrants from Bihar and UP in Assam (for instance, episodes in 2003 and 2007) (Kashyap 2007a). After the most recent killing, the vice-chairman of

ULFA, Pradip Gogoi, in jail for over eight years now, reportedly held New Delhi responsible for stopping peace talks, and "provoking our boys" (Kashyap 2007b).[10]

Through the 1980s ULFA carried out military attacks on the Indian state and was banned by the Indian government in 1990. Since then it has functioned underground, and carries out activities such as bombing of economic targets such as crude oil pipelines and freight trains; carrying out assassinations and guerrilla actions against government security forces. The AFSPA being in force in Assam, the armed forces of the Indian state act with complete impunity against the civilian population. In 2006 talks began between ULFA and the Government of India, but the latter has not addressed ULFA's core demand, the suspension of army operations, while the question of sovereignty for Assam is a distant one (Prabhakara 2006). The talks ended in a stalemate.

The extent to which the idea of Swadhin Asom still captures the imagination of the Assamese people is a matter of sharp debate. Scholars such as Udayon Misra at the end of the 1990s perceived the ranks of ULFA as expanding despite government repression. He felt that ULFA had succeeded in recruiting from all sections of Assamese society, including the tribes traditionally involved with tea plantations, immigrant Muslims, and plains tribals (Misra 2000: 147). In January 2007, however, extensive publicity was given in the media to a statewide poll conducted by an NGO called Assam Public Works, reportedly including family members of ULFA cadre, which claimed that 95 percent of the people polled (24.5 lakhs in nine districts), rejected the ULFA demand for Swadhin Asom (Kashyap 2007c).

Manipur In 1999, the Manipur People's Liberation Front (MPLF) was formed, bringing together the United National Liberation Front (UNLF), the oldest Meitei[11] insurgent group in the state, formed in 1964 with the goal of attaining independence from India; and the People's Liberation Army (PLA), founded in 1978.

The UNLF has training camps in Myanmar and Bangladesh. It is evident that political links between ethnic groups are being strengthened across national borders and that insurgent groups receive aid and training from the governments of Myanmar, Pakistan, and

Bangladesh, just as the Indian government allegedly does the same for insurgent groups from these countries.

Today in Manipur, there are up to thirty-five insurgent groups with various demands – independence, new states within India, greater autonomy, greater rights, territorial integrity, or simply development on their own terms. Some groups are powerful enough to run parallel governments – imposing taxes and running administrative and judicial systems.

A new phase of the unrest in Manipur was inaugurated in 2001 by the extension of the 1997 ceasefire agreement between the Indian government and the NSCN-IM to all the states in which Nagas live. By thus extending the geographical reach of the ceasefire to Manipur, the Indian government in effect recognized Nagalim (Greater Nagaland), which would spell the end of Manipur as a state. There was large-scale protest directed largely at the Indian and Manipuri governments (not at the majority Naga population) which was met by state repression. The movement has now grown into a powerful popular uprising against the AFSPA which shows no signs of waning even in 2006, its sixth year.

Two images of the struggle of Manipuris against the AFSPA:

> *2006* The calm, challenging face of Irom Sharmila, with a feeding tube in her nose – she is under arrest, being force-fed by the Indian state. Sharmila has been on a hunger strike from 2000, for six continuous years, demanding the repeal of the AFSPA. On the expiry of her fifth consecutive one-year sentence for "attempted suicide," she evaded police and flew out to Delhi, staging a *dharna* (sit-in) for several days, before being arrested again.

> *2004* A group of Manipuri mothers, having stripped themselves naked, confronting the armed soldiers at Kangla Fort in the capital Imphal, with a banner – Indian Army, Rape Us. The army had abducted a young activist, Manorama, and her raped and tortured dead body was found some days later. The image of the women's protest was to reverberate across the country, Prime Minister Manmohan Singh appointed a high-level committee to review the provisions of the AFSPA, and in 2006 the Jeevan Reddy Committee recommended that the legislation be scrapped. The deadly AFSPA

however, continues to remain on the statute books of "the world's largest democracy."

Ethnic identity and conflict

The second axis of conflict in the region is along the lines of ethnic identity. According to the 2001 census, about one-quarter of the population of the region is tribal, and in four states (Meghalaya, Mizoram, Nagaland, and Arunachal Pradesh), tribal people are in the majority. We have discussed the term "tribe" earlier.[12] It is a controversial one, because often it has a pejorative connotation of primitivism, head-hunting, and so on. It is also, however, the self-definition of politicized groups in this region, and an indicator of a claim to being indigenous, and therefore must be taken seriously. Levels of land alienation are very high among tribals, due to indebtedness or because it is sold for purposes such as educating children who remain jobless. Conflict over access to resources due to the high dependence on agriculture, high levels of land alienation, and lack of other avenues of work, has increasingly taken the form of ethnic conflict.

It is also important to note that the tension in the area between indigenous and non-indigenous peoples does not necessarily correspond to that between tribal/non-tribal. The non-tribal Assamese of the Brahmaputra Valley and the Meiteis of Manipur also assert their rights as indigenous people, while the Hinduized Assamese, in turn, face opposition from the Bodos, a tribal people from the plains of Assam who claim to be the original inhabitants (Baruah 1989: 2087).

The Manipur insurgency too has turned against "outsiders" – the minority Muslim Meitei, who became, in the 1990s, the target of a wave of progroms. They have in turn received support from Pakistani and Bangladeshi intelligence services in forming fronts such as the Islamic Revolutionary Front or Islamic National Front (Egreteau 2006: 64).

A long history of land acquisition by the Indian state for private tea estates, for the extraction of petroleum, uranium, and natural gas and for defence installations, as well as generally low levels of economic development in the neighboring region, has led to two phenomena: one, very high levels of migration into India's north east from other parts of India and from across the border, particularly from Bangladesh. The immigration is of two kinds, of laborers (Bangladeshi immigrants are largely illegal and mainly laborers), and of educated middle classes, the latter forming powerful immigrant communities in supposed ethnic homelands – for example, Bengalis in Assam. The second phenomenon is the gradual transfer of land from the indigenous people to the wealthier immigrants.

Thus, as mentioned earlier, the claim to indigenous identity has come to play a central role in the politics of this region because of the need to lay claim to local resources. Every successive immigrant group, whether laborers, plantation owners, or north Indian and Bengali middle classes, are inevitably perceived as a threat to the culture, and to the political and economic claims of indigenous people. Different groups assert different dates as cut-offs to establish indigeneity – the British–Burma treaty of 1826; the year of Independence, 1947; or the date of the first census, 1951. Whatever the date for which recognition by the Indian state is sought, those who come afterwards are defined as alien, and ethnic conflict has become endemic here. Many conflicts such as the Naga–Kuki conflict in Nagaland and the Naga–Meitei conflict in Manipur are all about land and exclusive control over depleted resources, as land increasingly becomes the only reliable long-term capital (Fernandes 2006; Oinam and Thangjam 2006: 66).

Similarly, as we have seen above, the claim to a "greater homeland" for the Naga peoples, to bring all Naga-dominated areas in the north east under one administrative mechanism, comes into conflict with other ethnic groups in Assam, Manipur, and Arunachal Pradesh. These resist the "expansionist" politics of NSCN-IM. Until NSCN's demand for Nagalim, it had been the rallying point for other insurgent outfits of the region, but now there are violent clashes between NSCN-IM and its former allies, especially ULFA. On the other hand, the Indian government's decision to recognize Nagalim de facto through the extension of the ceasefire agreement, can only be seen as an attempt to further dissension among ethnic groups in the north east.

In Meghalaya, the politics of Khasi identity emerged during the

Assam Movement. The anti-foreigner thrust of the movement was taken up by the Khasi Students' Union (KSU, formed in 1978), but the focus was also on non-Khasis in general. In the 1980s and 1990s KSU led agitations around the core issue of control of the economy, polity and land by the "natives of Meghalaya," the Khasis. Naturally, this aroused suspicion and fear among other tribes (Jaintyas and Garos) and non-tribal communities living in the state. In 2005, a demand by the Khasi leadership to restructure the Meghalaya Board of School Education (MBOSE), whose head office is located in the Garo Hills, was opposed by Garo organizations. The protests culminated in police firing resulting in the death of nine Garo protestors. The apparently innocuous issue of restructuring the MBOSE is thus revealed to be implicated in the politics of ethnicity – the KSU demand for bifurcation would split control of MBOSE between the Garo and Khasi-dominated parts of Meghalaya. Not surprisingly, the conflict escalated into demands for the bifurcation of Meghalaya – one for the Garos, another for the Khasis and Jaintyas (Talukdar 2005).

One of the demands of KSU is the introduction of the Inner Line Regulation system to Meghalaya, which would restrict entry of "outsiders" into the state.[13] The system currently operates in three states: Arunachal Pradesh, Nagaland, and Mizoram. This demand on the part of KSU is of a piece with the increasingly xenophobic tenor of many groups in the region. The North East Students Organization (NESO), a joint platform of eight powerful student bodies (from all the seven states, including both the KSU and the Garo Students Union from Meghalaya) in 1992 presented the central government with a charter of demands to take strong action against illegal immigrants. The fears expressed are typical of homogenizing nationalisms on the way to becoming nation-states: "the sheer number of illegal immigrants in all the North-Eastern states threatens to undermine our societies – socially, culturally, economically, and above all, politically"; the immigrants marry local Naga girls, and the children of such marriages pose a serious threat to Naga life and culture; Myanmarese ethnic Mizos who enter Mizoram are responsible for "about 80 per cent of the crimes committed in the state."[14] The KSU is actively involved in eviction drives of Bangladeshi nationals and in

2006 NESO demanded the scrapping of the Indo-Nepal Friendship Treaty, which it claimed was a cover for illegal immgration.

At the same time, NESO is active in the campaign against AFSPA, and supports the formation of a north-east trade zone which would facilitate trade between the region and South East Asia, in particular China, Myanmar, and Bangladesh. Thus, it seems the movements in the region are replicating the logic of the nation-state and the notion of the sanctity and integrity of national borders, the very logic against which their struggles began in the first place. As Bimol Akoijam puts it, "the region called the North East of the postcolonial Indian state ... is a theatre" in which the actors can only "make sense of each other in terms of an intelligible shared world of colonial modernity" (Akoijam 2006: 117), that is, the world of clearly bounded, homogeneous nation-states.

In this context, even an ecologically sensitive political imagination can coexist with ethnic jingoism. Sanjay Barbora discusses the "crusading ecomilitancy" of an armed ethnic militia of the Karbi tribe which issued a two-year ban on felling of bamboo and the use of pesticides in the Karbi Anglong area. Yet this group has been allegedly behind violence between Karbi and Kuki farmers. Barbora sees this as the outcome of a dual process of impoverishment and militarization, where small communities have to arm themselves to prevent a complete assimilation of lifestyles, culture, and resources (Barbora 2006: 3808).

"Conflict management" in the north east

Apart from military repression and playing off different militant groups against one another, the Indian state has also been pumping disproportionately large sums of money into "surrender schemes," which are meant to bribe militants away from violence. This is not accompanied by any infrastructure development or long-term planning. These funds therefore feed into a flourishing underground economy created by decades of armed conflict and militarization, involving smuggling, extortion, counterfeit currency, drug-trafficking, and arms-dealing – a whirlpool into which everyday life in the region tends to get sucked.

The "management" of conflict in the north east has meant increasingly, argues Sanjay Barbora, policy interventions on the guidance of international funding agencies such as the International Fund for Agricultural Development. The new transformative concept promoted by transnational donor agencies is "ethnodevelopment," supposedly a model that addresses the specificities of ethnic cultures and encourages them to join the global market. In this region, ending the practice of *jhoom* cultivation is one of the goals. This means the ending of community ownership of *jhoom* land, understood by bureaucrats to be incompatible with any form of rational agriculture, and the institution of individual property rights. The outcome is bound to be greater inequality between people of even one ethnic community, apart from accentuating inequality between less and more numerous or powerful groups (Barbora 2002).

Similarly, experiments in coffee, tea, and rubber cultivation were initiated in the 1980s by the Indian government, which consolidated lands for plantations by getting villagers to pool in common land, which was then placed under the supervision of a manager, usually a non-tribal. In the late 1990s when the prices of coffee fell in the global market, the government bodies withdrew, leaving "ghost plantations" dotting the hills (ibid.).

The striking features of politics in the region, then, are continuing insurgency, extreme state repression, and consequent overall militarization, the bureaucratized micromanagement of the economy under the tutelage of international funders and the limitations of what Sanjib Baruah calls the "homelandist" imagination (Baruah 2005b).

Baruah makes an argument for an "alternative institutional imagination" to end the "durable disorder" of the north east. This alternative imagination would disentangle identity from a territorially and ethnically rooted collectivity. He urges that the ethnic homelands of the region be dismantled by giving citizenship rights to the large numbers of "illegal" immigrants, and, more importantly, that the north east develop its relationship with its eastern neighbors (ibid.). Currently such an alternative imagination is certainly not the dominant vision visible on the horizon, either of the Indian state or of the insurgent movements.

Jammu and Kashmir

Insurgency in Kashmir, as with many states of the north east, cannot be understood without going back to the question of accession to India in 1947. Jammu and Kashmir (J&K) is the only Muslim-majority state in India, being roughly half of the territory called Jammu and Kashmir before 1947. About a third of the pre-1947 J&K is under Pakistani administration; an area called, respectively by the Indian and Pakistani governments, Pakistan-Occupied Kashmir (POK) and Azad Kashmir (Free Kashmir). The remaining part is controlled by China – Aksai Chin and the Trans-Karakoram Tract (Shaksam Valley), which was ceded by Pakistan in 1963.

J&K has three regions with specific profiles in terms of religious identity – Kashmir Valley is predominantly Muslim, Jammu predominantly Hindu, and Ladakh largely Buddhist. This particular demographic feature of J&K is also increasingly becoming relevant to understanding its politics.

In August 1947, under the Indian Independence Act, the 600-odd princely states had three options: accession to India or Pakistan, or independence. Most acceded to India, but those that did not were annexed, as we saw earlier with Manipur. In the context of Kashmir, a Muslim-majority state with a Hindu ruler, it is instructive to consider the case of another princely state, Junagadh, a Hindu-majority state with a Muslim ruler, who decided to accede to Pakistan. On the grounds that a Hindu-majority state could not be part of Islamic Pakistan, however, the Indian government annexed Junagadh, and in December 1947, it held a plebiscite in which, predictably, the Hindu-majority population overwhelmingly voted to be part of India. The question of a plebiscite thus hung over Kashmir too, but India never considered one at this stage.

The ruler of Kashmir Hari Singh had ambitions of Kashmir being an independent state, and in this was backed by the largest political party in the state, National Conference (NC) led by Sheikh Abdullah. He had therefore not taken a decision on accession until August 1947. In September, however, Pakistan permitted incursions into Kashmir by tribesmen from the north-west frontier, soon afterwards backing them with regular forces. Hari Singh had to turn to India for assistance, which was given on the condition that he sign the

Instrument of Accession. Thus began the first war between India and Pakistan, which ended with a ceasefire in 1949, outlining what has come to be called the Line of Control (LoC), the de facto border between the two countries.

Two more wars were fought between India and Pakistan – in 1965 over J&K, and in 1971, when India militarily backed the formation of independent Bangladesh. The Simla Agreement that ended the 1971 war defined the LoC in Kashmir and committed both sides to future bilateral negotiations. At this point India took the position that the question of plebiscite was no longer valid, while Pakistan still formally insists on a plebiscite, as do some militant groups in Kashmir.

If we are interested in understanding Kashmir, however, we must go beyond treating it as merely a "territorial dispute" between two nation-states as they race for greater control in the subcontinent. What do Kashmiris want? And is it possible to arrive at any reliable answer, given the extremely vitiated circumstances in that troubled state?

The run-up to the 1990s The Instrument of Accession gave J&K special status. It has its own constitution, and its legislature must adopt laws passed by the Indian parliament for them to become applicable in the state. It was also guaranteed autonomy in all affairs except for foreign policy, defense, and communications. This autonomy, however, has remained on paper, and its special status has been gradually eroded by the Indian state through constitutional amendments.

By 1964, constitutional amendments were passed that brought J&K under the strongly unitary umbrella of Indian federalism, rendering void almost all the provisions of Article 370, which gave the state a large degree of autonomy. One of these amendments ensured that the governor of the state, hitherto elected by the state assembly, was now to be nominated by the center. While the governor is in principle under the control of the democratically elected assembly, the extension of specific articles of the Indian Constitution to J&K meant that as with other states of the Indian Union, the central government could dismiss the state government, impose President's Rule and run the state through the governor whenever necessary.

It is important to remember that the accession to India was conditional, subject to "a reference to the people" as soon as the invaders had been removed. According to Balraj Puri, this condition was necessary to overcome Hari Singh's reluctance to accede to India, and moreover, it was this principle of "the people's will" that enabled India to annex two other states, Junagadh, which we have discussed, and Hyderabad (Puri 1993: 14–15). In other words, the accession itself was conditional on the holding of a referendum. By 1957, however, the Indian government took the position that since the Instrument of Accession had been ratified by the state's constituent assembly and by two consecutive legislative assemblies, the required "reference to the people" had been conducted and J&K was now an integral part of India. This "ratification," however, must be seen in the light of the fact that in the two elections to the state assembly that took place during this period, parties supporting plebiscite were not allowed to participate, and it is generally accepted that there was large-scale rigging by forces propped up by the Indian government, to ensure a pliable legislature (ibid.: 45; Behera 2000: 114; Joshi 2002).

The logic of the nation-state operated in the realm of the economy as well, a feature we have discussed with reference to other aspects of Indian politics – in the north east and with big dams, for instance. J&K's rich natural resources in forests and water have served to develop Indian capitalism. Extensive deforestation served to provide cheap timber for the Indian railways, while Kashmir's water resources are fully under the control of the center. All the key power projects in the state were taken over by the National Hydel Power Corporation, so that while Srinagar would be without power three days in the week, power from the state was being provided to the northern grid of India, Delhi being the largest consumer. Investment by Delhi in the state has basically been in two fields – roads/communication and power generation/transmission – the better to ensure commercial exploitation and military control. There has been virtually no investment in the field of industry (DN 1991).

Through the 1950s and 1960s, the Indian state clamped down on all forms of democratic protest in the state, treating demands for genuine autonomy as secessionist, jailing Sheikh Abdullah in 1953, as well as many other leaders.

The political movement for plebiscite and for the release of Sheikh Abdullah continued unabated until, in 1974, the Kashmir Accord was signed between the NC and the Indian government. While it offered much less autonomy than the state enjoyed prior to the developments described above, it was nevertheless welcomed, especially as Sheikh Abdullah was released and he returned as chief minister. The revived National Conference won sweeping victories in the assembly elections of 1977 and 1983 (under Sheikh Abdullah's son Farooq), generally accepted as the fairest ever held in Kashmir. For a decade after the Kashmir Accord, groups that stood for *azadi* (freedom for Kashmir) and pro-Pakistan voices were marginalized.

The 1983 general elections, however, were marked by the general trend toward communalization becoming evident in India at that time. The Congress campaign in J&K overtly appealed to Hindu sentiments in order to marginalize the growing challenge offered by the Hindu Right, while Farooq Abdullah's victory in J&K had been crafted in an alliance with an Islamist party, Awami Action Committee. Although the agenda of the alliance was not Islamist but the "preservation of Kashmiri identity," Farooq Abdullah posed a challenge to the Congress because he presented the elections as a referendum on who should rule Kashmir – New Delhi or its own people (Behera 2000: 150). Soon afterwards, the NC hosted a conclave of opposition parties. Such insubordination was not to be tolerated, and in 1984 the Congress Party in power at the center dismissed Farooq Abdullah's government. The successor government, too, was dismissed in 1986, and President's Rule imposed on the state. By the time of the 1987 elections, Farooq Abdullah, having learned his lesson, entered into an electoral alliance with the Congress. The 1987 elections are a landmark in the history of J&K, and signal the beginning of a period of renewed insurgency and state repression that cannot be said to have ended even today.

Abdullah's compromise with the Congress Party was seen as a betrayal by Kashmiri voters, already disillusioned by the corruption and incompetence that marked his previous regime. There was growing support for a new party, the Muslim United Front (MUF), a coalition of Islamic and pro-*azadi* parties. The NC-Congress alliance, however, came to power through a process marked by mass arrests of MUF candidates and party workers, and vote-rigging on a massive scale. Electoral politics in Kashmir was revealed to be a sham, and as democratic forms of protest became impossible, thousands of young men crossed the border to Pakistan, received training and arms, and returned to inaugurate a new phase of large-scale violence.

Militancy in the 1990s and beyond From 1987 to 1990 the Farooq Abdullah government faced growing economic crisis and an overall failure of legitimacy. There was increasing opposition to his government not only from militants, but from the people of Kashmir, which was met with extreme police repression. The center appointed Jagmohan as governor and Abdullah resigned in protest, as Jagmohan had been involved in the earlier dismissal of his government. The state came under President's Rule again.

Navnita Chadha Behera outlines five phases of the insurgency from 1988 to about 1996 (ibid.). The first phase (1988–90) involved the underground militant movement which evolved into a mass political movement. The Jammu and Kashmir Liberation Front (JKLF)[15] with its agenda of an independent Kashmir, set up a unit in J&K in 1988. It successfully mobilized violent protests around issues that ranged from hikes in power tariffs to Salman Rushdie's *Satanic Verses*, protests that could paralyze the state apparatus and which widely delegitimized political institutions. Assassinations, attacks on police stations and officials, and attacks on NC members (seen as a pro-India force in the valley) were routine.[16] The 1989 elections were boycotted. The daughter of the union home minister, Mufti Mohammed Sayeed, was kidnapped, and the release of five JKLF militants demanded. The government met the demand, and the returning militants were met with an explosion of joy in the valley, the jubilant crowds certain that *azadi* was round the corner.

Governor Jagmohan's policy was to crush the movement with armed force. "The bullet is the only solution for Kashmiris," he said in an interview. He started his first day in office with thirty-five dead in police firings and over 400 arrested (ibid.: 169, 206). The infamous Gawkadal incident, in which large numbers of unarmed civilians were killed by security forces, transformed the underground militant campaign into a mass movement. There was a near-total uprising of the entire population. Tens of thousands, including children, marched daily on the streets to the cry of *azadi* – many of them government employees, often marching behind the banners of their departments. Shoot-at-sight orders and long spells of curfew, often lasting for weeks, became the order of the day (Puri 1993: 61). Refusing to recognize the mass character of the uprising, the Indian government termed it Pakistan's "proxy war," thus justifying the draconian measures it used to quell the rebellion.

The JKLF, at the forefront of the movement in this phase, represents a secular vision of Kashmiri nationalism which foregrounds *kashmiriyat* or Kashmiri-ness. Its aim is to liberate and reunify the state of J&K as it existed prior to Indian and Pakistani Independence.[17]

The second phase (1991–92) saw the JKLF losing its leadership role, partly because much of its leadership was killed or imprisoned by the Indian state, and partly because Pakistan began to withdraw support to it because of its agenda of independence. Instead, pro-Pakistan and Islamist groups were raised, the most prominent being Hizbul Mujahideen (HM), its political patron being Jamaat-i-Islami. HM, backed by Pakistan, attacked and depleted JKLF cadres and the uncomfortable alliance between JKLF and Pakistan fell apart. HM's women's front in Kashmir Valley, Dukhtaraan-e-Millat, publicly supported the ultimatum that Muslim women should wear a burqa,[18] issued by another such group Lashkar-e-Jabbar in 2000. HM's strict adherence to Islamic ideology, however, is not popular in the valley, where Sufi traditions are prevalent. In fact this Muslim-majority state has among the lowest enrollment figures in the country for madrasas, where traditional Islamic teaching is imparted (Rashid 2006).

From the early 1990s there has been a virtual exodus of Kashmiri Hindus (called Pandits) from the valley. While this is attributed by many to the questionable role of Governor Jagmohan, who encouraged their departure in order to sharpen the sense of crisis in Kashmir, there is no doubt that HM and other organizations are also responsible for creating an atmosphere of terror for the Hindu minority. Targeted killing of Hindus has been common since the 1990s. The BJP has contributed to this agenda of communal polarization by systematically sabotaging attempts at joint community initiatives to counter HM and, instead, creating armed "village defence committees" in Hindu-dominated areas.

The third phase began in 1993 with the siege by Indian security forces of Hazratbal mosque and the surrender of militants. It is around this time that the conflict in Kashmir begins to get inserted into the larger politics of global Islam. New connections begin to be made. Pakistan, too, presumably saw an opportunity here to encourage Afghan and other foreign mercenaries of global Islam to enter the scene. This changed the character of militancy in the valley. *Kashmiriyat* was relegated to the background and the struggle in Kashmir became just one part of a global Islamic movement. Among the prominent groups of this sort is Harkat-ul-Ansar, an international network of Muslims, whose members are committed Islamic militants.

The growing disillusionment of the people with these transformations of the militant movement led to the fourth phase (1994–95), in which there was growing opposition from the people to the Islamization of the movement and determined efforts to regain Kashmiri control. There were incidents of massive public reactions against HM's criminalization of Kashmiri politics and its attempts to suppress ancient Kashmiri practices and festivals (Behera 2000: 188, 191). For their part, Kashmiri militant groups made an attempt to regroup. The All Party Hurriyat Conference (APHC), comprising about thirty political groups, was formed. Led by the Mirwaiz,[19] whose father had been assassinated by HM, the Hurriyat has an Islamic orientation, and its constituents' demands ranged from independence to union with Pakistan. Like the JKLF, it rules out a settlement within the framework of the Indian Constitution, is for plebiscite, and its constitution is committed to a peaceful struggle for self-determination.

The Hurriyat split in 2003 into what in India is called the "moderate" faction under the Mirwaiz, which has links with JKLF, and the more "hardline" pro-Pakistan faction led by S. A. S. Geelani.

In 1994, the JKLF leader Yasin Malik was released, and he announced that JKLF would renounce violence and henceforth adopt Gandhian means. He announced a unilateral ceasefire and his preparedness to hold talks with the Indian government. Malik also declared Kashmiri Hindus to be an integral part of Kashmir, and urged them to return (Sharma 2004).[20]

India and Pakistan in Kashmir By 1995–96 the Kashmiri component of the movement was in decline, and the Indian government was successful in initiating counter-insurgency through surrendered militants as it has in the north east. From 1990 there have been laws in place – the Armed Forces (Jammu and Kashmir) Special Powers Act and the Jammu and Kashmir Disturbed Areas Act – that give armed forces and security agencies unlimited powers of detention and interrogation. Human rights violations on a massive scale have been extensively documented – summary executions, custodial killings, torture, "disappearances," arbitrary detentions, regular warrantless searches usually in the middle of the night, attacks on civilians as retaliation for militant attacks, indiscriminate firing on unarmed demonstrations.[21]

Meanwhile, foreign mercenaries operate openly out of Pakistan, seldom claiming responsibility for attacks and kidnappings, many of which have been on civilians, often foreigners. It is common for them to change their names periodically, particularly after they are banned (Human Rights Watch 2006: 23–4).

In 1999, in the escalation of tensions following India's nuclear explosion in 1998, Pakistani troops and militants occupied parts of Kargil in J&K. The Indian state responded with force, and the Clinton administration stepped in to defuse the situation, getting Pakistan to withdraw. Later that year, militants hijacked an Indian flight to Afghanistan and secured the release of three Pakistani militants. Since September 11, 2001, Pakistan has been successfully pressurized by the USA to withdraw support to militancy in Kashmir and, according to Indian sources, there is a trend of decreasing infiltration over the years since then.

The 2002 elections In 2002, elections to the J&K state assembly were held, whose conduct was perhaps the fairest in its history, partly because they were held in full international and national glare, with observers from the European Union as well as scores of citizens' groups from the rest of India, monitoring them. Since Kashmiri nationalists and separatist groups refused to participate in elections under Indian supervision, however, the extent to which the current government, a coalition led by Mufti Mohammed Sayeed of the People's Democratic Party, represents the will of the people is in question. The voter turnout was only 48 percent (the national average is about 65 percent), but Praful Bidwai suggests that the picture is more complex than the rival claims made by India and Pakistan. The NDA government's claim was that that the successfully conducted elections were a victory for India's refusal to talk to hardliners, while Pakistan dismissed the elections as a farce. Bidwai argues against the Pakistani view by pointing out the high level of interest in the elections, with crowds of thousands turning out for campaign meetings. It is also significant that the voter turnout was as high as 77 percent in the overwhelmingly Muslim-majority districts near the LoC. The number of candidates filing nominations rose by 30 percent from 1996, and a host of small parties, focusing on local issues, participated. In response to hawkish pronouncements from India that these elections showed there was no longer any need for dialogue with Pakistan on Kashmir, however, Bidwai points out that contesting these elections cannot be seen as supporting New Delhi's policies because many candidates stood on a platform of *azadi*. But more importantly, he cites a report of the Coalition of Civil Society, a group of NGOs that monitored the elections, which asserts there was widespread coercion by security forces to ensure voting, although not to vote for a particular party.

Based on observers' reports and informal interviews, Bidwai concludes that while the elections were not seen by the Kashmiri people as a referendum on the Indian government's policies, Kashmiris are exhausted by the spiral of violence produced by externally sponsored militants and the Indian state. Many believed that a new J&K government could protect them from growing confrontation between these, while addressing everyday grievances about water, roads, and jobs. In addition, Farooq Abdullah's NC had lost all credibility, being widely seen as corrupt, unresponsive to people's basic needs, and opportunist in allying with the BJP. Many may have voted just to remove the NC from power. Says Bidwai, "Islamabad is thus wrong to dismiss the elections. And New Delhi is equally mistaken to see them as a *substitute* for a genuine broad-based dialogue both within India and with Pakistan" (Bidwai 2002).

In 2003 India and Pakistan announced a ceasefire at the LoC, ending almost a decade of continuous exchange of fire. The previous PM of India began talks with general Musharraf of Pakistan, and the current UPA government is also committed to the peace process.

Regional autonomy and communalism within J&K Ascertaining the "will of the people" of J&K is complicated by growing differences between the three regions of J&K. Since the demography of these regions also corresponds to religious identities – Kashmir Valley has a majority of Muslims (95 percent), Buddhists comprise 50 percent of the population of Ladakh and 66 percent of Jammu is Hindu – demands for trifurcation of the state along religious lines have of late been propagated by Hindutva forces. Fighting elections on this plank, however, the BJP and the RSS–Jammu State Morcha alliance were trounced in the 2002 elections.

But demands for greater autonomy made by Jammu and Ladakh have a longer history independent of national-level communal politics, which can be traced back to the 1950s (Behera 2000: 215–47). There was disappointment in these regions after the 1987 elections, when the NC failed to keep its commitment to appoint a commission to look into regional autonomy (Puri 1993: 54). After its victory in the 1996 elections, the NC once again promised to build a federal structure, with regional autonomy for Jammu, Ladakh, and Kashmir, and "sub-autonomy" for ethnic and religious groups in these regions. The controversial report of the Regional Autonomy Committee (RAC), however, set up by Farooq Abdullah in 1999, recommended the sharp division of each region along religious lines with no real devolution of power. This was widely perceived both as a communal move and as a tactic to stall the process of internal autonomy.

It would be naïvely optimistic not to recognize the communalization of regional aspirations in J&K, especially since 1989, in keeping with general developments in the subcontinent. Ladakh has witnessed the emergence of modern communal politics at the electoral level, as well as violent clashes between the Buddhist and

Shi'a Muslim communities. In 1990 some Kashmiri Pandits formed the organization Panun Kashmir (Our Own Kashmir), demanding a secure zone in the valley in which the Hindu population could be concentrated. This would be a homeland, they claim, for internally displaced Kashmiris, who "mostly happen to be Hindus," who have "faced oppression for centuries" (Behera 2000: 231). This demand is not supported by the Pandit community as a whole, however, who are spread out throughout the valley, and do not wish to be herded into a "homeland." Nor is Panun Kashmir the only organization representing the community. Although most organizations of Kashmiri Pandits are understandably formed on a platform marked by the enforced departure of the community from the valley, at least one organization of Pandits, the older All India Kashmiri Pandit Conference, has recently begun initiatives to work with Kashmiri organizations such as Hurriyat towards bringing about peace in the state (PTI 2002).

In addition, the Kashmir Valley has seen, over the last decade, the development of Islamic sectarianism that has taken violent forms. Following an attack on a saint in 2005 and the killing of worshipers in 2006, an initiative has been taken by the Jamaat-i-Islami to start dialogue among different sects, so that their differences may not be "exploited for political ends." The fact that the initiative has come from the Jamaat is perceived as significant because it has stood so far for strict Islamic practices.[22]

Despite the emergence of communal politics, however, there is undoubtedly a need for genuine autonomy for the regions in keeping with federal principles. An alternative proposal was formulated by Balraj Puri, who had initially been appointed working chairman of Farooq Abdullah's Regional Autonomy Committee and later dismissed. Puri recommended the recognition of regional identities as the best guarantee of secularism, and recommended a five-tier system that included devolution of power from state to region to district, block, and village level (Chowdhary 2000). Significantly, JKLF too envisages a democratic and federal system for independent Kashmir in which each of the five federating units (Kashmir Valley, Jammu, Ladakh, Azad Kashmir, and Gilgit & Baltistan) would enjoy internal autonomy. Indeed, under the present circumstances, many feel that regional identities can be "an alternative rallying point" to communal identities (Watt 2002).

The "Kashmir Question" at the end of 2006 In 2005, according to the terms of the Congress–People's Democratic Party (PDP) coalition that won the 2002 elections, Ghulam Nabi Azad of the Congress Party became the chief minister of J&K, replacing Sayeed of the PDP. By the end of 2006, the coalition appeared to be in trouble, with PDP declaring itself ready for mid-term polls. The tussle over leadership is at one level a reflection of regional differences – Azad being from Jammu and Sayeed from the Kashmir Valley. But there are more fundamental differences between the two parties on autonomy for J&K – the Congress wants the 1975 Kashmir Accord as the framework, while the PDP turns to the pre-1953 status. The PDP is thus committed to talks with separatist forces such as the Hurriyat Conference, which the Congress will not accept.

During the two round-table conferences on J&K called by the Indian government in 2006, no attempt was made by Indian authorities to involve groups that question accession to India. Indeed, the prime minister's opening statement made it clear that "a common understanding on autonomy and self-rule in Jammu and Kashmir" would have to be evolved *"within* the vast flexibilities provided by the constitution" (Navlakha 2006: 947, emphasis added). Such intransigence on the part of the Indian state accompanied by the continuance of extraordinary laws empowering security forces, does not bode well for a democratic resolution that represents the will of the people of J&K.

Today the Kashmir Valley remains a heavily militarized area with the visible and intimidating presence of hundreds of thousands of army, paramilitary, and police forces. The pressure on these men, too, is evidently close to unbearable – since 2002, there have been about 400 suicides by soldiers, while about a hundred have been shot by colleagues in "fratricidal" fights related to stress (Special Correspondent 2006b, 2006c).

In Arundhati Roy's words, "... Kashmir is a valley awash with militants, renegades, security forces, double-crossers, informers, spooks, blackmailers, blackmailees, extortionists, spies, both Indian and Pakistani intelligence agencies, human rights activists, NGOs and unimaginable amounts of unaccounted for money and weapons ... Truth, in Kashmir, is probably more dangerous than anything else" (Roy, A. 2006: 74).

Roy raises the question of truth in the context of the current controversy over the Supreme Court's awarding of the death sentence to Afzal Guru, implicated in the attack on the Indian parliament on December 13, 2001. The attack was foiled by security forces. Six policemen and a gardener were killed in the exchange of fire, as were all five militants, alleged to be linked to Pakistan-based organizations active in Kashmir. India began to deploy troops to the border, as did Pakistan. As nuclear conflict loomed, international pressure pulled back both sides. The attack enabled the NDA government to repromulgate the draconian Prevention of Terrorism Ordinance and subsequently to pass it in an extraordinary joint session of parliament as the Prevention of Terrorism Act, in March 2002. This legislation had been severely criticized for its violation of civil rights, and influential public opinion had been building up against it prior to December 13.[23]

Questions began to be raised by concerned citizens about the timing of the attack on parliament, the unsustainability of the prosecution argument and the callous disregard for the rights of those accused of participating in the conspiracy (the actual perpetrators were, of course, all killed). In an article published in 2004, later extended into a book, a Delhi University professor, Nirmalangshu Mukherji, raised serious doubts, meticulously documented, about the genuineness of the attack itself.

Afzal Guru is a surrendered militant who was in constant contact with, and under the surveillance of, the Special Task Force of the J&K police when he was arrested for the parliament attack. After he received the death sentence in 2006, a public campaign to reveal the truth about December 13 has grown in strength. The barely veiled question being asked with greater confidence is: was the attack actually stage-managed by the Indian security forces with backing from the political leadership, who used the incident as a pretext to carry out massive military mobilization on the Indo-Pakistan border, pushing the subcontinent to the brink of nuclear war? This question becomes stronger in the face of extensive documentation of the collusion of influential visual and print media in purveying police versions discredited by the courts.

The campaign includes a petition for clemency for Afzal, not only because the campaigners are opposed to the death penalty itself, but because the Supreme Court judgment clearly concedes there is no evidence against Afzal. Despite this, the judgment goes on to say, "The incident ... has shaken the entire nation, and the collective conscience of the society will only be satisfied if capital punishment is awarded to the offender" (Mukherji 2004, 2005; Roy 2006; Noorani et al. 2006).

Public opinion in the country is thoroughly polarized on the issue. For many, those who want clemency for Afzal represent nothing less than the enemy within. The family members of the policemen who died on December 13 have returned their medals for gallantry in protest at the sentence having been deferred. That Afzal – representing a state and a people that have doggedly eluded the grasp of the Indian nation – should be still alive at the end of 2006 has become, for many, a symbol of the deepest injustice. When a demonstration by visually handicapped people in Delhi for their demands was lathi-charged[24] by the police, their posters the next day read, *andhon ko lathi, Afzal ko maafi?* – beatings for the blind but pardon for Afzal? Here is a tragic irony – the blind competing with the "terrorist" for the mercy of the state – the one utterly marginal to the nation, the other central to its self-legitimation.

December 13, 2001 and its aftermath represents another moment in that never-completed project of producing a nation. Another attempt to assuage what Ranabir Samaddar terms a "particular kind of post-colonial anxiety" – the anxiety of "a society suspended forever in the space between the 'former colony' and the 'not-yet nation'" (Samaddar 1999: 108).

7 | India in the world

The 1990s, as we have seen, followed a specific trajectory sparked by a set of *internal* developments within India, but this trajectory was framed in the specific *global* conjuncture inaugurated by the collapse of the Soviet Union and the advent of a neoliberal dispensation.

The cold war era

The "end of the cold war" meant for India a very significant material loss, for it encountered the phenomenon not simply as the thawing of relations between the superpowers – it was the loss of an entire world. The USSR and the Soviet bloc had constituted India's most reliable fall-back option, in economic terms as well as in political support, despite India's declared policy of non-alignment.

India, it is well known, had been one of the chief architects of the non-aligned movement and had charted out a relatively independent path for itself that steered clear of global power blocs, especially military alliances. There is a complicated dynamic to the way India's external relations evolved during the 1950s. Despite Nehru's professed "socialist inclinations," he did make attempts to develop close relations with the West, including its former colonial ruler Britain, retaining India's membership of the Commonwealth (Stein 1969: 27). The later tilt toward the Soviet bloc can be understood at one level as a result of the insistence of the Western powers that the Kashmir issue be resolved in terms of the original understanding of accession through a plebiscite, while the USSR supported the Indian position (ibid.: 28, 29).[1] At another level, India's internal economic compulsions and the need to acquire self-reliance through import-substituting industrialization dictated that India not put all its eggs in one basket. Here the unequivocal support received from the USSR in developing the Bhilai steel plant and the heavy machine plant in Ranchi was critical. Moreover, support from the USSR was often backed by support from other East European partners. In Bhilai, for instance, Czechoslovakia and Poland also contributed to the development of the plant (ibid.: 173, 178). Over time, this relationship was gradually fortified through a series of developments culminating in the Indo-Soviet Friendship Treaty in 1971.

One of the important factors behind this strengthening of Indo-Soviet relations was the growing closeness toward the end of the 1960s, between the United States and China. Given the fact that China had already been supportive of Pakistan's claims on Kashmir and had opposed the liberation of Bangladesh, dubbing it the dismemberment of Pakistan, this new development gave credence to the idea of a Pakistan–USA–China axis. Pakistan, of course, has never ceased to haunt the Indian establishment and has therefore functioned as a fundamental determinant of foreign relations in many respects. With China, too, India has had a longstanding and unresolved border dispute. All these combined to give the USSR a massive edge as a possible ally. Thus it was that within a month and half of Henry Kissinger's disclosure in July 1971 that the USA and China "had been engaged in secret negotiations," India and the Soviet Union signed the Indo-Soviet Friendship Treaty (Vanaik 1995: 30).

The new unipolar world

Thus not only did the collapse of the USSR make non-alignment irrelevant, India suddenly lost its primary anchor in international politics. Its first test, as it were, came with the first Gulf crisis in 1990–91, with the Iraqi invasion of Kuwait followed by the US invasion of Iraq. By and large, until that point, India had maintained friendly relations with most West Asian countries, including Iraq. It had also ardently supported the Palestinian cause. It has been observed that "the Gulf war served as a catalyst for a reassessment of Indian foreign policy and a recognition of the realities of the post-cold war era" (Hardgrave and Kochanek 1993: 405). Already by the end of 1991, the Indian government was moving closer to US positions in many international issues. Notable among these is the fact that it voted, in December 1991, for the repeal of the UN resolution equating Zionism with racism – a resolution it had championed in earlier times. In

January 1992, it voted with the USA in "condemning Libyan support for terrorism" and in February, it established diplomatic relations with Israel (ibid.). It is important to recognize that this shift took place while the Congress, the architect of the earlier policy, was in power and not the right-wing BJP, which was always more inclined toward Israel. Within a decade of establishing diplomatic relations, and especially under NDA rule, Israel emerged as India's second biggest weapons supplier and biggest trading partner in the region (Chiriyankandath and Wyatt 2005: 205).

This rapid shift was undoubtedly motivated by considerations of realpolitik and a realization that India was now dealing with a different world. But there were specific internal developments that spurred this shift, too. The closeness to the USA was accentuated after the BJP-led NDA's accession to power, after initially deteriorating when the government went in for a nuclear explosion in May 1998. The NDA government soon started making serious efforts to get back into America's favor. Within a matter of three years the events of 9/11 in New York and the subsequent War on Terror accentuated this trend.[2] The obsessive anti-Islamism of the NDA regime meshed very well with Bush's War on Terror, and came in handy for the Bush administration as it launched its attack on Afghanistan and Iraq.

Even after the end of the NDA regime and under the Left-supported UPA government, the tilt toward the USA has continued, despite opposition from the Left. During this period (post-May 2004), the Indian government has succumbed to US pressure on Iran, voting against Iran in the International Atomic Energy Commission (IAEA) while it simultaneously negotiated the controversial Indo-US nuclear deal.

The Indo-US nuclear deal

Two key features of the Hyde Act as passed by the both Houses of the US Congress, which will be the basis for the final version of the Indo-US nuclear deal, have come in for criticism across the board from Left to Right. One, the clause requiring the US president to certify that "India is fully and actively participating in the United States and international efforts to dissuade, sanction and contain

Iran for its nuclear program consistent with United Nations Resolutions." This clause essentially ensures that the US government will decide Indian foreign policy. The point made by even ideologues of the Hindu Right such as Arun Shourie, with no predilections toward Iran, is that Iran specifically is not the issue – the question is of national sovereignty (Shourie 2006). The second feature of the Indo-US deal that is criticized by both Right and Left is the limitation on transfer of technology, material and equipment that would help India develop a civilian nuclear energy program. This feature arises from the Nuclear Non-Proliferation Treaty (NPT) which enables the USA to refrain from directly or indirectly assisting other states in the development of nuclear weapons and, as is well known, the line between civilian nuclear energy programs and the development of nuclear weapons is very thin.

The concern of both ends of the political spectrum, then, has to do with the fact that the Hyde Act places India in a subordinate position to the world's sole remaining superpower (Jayaraman 2006; Kulkarni 2006).[3]

In the sound and fury of this debate that has mobilized all the familiar and widely popular tropes of nationalism and sovereignty, a crucial voice has been relatively marginalized. This is the perspective that is committed to global disarmament and universal nuclear non-proliferation. From this point of view the real concern is that the deal "will actually promote the continued acquisition of weapons of mass destruction and impede nuclear disarmament."[4] The fact that the deal leaves India's "eight unsafeguarded reactors, two fast breeders and all dedicated military nuclear facilities out of IAEA inspections," thus leaving open possibilities for development of weapons, is of great concern to peace activists (Bidwai 2006). Further, there is no doubt that the deal will accelerate the arms race between India and Pakistan. This set of scholars and activists, which considers itself as part of the global anti-nuclear peace movement rather than as representing nation-states, believes it would be wiser for India and Pakistan to negotiate a fissile cut-off pact which may create "positive ripple effects" in China and the USA (Hoodbhoy 2006).[5]

Seven

Pakistan and India

At the regional level, the mutual suspicion and hostility between the Indian and Pakistani states continued till about the mid-1990s. A change was initiated in 1996 with the advent of the United Front government and its commitment to what has come to be known as the "Gujral doctrine," after Inder Kumar Gujral, who took charge of India's foreign policy and also became prime minister of the UF government later. The "Gujral doctrine" basically called for a generous and accommodating approach to neighbors, including Pakistan. Although it was criticized at that time as being too "soft," even hawkish analysts see it as a policy that was "aimed at liberating India to play a larger role in the world" (Raja Mohan 2003). In many ways this process continued even after the fall of the UF government and the accession to power of the BJP-led NDA, even though relations initially deteriorated rapidly after the nuclear bomb blasts in May 1998. Within a month, Pakistan tested a nuclear device too, and in less than a year, the first war between the two countries in thirty years took place in Kargil. The fact that this time the military conflict was between two "nuclear powers" hastened the diplomatic intervention of the USA.[6]

The period of NDA rule (1998–2004) was a period full of contradictory pulls in this regard, given that its shrill anti-Pakistan and anti-Islam rhetoric went hand in hand with attempts to deal with an entirely new situation in which normalization of relations with neighbors was important for "playing a larger role in the world" at large.

In the meantime, since 1993, another semi/non-official line of communication between the two countries was opened under the rubric of something called variously "People to People" contact, Track II diplomacy, or CBM, the last sounding ominously like another missile, but which expands to the utterly benign "Confidence Building Measures." The border between the two countries has become considerably more open and there is regular two-way traffic by air, bus, and train, despite continuing problems with getting visas and the occasional bomb blast. It is important to remember that large numbers of families (mostly Muslim, but some Hindu) are divided by the border, and for them, crossing the border is no political statement but a deeply emotional and personal journey. Anti-nuclear and peace groups have collaborated in organizing joint meetings and student and scholar exchanges, and the Pakistan India People's Forum for Peace and Democracy, formed in 1994, has regularly held annual conventions in both countries, in which over a hundred participants from each country visit the other. For the latest convention, though, scheduled to be held in May 2007 in Lahore, the Pakistan government refused all 250 visas for Indian participants. This time, however, the reason had less to do with India–Pakistan relations and more to do with the ongoing massive internal popular upsurge against military rule in Pakistan. The Pakistani government claimed it could not guarantee the safety of Indian citizens under the disturbed conditions prevailing.

"Looking east"

What has really transformed the terrain of the Indian elites' relationship with the rest of the world, in some fundamental ways, is the new economic logic of globalization. It has forced them to look beyond age-old preoccupations and consider a series of economic and trading blocs at regional levels with neighbors, in the search for a more secure place vis-à-vis the Western industrial countries.

The "Look east policy" of the Indian government, launched in 1992, was in a sense a direct consequence of the collapse of the Soviet Union and went beyond what is conventionally understood to be foreign policy – exploring synchronized development within a larger Asian universe. The policy began with Prime Minister Narasimha Rao's visits to China, Japan, South Korea, Vietnam, and Singapore and led to India becoming a summit-level partner (on par with China, Japan, and Korea) of the Association of South East Asian Nations (ASEAN) in 2002 (Kuppuswamy 2006). Other sub-initiatives within this Asian venture are the Bay of Bengal Initiative for Multi-Sectoral Technical Cooperation (BIMSTEC) with Bangladesh, Myanmar, Sri Lanka, and Thailand, which is to be developed into a free trade area; and the Mekong Ganga Cooperation Project which includes India, Myanmar, Thailand, Laos, Cambodia, and Vietnam and aims at developing overland trade, tourism, transport, and communications (ibid.). Trade between India and ASEAN has gone up ten times in the short period since the "Look east policy" was initiated (Venu 2007). This, along with vastly improved relations with China, is expected to transform the nature of Asian economic cooperation over the coming years.

The project of a gas pipeline from Iran to Pakistan and India (via Pakistan), negotiations on which continue, is another such instance likely to radically transform relations between traditional enemies – foreshadowing, as it does, the necessity of future economic collaborations. Once this pipeline, stretching over 2,700 kilometers, comes into operation, it will provide 90 million cubic meters of natural gas to Pakistan and about 60 million to India.[7] Reports suggest that all sides have come to an agreement over the price formula and have also "rejected the possibility of US pressure influencing the future" of this project.[8]

Going beyond "Looking east," there have also been attempts to find common ground against the rich G-8 countries by forming a trading-cum-political bloc along with Brazil and South Africa.[9]

Thus, at the international level the Indian elite negotiates its position in the unipolar world by exploring avenues of the kind that we have seen above, which might give it some leeway in terms in retaining a degree of autonomy.

India and "Southasia"

In its neighbors' opinion, India has "alternated between being the regional bully (remember Farakka[10]) and the munificent squire (the Gujral Doctrine)" (Dixit 2007: 21). It is important to understand that the Gujral Doctrine, with one of its principles being that no South Asian country will allow its territory to be used against the interest of another country of the region, has also worked to strengthen undemocratic regimes against democracy movements. This has affected, for instance, Bhutanese democracy activists using Indian territory for transit back into Bhutan. These activists can, under the Gujral Doctrine, be handed over by Indian border police to the monarchical regime they are challenging.

The Indian state, by and large, has acted to shore up other existing regimes in the region. In 1987 it sent the Indian Peace Keeping Force (IPKF) to help the Sri Lankan government in the civil war with the Liberation Tigers of Tamil Eelam (LTTE). The IPKF was intended only to guarantee and enforce the cessation of hostilities between LTTE and the Government of Sri Lanka, but it very soon was engaged in full-fledged war with LTTE. The IPKF stands indicted of a number of rights violations involving rape and torture of LTTE militants and the Tamil civilian population. The IPKF withdrew in 1990. The rage generated against India by the IPKF operations led to the assassination in 1991, by a suicide bomber, of Rajiv Gandhi, under whose prime ministership the India–Sri Lanka Accord had been signed, which brought the IPKF into being. As we saw in Chapter 6, though, the LTTE has considerable sympathy and support from the state of Tamil Nadu, to an extent that amounts to sedition in the terms of the Indian government.

With regard to Myanmar, in the second half of the 1990s, the Indian government started to modulate its earlier wholehearted support to the democracy movement under the imprisoned Aung San Suu Kyi, who is an icon of defiance to power for democratic struggles in the region, including India. Indian state policy has shifted toward extending economic and political support and military training to the repressive military junta in Myanmar. This attempt to befriend the military regime has several reasons behind it. India plans to buy natural gas from Myanmar, it hopes to limit China's presence in the region, and to gain the support of the regime in order to break up the military bases in Myanmar of insurgent groups from the north east of India (Myint 2007).[11]

With Nepal, India has had a longstanding treaty that allows for open international borders. Sections of the Indian political class have had close relations for many years now with the Nepali Congress and the Communist Parties of Nepal and they have been generally supportive of the long struggle for democracy in the erstwhile kingdom. In 2005, however, as the powerful underground Maoist movement also came forward to join hands with the Seven Party Alliance that overthrew the monarchy, the Indian government sent an emissary to save the tottering monarchy when it was on its last legs. This move had to do with the Indian elites' perception of the Maoist threat within the country, as we have seen in Chapter 5. The Indian emissary not only got the Indian embassy to convene a meeting of Nepalese political parties to find a compromise solution, he met King Gyanendra to put to him the same proposal after it had been rejected by the parties. Fortunately, due to the influence of the Left parties in the UPA, the Indian government ultimately established relations with the democracy movement (Dubey 2006).

The idea of "Southasia," the term used by the influential journal *Himal Southasian* in preference to "South Asia," seems to indicate more than a geographical region. It indicates the potential for an identity that transcends the national borders of the region, that is, at the same time, resolutely opposed to Indian hegemony. Kanak Mani Dixit, the editor of *Himal*, points out that the Indian government and Indian elites have come only recently even to the term South Asia. They used the term "Indian subcontinent" to refer to the region for a long time, moving to "Subcontinent," until finally just before the fourteenth summit of the South Asian Association for Regional Cooperation (SAARC) in March 2007, the entity of South Asia was recognized, a term used by other countries in the region since the 1980s. The newfound comfort of "New Delhi's power elite" with the term, Dixit believes, has to do with the economic progress made by India in the recent past. This confidence has led to India recognizing the Himalayan ridgeline as a porous economic frontier rather than a strategic buffer, as evidenced by the improved relations with China, the release of Bhutan from Indian control over its foreign policy, the project to improve highways in the border points, and a willingness to allow border states to develop their own relationships with neighboring countries (Dixit 2007: 21).

"Southasia" as opposed to the SAARC model indicates a "many-layered entity," constituting "the cumulative total of bilateral relationships," including the cross-border relationships between India's border states and their immediate neighbors. Such a version of regionalism would, Dixit believes, "in one stroke also make irrelevant the biggest knot in the evolving Southasianism: the overwhelming asymmetry presented by the sheer geostrategic and economic power, physical expanse and population of India – a country in the centre of the region, bordering all other countries, none of which adjoin the others" (ibid.: 23).

Of course, there is also the recognition that India's discovery of

Southasia is, to a great extent, an attempt to infiltrate the neighborhood's economies for the benefit of Indian multinationals. "Pakistan is wary of being swamped by Indian goods; and Bangladesh, which is already seeing a strong Indian multinational presence, may be alarmed enough to implement harsh protectionism" (ibid.).

It is important to note that the borders of India are becoming more porous only for the movement of goods, not people – at least, not legally. Thousands of poor immigrants from Nepal and Bangladesh cross the border into India looking for work. They lead precarious existences, on low-paying exploitative jobs, including sex work, while Bangladeshis additionally live with the imminent threat of deportation. South Asia is a region of widespread homelessness and migration, the mass movement of populations necessitated by political disturbances, ethnic/communal violence, ecological degradation, large-scale "development" projects, and structural adjustment policies. Of course, as Ranabir Samaddar points out, the social reality of migration is also often "a distorted version of natural human flows through the centuries" – distorted, that is, by the emergence of nation-states cutting across ethnic and tribal groups, and across lands that people once ranged freely (Samaddar 1999: 40). The "spectre of hordes of illegal immigrants" (ibid.: 17) is therefore one that constantly haunts the Indian nation-state.

Conclusion: a heterogeneous present

Globalization and growth

The advent of the Congress-led UPA government has introduced a new set of complexities, while older trends continue. To begin with, there is the logic of globalization and the desperate desire to catch up with the West, as we have discussed at length in the book. For the third successive year, India's economy has registered an impressive growth – the average growth rate between 2003–04 and 2005–06 was 8 percent. The global financial services firm Goldman Sachs has predicted that India can sustain this growth rate till 2020 and is likely to overtake UK as the world's fifth largest economy by the middle of the next decade.[1] The picture of this rapid growth, as we have seen in Chapters 3 and 4, is quite complex. While new avenues and opportunities have opened up, enormous long-term costs are being paid for this growth – and not by the classes benefiting from it.

The UPA, the Left, and social movements

Another level of tension has to do with the nature of political alliances that have come together around the present UPA government. While it is a Congress-led government of the same kind of regional parties that constituted the NDA, it is crucially dependent on the support of the Left parties for its survival. More significantly, at a less visible level, this government is configured through its relationship with a wide array of social movement groups and a broadly non-party, left-wing intelligentsia.

This configuration emerged on the eve of the 2004 parliamentary elections, produced by six years of NDA rule, which had brought together, in opposition to it, a range of political parties, social movements, citizens' initiatives, NGOs, and individuals attempting to articulate a different vision from that of the Hindu Right. Even though these forces continue to have serious conflicts with the government on economic policy issues, there have also emerged important sites where at least some segments of the ruling alliance can function with movement groups.

This conjuncture has produced the UPA as the site of significant new contestations of recent times, of which we briefly discuss four below.

First, the *debate around school textbooks*, which has led to one of the most productive pedagogical exercises since Independence. The National Council of Educational Research and Training (NCERT), which produces school textbooks for all levels, has in the past been dealt with in a highly partisan manner by successive governments. Pedagogical questions were never debated and the textbooks reflected the politics of particular governments in power, even when they articulated a once common secular–nationalist consensus. Once the Nehruvian Consensus broke down and the Hindu Right came to power, as we saw in Chapter 2, textbooks were changed to introduce an openly Hindu and anti-minority bias. Since the Hindu Right and the NDA never had the intellectual resources of its predecessors to produce academically competent books, the "saffronized" books were, as a rule, instances of cavalier, if not shoddy, scholarship.

With the advent of the UPA government there was a change in the way the exercise was undertaken, largely as consequence of the new configuration that surrounded the government. The new director of the NCERT, Krishna Kumar, a well-known senior educationist, was given considerable autonomy in this respect. Many in the Left simply wanted a return of the old textbooks, though these were quite outdated in terms of the disciplinary developments in respective fields. A vigorous debate ensued, involving large sections of the academic community – not merely on the content but also on pedagogical questions. For the first time since Independence, the pedagogical focus is on the child, rather than on "nation-building," a shift that many in the mainstream Left are very uncomfortable about.[2]

The other important development of this period is the enactment of the *Right to Information Act 2005* (RTI). This legislation was the result of a prolonged public campaign initiated by the Mazdoor Kisan Shakti Sangathan of Rajasthan, which had made use of the idea at the local level in order to ensure payment of daily wages to casual workers. The RTI Act was perceived as a threat by many bureaucrats, and there have been attempts to dilute some of its provisions, especially to exempt "file notings" from its purview, which are often crucial in terms of ensuring accountability. For instance, Parivartan, a voluntary organization, used the RTI to obtain file notings regarding the privatization of water management in Delhi, in 2005. The notings revealed serious malpractices on the part of the World Bank, and Parivartan was able to block the deal that could have raised water rates by ten times for Delhi citizens (Sridhar 2007).

Another significant development was the passage of the *Scheduled Tribes (Recognition of Forest Rights) Act 2006*. The Left parties actively pushed the government to pass this legislation, which was supported by indigenous people's organizations and other movement groups. Since the advent of colonial rule, the usufructory rights to land, of millions of tribals and forest dwellers, has remained disputed or unacknowledged due to lack of records of land rights.[3] A Supreme Court judgment in 2001 put the final seal on the extinguishing of such rights when it issued a stay on the regularization of tribal villages in forest areas. The legislation was thus brought about in order to recognize and formally codify these rights.[4]

A fourth development is the passing of the *National Rural Employment Guarantee Act* (2005). This legislation guarantees 100 days of paid employment in the rural sector, and has the potential to make a dent in rural poverty, especially if movements use it in tandem with the RTI Act discussed above.

All these initiatives, despite their weaknesses, are landmarks in acknowledging citizenship rights at different levels.

Hindutva and caste politics

Meanwhile, in the wings, the Hindu Right mobilizes its forces. In early 2007, the BJP won the Delhi municipal elections and the election to the legislative assembly of the state of Uttarakhand. As we saw in Chapter 2, the BJP has decided to recover its edge by sharpening its Hindutva platform. Violence against minorities has risen, especially in the states in which it wields power – the fear that states such as Karnataka and Rajasthan will be "the next Gujarat" is very real. Years of Hindutva's campaigns and six years of BJP rule at the center have so substantially transformed the political culture that recently, when two Christian priests in Rajasthan were beaten up by VHP supporters, supposedly for converting Hindus, it was the pastors who were arrested and not the attackers (Vardarajan 2007: 11). Similarly, in May 2007, when Hindutva forces attacked an art exhibition in a university in Baroda (Gujarat), and one student in particular, for drawing "obscene" images, it was the artist who was arrested, while the dean of the faculty who refused to apologize for allowing the exhibition has been placed under suspension (Khan, A. 2007: 1). Similarly, a local court recently ordered that the property of India's most well-known painter, M. F. Hussain, be attached by the state. This follows a case filed against him by a lawyer for painting "mother India in the nude."[5]

It would be a mistake, however, to attribute recent electoral victories of the BJP and its allies simply to growing communalism – as we have argued earlier, elections bring into play a wide range of local factors. In Delhi, for instance, the defeat of the Congress was due in no small measure to its inability to stand up to Supreme Court orders to implement the outdated and inequitable Delhi Master Plan, leading to mass dislocations and loss of livelihoods (Menon and Nigam 2006).

On the other hand, in a very significant development from the long-term point of view, the recent election results from Uttar Pradesh (May 2007) reveal a severe setback for Hindutva. The Dalit party BSP, under Mayawati's leadership, emerged as the majority party; this is the first time a single party has got a majority in fourteen years in UP. For the BSP, too, this was unthinkable till some time ago, given that Dalits comprised only about 25 percent of the population in the state. The secret of this new development lies in a factor we discussed in Chapter 1: the sharp conflicts between the powerful OBCs and the Dalits. Over the years of OBC dominance, embodied in the Samajwadi Party's rule in UP, the upper castes had been alienated, and the BSP skillfully used this to forge an alliance which was largely accomplished at the cost of the BJP, whom these castes had supported earlier. This development also underlines the extreme fluidity as well as heterogeneity of the contemporary dynamic of caste politics.

The caste question continues to simmer on the reservation issue as well. The Supreme Court recently issued a stay order on the implementation of Mandal II on the grounds that the OBC communities have not been properly identified. As the UPA government readies itself to challenge the stay order, the Tamil Nadu government has demanded to be impleaded in the case so that its experience of implementing such reservations may be taken on board.

Violence against women and feminist initiatives

The women's movement in its various forms – women's wings of Left political parties, non-funded groups, NGOs, and feminist initiatives in institutions such as universities – continues to take up issues, apart from those already discussed, that have long remained on the feminist agenda. A serious issue is the alarming decline in the sex ratio (the average for the country was 927 females to every thousand males in the 2001 census, with a greater decline at the 0–6 age level), and the widespread use of technologies of sex-determination to selectively abort female foetuses. Another issue that continues to be on the feminist agenda is sexual harassment and sexual violence. In 1997, the Supreme Court, in response to a petition by some NGOs, issued guidelines against sexual harassment at the workplace. Known as the Vishakha judgment, after one of the petitioners, it has formed the basis for feminist initiatives to formulate policy in several institutions, especially universities. There has been a decade-long effort by feminist groups, countrywide, to amend the criminal law on rape, which recognizes only penile penetration of the vagina as rape, deeming all other forms of sexual violence to be less harmful, and deserving of lesser punishment (section 377 is a separate case, discussed in Chapter 5). The recently passed Domestic Violence Act (2005) is the result of a longstanding feminist effort to ensure that women have a right to their matrimonial home. This act also recognizes marital rape, which the existing law on rape does not. In one of the earliest tests of this law, however, a Supreme Court judgment (2006) restricted the scope of what may be considered to be a woman's "matrimonial home."[6]

Conclusion | 181

Resistance to corporate globalization

Special Economic Zones and large-scale land acquisitions for corporate purposes face determined resistance across the length and breadth of the country. The struggle of the Kalinganagar tribals in Orissa against land acquisition for the Tatas, leading to police firing and the death of twelve people (January 2006), has now burgeoned into a countrywide movement. The peasants of Raigad, in Maharashtra, determined to stop an SEZ in their area, told a journalist that they were prepared to kill rather than die – in an allusion to the widespread reports of farmers' suicides in the state. An unexpected and successful electoral alliance here on this issue was between the Peasants and Workers Party and the Hindu right-wing Shiv Sena.[7] Nandigram in West Bengal, of course, has become the symbol for militant resistance to land acquisition across the country, and the same sort of broad alliances seen there seem to be forming everywhere, with the single-point agenda of resisting SEZs, regardless of often serious differences on other issues. In the state of Jharkhand, close to forty industrial projects whose MOUs (Memoranda of Understanding) have been signed, are held up in the face of popular resistance to land acquisition. There is also an emerging nationwide resistance from traders' and vendors' organizations, to Indian and foreign MNCs' plans to open retail chains across India.[8]

Of course the moment is complex and unpredictable, as is any moment in history. We admit, nevertheless, to the "undaunted optimism" the *Economist* reviewer so deplored,[9] an optimism generated by the fact that in India, as elsewhere in the world, the contestations to the power of Capital and Nation are so many, so varied, and so relentless.

Epilogue June 2014

Two General Elections have taken place since *Power and Contestation* went to press in late 2006. The latest, in May 2014, put the 16th Lok Sabha in place with Narendra Modi as Prime Minister. The BJP is the single largest party with a clear majority (282 seats), and with its allies, the NDA has 336 seats. The Congress has been decimated (44 seats), and the Left is in complete rout (CPI has 1 seat; CPI-M, 9). The Bahujan Samaj Party got no seats at all. Regional parties have done relatively better, to the extent that their representation remains the same as in the 2009 elections, at 212 seats.

It may also be relevant to note that the vagaries of the First Past the Post system that advantages bigger parties and marginalizes smaller parties and radical agendas, has resulted yet again in a lack of fit between vote share and seats. The BJP has got a majority (282 out of 543 seats) with only 31 percent of the votes; with its allies, the vote share goes up to only to 38.5 percent. It has been pointed out that in 1977, in the post Emergency election which saw a decisive defeat for the Indira Gandhi regime, her party, the Congress (I) got 34.2 percent of the vote share, which is 3 percent more than the BJP has managed to get in 2014. In other words, this government is less representative than the discredited and defeated Congress of 1977 (Sengupta 2014). It is also the first party with a majority on its own which does not have a single Muslim MP in the Lok Sabha. It did field 7 Muslim candidates, but they all lost.

Nevertheless, this majority for the BJP marks a break from the pattern of the past three decades where no party had been able to get a majority on its own. Moreover, this unprecedented victory of the Hindu Right has been accomplished under the stewardship of Narendra Modi, the former chief minister of Gujarat, who is widely perceived to have presided over the 2002 carnage in which close to a thousand Muslims were killed (Chapter 2). The persona of Narendra Modi has since emerged as the single most divisive figure in Indian politics and carries an ominous meaning for the minorities.

It has been barely a month since Narendra Modi took oath of office, and already the storm troopers of the Hindu Right have attacked Muslims and their property in several places in Karnataka during BJP victory processions;[1] gone on the rampage in Pune (Maharashtra) over supposed slights on Facebook to Bal Thackeray, the late Shiv Sena supremo, killing one 'Muslim-looking' youth and destroying property;[2] violent clashes between Hindus and Muslims broke out in Ahmedabad (Gujarat) when two cars from the different communities crashed in an accident during a marriage procession;[3] and in Gurgaon (Haryana), the death of a man in an accident triggered communal 'riots'.[4] As we pointed out in Chapter 2, the term 'riot' is a deliberate misnomer, which suggests spontaneous and unpredictable mass action. In fact, most 'riots' in India are far from spontaneous and involve what Paul Brass has called 'institutionalised systems of riot production, in which the organizations of militant Hindu nationalism are deeply implicated', which are activated during political mobilization or elections (Brass 2006: 65). In such systems, Brass sees a central role as being performed by 'conversion specialists', whose task is to decide when a trivial everyday incident will be exaggerated and inserted into the communal discourse, and allowed to escalate into communal violence (2005: 32).

Of course, Modi himself had nothing to do with the incidents described above, and he specifically deplored the violence in Congress-ruled Gurgaon and Pune as 'communal', while the state governments tried to pass them off as 'law and order' situations. It is this kind of manipulation of minority community fears and potential minority votes by all parties that makes 'secular' a term impossible to apply to almost any mainstream party. In Chapter 2, we have discussed the complex imbrication of caste politics in the secular/communal equation, and the need to distinguish between secularism as a value (of non-discrimination, acceptance of difference, mutual respect) and secularism as a principle of state-craft. We have argued for the need to continue to call ourselves secular in the first sense while mounting a critique of the practice of secularism by the Indian state and political parties.

In Muzaffarnagar in Uttar Pradesh, the 'institutionalised system of riot production' was very much in evidence in the run-up to the recent elections, where Narendra Modi's close aide Amit Shah was sent 11 months before the elections to turn things around. At the time, the BJP held 10 seats in UP and its cadres had been in disarray for years. In September 2013, a petty incident led to the worst communal violence in the state; the ruling Samajwadi Party (SP) was both ineffective and cynical in its handling of the situation, successfully alienating both Hindus and Muslims; and in the communal polarization that broke SP's links with large sections of its voters, the BJP ended up winning 71 seats.[5]

A documentary film, *The Killing Fields of Muzaffarnagar*, by Gopal Menon, has live footage showing that the violence was instigated by right-wing Hindu politicians very much under the influence of Amit Shah. The Supreme Court has taken into cognizance Menon's documentary as evidence, in considering pleas by petitioners seeking punishment for perpetrators of the violence. Menon also claimed to have spoken to a local group called 'Narendra Modi Army' that was active during the violence.[6]

Despite all of this however, to read the victory of the BJP and the NDA as a victory for Hindutva would be a big mistake. While the street gangs of the Hindu Right clearly feel emboldened with the ascent of Narendra Modi to the highest office in the land, Modi himself fought the election on a platform of Development, distancing himself from his image as an anti-minority, violent, Hindutvavaadi. What then, are the implications of Narendra Modi becoming Prime Minister? We put it in this way advisedly, rather than asking what the implications are of the BJP being in power. In order to explain this distinction, we need to briefly take a look at the 2009 General Elections and the scenario that unfolded between then and 2014, to get a more complete sense of the current situation.

General Elections 2009

Return of the UPA In the General Election of May 2009 the Congress-led United Progressive Alliance (UPA) came back to power with a new and overwhelming mandate. Contrary to all poll predictions of a hung Parliament, the verdict was decisive. Far from being a photo finish between the two contending formations, namely the UPA and the BJP-led National Democratic Alliance (NDA), the Congress party returned as the single largest party with 206 seats in the 543 member parliament, crossing the 200 mark for the first time since 1991. The strength of the BJP led-NDA was reduced to 159 from 271 while that of the Left bloc also came down dramatically from 61 to 24 seats.

Decline of the Left Some months before the elections, the Left parties had withdrawn support from the ruling UPA over the contentious issue of the Indo-US Nuclear Deal (Chapter 7). They were however, unsuccessful in forging an alternative, a third electoral front, leaving them isolated from other parties and from the electorate. The fear of the BJP coming back to power meant that the support of the minorities and secular forces went to the Congress, while what may be termed the Nandigram Effect (Chapter 5) decimated the CPI(M) in West Bengal, a state it had ruled for over thirty years. The CPI(M)'s 'anti-imperialism' remained limited to opposing the nuclear deal with the US, for in West Bengal it simultaneously implemented neo-liberal policies aggressively.

But this is only a part of the story of the defeat of the Left. The other part is equally serious. What Singur and Nandigram did was not simply to raise the question of land. Those struggles broke the daily, unspoken fear that stalked rural West Bengal, where CPI(M) had ruled for three decades with an iron hand, and it was faced with a sudden exodus from its ranks.

Decline of the Hindu Right Another key feature of the 2009 elections was the further decline of the Hindu Right. As we saw in Chapter 2, after BJP lost the 2004 elections, it launched into an aggressive Hindutva policy, deepening the communal divide and creating an atmosphere of violence. This appeared to have been the wrong lesson to have learnt from their previous defeat. The party lost voters across the country with the exception of two states, Himachal Pradesh and Karnataka.

This despite the fact that in many ways, the atmosphere was ripe for a massive return of the Hindutva agenda. The 2009 elections took place against the backdrop of a series of bomb blasts and terrorist attacks, including the attacks in Mumbai on 26 November 2008. In what now seems to be quite clearly an operation planned and executed with the backing of the Pakistan military establishment, terrorists entered an elite hotel, taking hostages who were later killed – apart from indulging in indiscriminate killings in a crowded train station. These attacks were followed by angry demonstrations by the upper classes against the government and politicians in general, and even calls to refuse to pay taxes (Menon 2008)

Prior to this, Delhi had been rocked by bomb blasts in September 2008. Caught completely unawares and clueless, sections of the police and government later staged what was widely suspected to be a fake encounter in the largely Muslim residential locality of Jamia Nagar in Delhi, in which two students died. One police officer also lost his life in this 'encounter'. This entire episode aroused suspicions among all sections of the democratic rights community (JTSA 2010).

For the BJP and other organizations of the Hindu Right these were ideal circumstances. Unsurprisingly, all these situations were played up and no effort was spared to turn the feelings of anger and insecurity arising from them into a communal polarization. A strong national security state was advocated, and the UPA and the Congress government accused of being soft on terrorism, ably aided by the media that went into an overdrive of war-mongering hysteria.

But even in Jammu and Kashmir, the swing away from the BJP was 4.4 percent. Since Muslims in the state are unlikely to vote for the BJP, this decline in votes has to have happened mainly among the Hindus of the state, who had very recently been massively mobilized around the Amarnath shrine sacred to Hindus. The Governor of Jammu and Kashmir, a BJP appointee, decided to transfer 100 acres of forestland to the Shri Amarnath Shrine Board (SASB) in violation of the Forest Conservation Act. This allocation of protected forest land for Hindu pilgrims was protested by the Hurriyat leaders and the JKLF (Jammu and Kashmir Liberation Front), as a strategy to settle Hindus in that Muslim majority area. The land transfer was then revoked by the Congress-led government, providing the opportunity for unprecedented mass mobilization of Hindus by the BJP. What is striking is that in the 2009 elections, the BJP candidate Leela Karan Sharma, the main leader of the Amarnath agitation, lost to the Congress candidate by a huge margin of over 1.2 lakh votes, indicating that the overall effect of such militant mobilizations had a negative effect on the electorate in 2009.

Even after a term out of power – and therefore no 'anti-incumbency' to deal with – the BJP's losses ranged between 4 to 7 percent in many states and were as high as 12 percent in Rajasthan, which, along with Karnataka, was widely seen as the Hindutva laboratory (to reproduce Gujarat) in the BJP-RSS game plan. Thus the BJP's decline over the period 1999–2009 showed a continuing trend, irrespective of whether it was in power or not.

It is legitimate then, for anyone interested in India to ask how we managed to arrive at this point in our collective life in just about five years.

The UPA and contestations over development

Many analysts attempted to interpret the 2009 election results as a vote for 'development' and against the sectarian politics of the Hindu right. This is partly true but we must be clear what we mean by it. If 'development' means land acquisition for industry, dispossession of the rural poor, demolitions of slums and expulsion of the urban poor from cities to make way for shopping malls and multi-level air conditioned car parks, or the replacement of vegetable and fruit vendors with retail chains (Chapter 3), then the vote was not for development. But the Congress and UPA did not understand this, interpreting the results as a license for unbridled neo-liberal reforms, a game that they could never play as well as a Narendra Modi-led BJP.

They did not understand that against the 'India Shining' neo-liberal slogan of the BJP, they had reaped the benefits of a contradictory set of developments – the enactment and implementation of important pro-people laws like the National Rural Employment Guarantee Act (NREGA), the Right to Information Act (RTI Act) and the Forest Rights Act (discussed in the Conclusion). The RTI Act has enabled a more transparent implementation of the provisions of the NREGA and a check on corruption on that front. Here we reiterate the argument we made in the Conclusion, that these initiatives were not the outcome of the Congress party's vision so much as the fact that the UPA had emerged as a heterogeneous space where social movements also had some voice. The involvement of individuals like Aruna Roy, Jean Dreze and other representatives of social movements, as well as the fact that the Left parliamentary bloc was supporting the government, had transformed the UPA into a space full of diverse possibilities that could simultaneously undertake steps that were oriented towards welfare of the poor.

Overall, despite the contrary pulls, UPA I actually kept up a growth rate of 8 percent per annum, while simultaneously maintaining a poor-friendly face. (Ghatak et al. 2014: 36)

Many Special Economic Zone (SEZ) projects were put on hold and the state governments of Maharashtra and Goa made it clear that they would refrain from acquiring land for industrialists, leaving it to them to negotiate directly with the farmers. In 2011 Rahul Gandhi started actively supporting the struggle of the farmers of the twin villages of Bhatta and Parsaul in UP, in the outskirts of Delhi. Their struggle against land acquisition for the Yamuna Expressway, became a major issue and reached the courts (Polanki 2012). Even the Supreme Court started taking the land acquisition question more seriously, especially with respect to the claims of land owners dispossessed as a result of the acquisition.[7]

Over the 1990s, high economic growth and opening out of new opportunities outside the conventional frame of government jobs, resulted in an explosion of desire and aspirations, as we discuss in Chapter 4. While the urban lower middle classes went for a range of reasonably paid infotech enabled industries, the rural poor initially came into jobs that ranged from those in informal sector construction work and small scale industries, to other kinds of factory employment. But their imaginative horizons had changed. They would eventually move out into other trades. Work in the unorganized sector, with a toehold in the city, is often the first step towards saving and moving on. This is a story one often encounters in the bigger cities and towns.

Even though the global recession affected this expansion in a big way, there is little doubt that the impact of the economic crisis has been relatively cushioned in India. India managed to escape the worst effects of the recession at least partly because of its network of public institutions, especially the nationalized banks.

Parenthetically, we may note here the alarming recent report of the P. J. Nayak Committee (2014) set up by the Reserve Bank of India, which implicitly advocates privatization of public sector banks (Ram Mohan 2014).

Long before the time of UPA II, however, despite the space for Left-wing social movements to intervene in government policy, neo-liberal wisdom had become the dominant consensus among the political elites from Left to Right, even though it was being constantly and severely challenged by the growing force of movements and struggles both local and national. By the time of UPA II then, the constraints placed on the UPA by the environmental and equity concerns of social movements had already begun to irritate sections of the Congress as well as of course, corporate interests. Struggles around land acquisition, the pressures for environmental clearance that held up corporate projects, social welfare programmes that came in the way of unbridled pursuit of profit, and subsidies that supposedly introduced 'market distortions' – all these had been greatly troubling the corporate sector and their ideologues in the media. A campaign was initiated to install a strong leader with a solid majority, who would give the bourgeoisie a free hand.

It may not be an exaggeration then, to say that the election of 2014 is nothing short of a peaceful counter-revolution (Nigam 2014a) or as *Economic and Political Weekly* put it, 'the biggest corporate heist in history' (EPW Editorial 2014). Counter-revolution, not because there was an imminent threat of revolution that has been put down, but because the big bourgeoisie has for the time being, decisively blocked the challenge from mass struggles that corporate interests had been facing.

Congress and crony capitalism

Meanwhile, the Congress enthusiastically participated in its own demise by its pursuit of the worst kind of crony capitalism during UPA II. Already, towards the latter part of the UPA I regime what has since come to be known as the '2G Spectrum scam' took place. 122 licenses were issued in 2008, during the tenure of Communications and Information Technology Minister A. Raja, which favoured some telecom companies and cost the public exchequer dearly. Estimates made by the Comptroller and Auditor General (CAG) put the loss at Rs 1,75,000 crores (approximately US$ 30 billion) while the charge-sheet filed by the Central Bureau of Investigation (CBI) put it at Rs 30,984.55 crores (US$ 5.2 billion) (Mahapatra 2011).[8]

Within a year and a half of the UPA government coming to power, in November 2010, the *OPEN Magazine* published some transcripts of telephone conversations of lobbyist Niira Radia with politicians, mediapersons and corporate officials that signaled a far more serious violation of democratic principles.[9] The tapes indicated that the corporate houses were not merely bribing their way into getting lucrative contracts at the cost of the public exchequer; they had also been involved in fixing specific people in particular ministries. Later many more tapes were to find their way into the public domain and it was evident that Radia had been acting at the behest of corporations like Tata Teleservices and Mukesh Ambani's Reliance Industries. The conversations had been recorded by the Income Tax Department between 2008 and 2009 and they suggested that at least some corporate houses were not averse to subverting the political process through such behind-the-scenes machinations.[10]

In March 2012, the CAG further indicted the government for allocating 194 coal fields, over the period 2004–2011, without going through a process of competitive bidding, leading to what it referred to as a 'windfall gain' of Rs 1.86 lakh crores (approximately US$ 31 billion) for the beneficiary companies – and a corresponding loss to the government. The beneficiary companies included Essar Power, Hindalco, Tata Steel, Tata Power and Jindal Steel and Power.[11]

We may reiterate here that thus, even during the period that the constellation of the Congress, Left and social movements was in place, the corporate and neo-liberal agenda was being pushed regardless. However, it was only during the UPA II regime that this high degree of corruption began coming out in public. The apogee of Congress corruption was the complete fiasco of the Commonwealth Games in 2010 – which highlighted the levels of corruption in everything associated with it. For people living in Delhi, every day in the run up to the games became a nightmare. This started with the large-scale demolition of settlements of the poor throughout the city – a process whose earlier history is already recorded in Chapter 3. The extent of corruption visible in the city involved practically everything from the commissioning of street lighting systems to digging up and redoing roads and pavements that needed no work done on them, from installing a Timing and Scoring Results system for the games, to the construction of the CWG village apartments. Everything reeked of corruption.[12]

The anti-corruption movement

It was against this background that the Anti-Corruption Movement took shape. The beginnings of the movement can be traced to November 2010, when Arvind Kejriwal, a former bureaucrat turned RTI activist, convened an all-faith rally in Delhi's Ramlila Maidan. At this point the demand was for a law that would put in place an Ombudsman type of institution to tackle questions of corruption. This was to remain a key demand, but gradually a mass movement of unprecedented dimensions in urban post-Independence India, developed around it. On January 30, 2011, a huge rally was held in Delhi in which several social movements also participated around the demand for the new law – the Jan Lokpal Bill. In April 2011, Anna Hazare, an eminent Gandhian who runs a 'model Gandhian village', Ralegan Siddhi in Maharashtra, entered the movement to lead it, at the request of Arvind Kejriwal (Jeelani 2011). Initially, the movement had included right-wing elements such as the RSS and a 'godman' Baba Ramdev, but it also attracted 'outside support' from student organizations of the Left such as All India Students' Association, affiliated with CPI (ML). Over time, the movement changed character, with right-wing elements breaking away.

The term 'corruption' as it played out in the movement, condensed within it a range of discontents – an accumulating anger over repeated betrayals of democratic expectations over years, but especially over the decade that had passed. The immediate trigger of the movement was the series of instances of looting of the public exchequer mentioned above – the Commonwealth Games, the 2G Spectrum scam, the Niira Radia tapes that exposed how ministers were being fixed to benefit particular business houses, and so on. But corruption is also an everyday matter for the poor – the *thelawala* (street vendor) paying *hafta* (weekly bribe) to the beat constable; the labourer whose muster rolls are faked, the agricultural worker whose NREGA payment is swallowed up, undertrials in jail on trumped up charges, the aspirant to own an auto rickshaw costing

1 lakh, who ends up paying more than a car costs, and drowns in debt; the farmer whose land is seized to be passed on to corporates – this last an issue mentioned by Anna Hazare in his speech at Ramlila Maidan (*kisanon ki zameen zabardasti chheeni ja rahi hai* – farmers' lands are being forcibly snatched) (Menon and Nigam 2011).

In our opinion, 'corruption' acquired in the course of this struggle, the emotive charge of 'salt' of the Dandi March. It touched everyone, and it highlighted the oppressiveness of the state. Holding government and the bureaucracy accountable for corruption, highlighted corporate corruption too, because corporations circumvent the law by bribing the former.

It is also important to remember that the Lokpal Bill has a long history before the anti-corruption movement. The institution of a Lokpal (Ombudsman) was first suggested in 1966 by the Administrative Reforms Commission, and the first Lokpal Bill introduced in 1968. Since then it had been introduced nine times, and never been passed. Thus the history of the Lokpal Bill had been one of betrayal, and it had been over forty years in the making. The anti-corruption movement that formally began April 2011 was really the crystallization of a long process that began in the villages, initiated by the campaign around the Right to Information. The RTI Act (2005), instrumental in exposing corruption in a range of spaces from NREGA to municipal schools, was the culmination of one phase of the movement; the establishment of an Ombudsman or Lokpal was always planned as the next stage.

Corruption is tied fundamentally to the RTI Act that exposes it, so effectively that about 50 RTI activists have been killed since 2008, and hundreds are routinely assaulted and harassed by the nexus between corporates and politicians.[13]

A systematic analysis of the anti-corruption movement and its significance is not possible here for lack of space, but it is important to note the key shift that it marked in political action in India. Many powerful mass movements have addressed the state directly, as we have seen through the book, but this movement was different in two ways. First, it was an urban movement, and apart from Delhi, which was its centre, its reverberations were heard in other cities and towns like Mumbai, Kolkata, Thiruvananthapuram, Hyderabad, Jaipur, Chennai, Patna, Bhopal, Ahmedabad, Ranchi and Pune. Second, and this is the more significant shift – while at one level, the movement did not challenge the state's legitimacy in any way, demanding rather, that the state put in place a law that would oversee its own operations; the *form* of the struggle posed fundamental challenges to the idea of representative democracy as one in which The People have been tamed to enter the stage of action briefly, once every five years.

Especially over the twelve days in April while Anna Hazare was on fast, the city of Delhi, in which protests had been confined to the museumized space around Jantar Mantar, was reclaimed for protest by a crashing tide of humanity so huge, so peaceful and non-violent, that it simply took back the city. It was in many ways, a celebration of the pure ideals of democracy – of the idea that 'we the people' are sovereign, that politicians are the servants of the people, that laws must originate in the needs and demands of the people.

Thus, while the Congress and mainstream political parties, as well as many commentators of the Left, criticized the anti-corruption movement as an attack on democracy itself, as anti-political, 'middle class', right-wing and even as fascist (Sengupta 2011; Chatterjee 2011; Appadurai 2011), we see it as having decisively opened up the question of democracy and the will of the people. What the movement did, was to make it legitimate to say that we have a right to the information that will enable us to arrive at a conclusion regarding law-making and state functions. For instance, a young law student in the protests stumblingly explained before a TV camera in English, which was clearly not his first language: 'They say the Parliament is sovereign. No. They should read the Constitution. The people are sovereign.'

This understanding is neither anti political nor anti political classes – it is the exact opposite. It is the insistence precisely that 'we the people' are political, we demand accountability from those whom we send to Parliament.

It was far from being exclusively 'middle class', a fact that these commentators refused to note. If the lakhs of people who participated in the protests over twelve days in Delhi alone, were all 'middle class', then India must have been Shining after all! Anybody who moved around where protests were happening could have seen that the large majority of participants were lower middle class to working class people. In Delhi, local protests happened everywhere, far away from TV cameras – in middle class housing societies, working class 'unauthorized' colonies, around local mosques in poor localities, small temples.

It is by now established that there was substantial Muslim and Dalit participation despite their leaders' disapproval. We also know from newspaper reports that there was growing participation of workers throughout – railway workers affiliated to AITUC; 1800 temporary-for-years Delhi Transport Corporation workers who were sacked for going to Ramlila Maidan; dabbawalas in Mumbai who have not struck work for 140 years; sections of auto drivers; Maruti workers from Manesar in Haryana.

The other argument made against an anti-corruption law was that corruption provides a little shade to the poor (Roy 2011). As skeptics about the law and the state, we recognize the freedoms made possible by going under the radar of the state. But how to understand the poor and working class who thronged the movement? Perhaps 'corruption' is precisely not to be in the shade, to be forced into engaging with the force of Law, but outside the protection of the law. Perhaps the 'corrupt' people protesting corruption would like to live a life in which they wouldn't have to be corrupt just to survive every day?

Any mass movement brings together disparate and sometimes starkly contradictory tendencies. The huge movement in Goa that succeeded in scrapping the SEZ Bill was composed of precisely such a broad formation – from the Church to the Hindu Right, to Left-wing organizations. They came together, they went their separate ways once their campaign succeeded. Nandigram saw a similar formation. Many non-party non-funded citizens' forums have too. The Narmada Bachao Andolan is another broad alliance coalescing on a single issue. For that matter, at Tahrir Square there were Islamists (Muslim Brotherhood), and people and groups who stand for full-scale capitalism apart from secularists and feminists and workers and trade unions. Now it's a struggle of secularists against the Muslim right-wing in Egypt, but that is a historically contingent, not necessary or inevitable development.

It is the logic of the development of a mass movement in all its messiness that a Left perspective today should seek to understand. Any student of mass movements anywhere in the world knows that mass movements of this scale only arise around issues where the largest sections of the people feel affected by it. The question really is of the *potentiality* of the movement rather than what it *is*, at any given point. It will only be inclusive to the extent that it is able to draw in the largest number. Different sections will of course have to part ways at some point to fight their separate battles, but they can come together for a specific limited goal.

As for the Lokpal, the Central Government finally passed the Lokpal and Lokayuktas Act in 2013 – a legislation with limitations – but overall seen as a welcome step (Ajith 2014).

Anti-rape protests in Delhi and legal reform

The experience of the mobilizations around corruption was revived in the massive protests around the Delhi gang-rape (December 2102 to January 2013). This time, the voices of critique were muted, although some critics still immediately termed the protests upper class. But again, this was not the case. The protests were sparked off by the rape of a girl on a bus at 9.30 at night. She could have been anybody – she was not in a car, or even an auto rickshaw. Nobody knew her caste – later it turned out she is from a very poor family and from the Kurmi caste, which is one of the

Backward Castes – but the point is nobody actually knew who she was – she was Everywoman.

And again, people did not have to be mobilized by any organized left wing, right wing or feminist groups, although all of these tendencies were very much present in the protests. The feminist understanding was being articulated not only by people calling themselves feminists, but by many who may not have considered themselves to be very political at all. The Congress government in Delhi treated the protests for days as criminal activity – the largely young women and men faced the full force of police action, from lathi charges to water cannons, only for demanding an immediate investigation of the rape and murder, and calling for better public transport and safer public spaces. Belatedly, the Central Government then set up the Justice Verma Committee (JVC). There were thousands of submissions to the JVC, many of these from otherwise non-political people, from Residents' Welfare Associations and so on, asking for changes in the broader patriarchal context of society, raising issues such as women's safety in public and police sensitivity.

Over the decades from the Open Letter by four law professors protesting the infamous judgment on Mathura's rape by the Supreme Court (Baxi et al. 1979), innumerable draft legislations on sexual assault have been prepared by different sections of the women's movement, none of which were taken seriously by the legislature. These drafts, arising from intense discussion within the movement, tried to redress the utterly patriarchal law on rape that recognized only penile penetration of the vagina as rape, while other forms of penetration came under 'outraging a woman's modesty', a considerably lesser crime. In one case of a three-year old being penetrated by a finger, judges debated whether a small child could be held to have modesty at all!

These debates since the 1980s have not been restricted to seminar rooms, nor did they originate there exclusively. In a recognizable dialectic between theory, practice and everyday life, the transformative collective power of challenges to patriarchy, misogyny and heteronormativity have percolated to ground level. The decades since the 1980s have been marked by a range of interventions. Workshops in rural areas, mass political struggles on varied issues, discussions in urban classrooms – all of these have been the medium of circulation of such ideas, carried by activists, students and teachers, writers, parents and children of all genders.

The electrifying and massive protests that galvanized the country in December–January 2012 then, were a dramatic manifestation of this ground level transformation at least within a section of the people. Slogans and statements, (not in English only), revealed feminist understandings about the autonomy and mobility of women. The young women on the street were militant and unafraid, there were as many men as women expressing their anger, and in their class composition the protesters seemed to range from lower middle class to middle class – they were by no means 'upper class' or elite.

This suggests that there has been a ground level shift among a section of the people reflecting decades of feminist intervention at different levels, but there is a real disconnect between the people and politicians. Feminist understandings have caught on in the ordinary public but this is not matched by the understanding of state agencies. Not only was a feminist position *not* articulated by anyone in a position of power or any political organization in a consistent way, most politicians from Left to Right came out with the most misogynist and regressive statements about women and about sexual violence.

This moment yielded two historical documents – a visionary report and a very disappointing piece of legislation. The Justice Verma Committee (JVC) Report of January 2013 was widely recognized as a paradigm shift in understanding sexual violence, reflecting the inputs of the women's movement and queer movement among others. The Criminal Law (Amendment) Act 2013 that followed is marked by an arrogant blindness towards the entire charged debate that preceded it, and deliberately ignores the JVC Report.

The JVC Report recommended recognition in law of marital rape, new provisions on the offence of breach of command responsibility and permitting the prosecution of members of the security forces accused of sexual assault and rape. The determination of 'consent' to any sexual act, it held, was not to be affected by the previous sexual experience of the victim or the relationship between the victim and the accused.

The definition of rape changed. The crime of rape was retained as a separate offence but was expanded to include any non-consensual penetration of a sexual nature. The Committee recommended that non-penetrative forms of sexual contact should be regarded as sexual assault, the sexual nature of an act to be determined on the basis of the circumstances. New offences were to be recognized, such as verbal sexual assault and acid attack. Most importantly, the JVC recommended gender-neutrality of the victim, but not of the perpetrator except in cases of custodial rape or rape in the context of a clear power-differentiated situation. That is, women in authority or with custody over others could be accused of sexual assault/rape.

The Criminal Law Amendment Act 2013 is entirely different. It does not recognize marital rape, protects members of security forces from prosecution for sexual assault, and introduces the death penalty for rape, which was rejected by the JVC. It does accept the expanded definition of rape, but retains sex specific perpetrator (male) and victim (female). The interim Ordinance this law replaced had swung to the other extreme – it had established the gender neutrality of the perpetrator too, which, in a misogynist society with high levels of violence against women, would only further make women the target of the law rather than offering them protection. However, going back to seeing victims as only female means that the new law refuses to recognize sexual assault on men and transgender people, and is deeply troubling from a queer feminist perspective.

Sexual violence, class, caste and community

Meanwhile, sexual violence in the country continues to be on the rise and there have been hundreds of rapes and gang rapes reported since December 2012. Particularly significant has been a rise in the systematic rape of Dalit women and school girls, in North Indian villages in particular – Haryana and Uttar Pradesh have reported some of the most brutal rapes and murders of Dalit and lower caste women by Yadav and other OBC men. It is relevant that the caste divide also generally maps on to class – upper and intermediate castes own land, lower castes and Dalits are landless, agricultural workers.

Feminists have always termed rape an act of power, not sex, and rising incidents of rapes, assaults and humiliation of lower castes, especially Dalits, must be seen as acts of power designed to deal with rapidly changing rural settings in which the latter are more defiant, upwardly mobile and organized. It is common for the rural landed elite to use rape to stifle assertions of the rural poor in sharecropping disputes, reclaiming lost land, or in demanding the payment of minimum wages (Chakravarti 1982).

Sexual assault of women is common also in communal violence, as we have seen in the innumerable 'communal riots' in India since Independence, the most recent being in Muzaffarnagar in September 2013 (Singh 2014; Citizens' Report 2013). Here too, the point is to assault the community's honour and sense of identity through its women.

The rising graph of violence against women must also be seen in the background of the rapid escalation of stark inequality in urban spaces over the last two decades that we drew attention to in Chapter 3 – the glittering malls, hotels and other spaces of conspicuous consumption visible to, but brutally inaccessible for, the hundreds of thousands of dispossessed migrants that throng the city. The arrogance and blindness of India's consuming classes towards the poor and the violence they routinely practice on those who work for them, can only exacerbate the situation. (The

National Commission for Women receives complaints of eight cases of murder of household help every day from all over the country!) (Dixit 2014)

The big city in India is becoming a very violent, masculinized space, and it is futile to think of sexual violence in isolation from this phenomenon.

Aam Aadmi Party

The formation of the Aam Aadmi Party (Common Man's Party – AAP) in November 2012 must be seen against the broad backdrop of the anti-corruption movement and the anti-rape protests discussed above. Essentially, the AAP emerged as the distilled essence so to speak, of the anti-corruption movement. The energies that the movement had unleashed, reverberated through the myriad protests that took place in Delhi and neighbouring regions over the next year. The anti-corruption movement in the meanwhile, had reached a dead-end with no other form of action in its inventory except periodic fasts by Anna Hazare. It had to undergo some rapid change if it wanted to channelize the energies produced by the movement. It was at this stage that the idea of forming a 'political party' took shape – though Arvind Kejriwal, the chief architect of the movement and now the party, has so far stuck to his position of treating AAP fundamentally as an open platform rather than a party.

The initial activities of the party remained focused on exposing the corruption of important political personalities by publicly releasing documents meticulously collected over the years. However, organizationally, the first year of its formation was also the time of setting up state level chapters in places where its campaign had drawn people towards it.

Within a year of its formation, AAP contested the assembly elections in Delhi that were held towards the end of 2013. It was a stunning performance for a debutante party, as it won 28 out of 70 seats and 29.5 percent of the vote polled. Its candidates, all of them completely new faces and from very modest backgrounds, defeated some of the most seasoned politicians of both the ruling Congress and the opposition BJP.

Something strange and interesting happened at this point. AAP had already created such a moral pressure on other parties that the BJP, despite being the single largest party with 31 seats, refused to form government in the state as it did not want to face AAP as an opposition. In any other context, given their past record, they would have gone on to form the government, even if it meant entering into unprincipled alliances with their opponents. On the other hand, so strong was the sentiment in favour of AAP that they now came under tremendous pressure to form the government. There was no way this would have been possible without support from the just dislodged and discredited Congress. The Congress was only too happy to extend support and trap AAP into a situation in which the latter would be unable to deliver on its promises, being a minority government. The AAP leadership was divided on this issue and so the party decided to go to its electors for their opinion. The result of the 'referendum' was overwhelmingly in favour of forming government. The AAP leadership decided to walk the razor's edge: it formed the government but without asking the Congress for support, and Congress support in the vote of confidence in the state assembly was unilateral.

Till this point, big capital and big media had also been broadly supportive of AAP, as were large sections of the middle class. AAP's tirade against corruption had seemed to be quite open-ended and expressive of an anodyne desire for 'clean governance'. Once in power, two things happened that decisively turned corporate capital and the big media against it. The middle class too, in such a situation, could not be far behind. First, the Delhi government took a position against Foreign Direct Investment in the retail sector, arguing that this would adversely affect livelihoods of a large number of common people. Second, in continuation with the agitation against high electricity tariffs that the AAP had been conducting, the government demanded that the private electricity distribution companies submit themselves to a CAG audit, failing which their contracts would stand cancelled. The companies, especially the one owned by Reliance, opposed this move but the matter went to the court and the Delhi High Court ruled in favour of a CAG audit. Further, AAP's stand against the proposed gas price hike, which clearly favoured Reliance Industries, was the third issue that was decisive in determining the line-up of forces in subsequent months. (For details of gas price controversy, see Guha Thakurta et al. 2014)

This was, in a profound sense, a turning point in the way the electoral battle panned out. For, from this point on, the media turned decisively against AAP as did the corporate sector. The fact that the party kept up its agitational style even in matters of government made it suspect in the eyes of vested interests. This high decibel agitational style also allienated progressive sections of support when it was deployed against African women suspected of being sex-workers in Khirki, an urban village in Delhi (Nigam 2014c). The multi-pronged attack on the party that emerged, along with obstruction by the opposition, led eventually to the resignation of the government in just forty-nine days. Although the resignation was legitimately over the thwarting of the Jan Lokpal Bill by Congress and BJP (Pandit and Lalchandani 2014), the major campaign plank against the party in the General Elections, assiduously purveyed by the media, was that it had abdicated and 'run away' rather than fulfilling its commitments. This hasty resignation by a government on which high hopes had been pinned, may well have been a fatal misjudgement on the part of AAP.

Nevertheless, in the 2014 general election, AAP has done surprisingly well, winning 4 seats in Punjab, and 2 percent of votes across the country, that is to say about 11 million votes. In Delhi, though it did not win a single seat, its vote share actually went up from 29.3 percent in the Assembly elections to 32.9 percent in the Lok Sabha elections. AAP was also second in every seat in Delhi, thus completing the rout of the Congress. Moreover, by taking on Narendra Modi in Varanasi, Arvind Kejriwal showed his ethical commitment to fight the corporate-Hindutva tsunami. Although he came second, the AAP campaign in Varanasi may have transformed the political landscape in the long term (Menon 2014).

But the more important development, with AAP entering the all-India electoral battle, was that it emerged as a point of articulation for a whole range of social movements. As the election battle unfolded, important figures like Medha Patkar of the Narmada Bachao Andolan, S. P. Udayakumar of the Kudankulam anti-nuclear energy struggle, Dayamani Barla, the feisty adivasi leader of Jharkhand, Soni Sori the school teacher from Chhattisgarh were arrested and tortured on suspicion accused of being a Maoist – and many others, joined the electoral battle as AAP candidates. AAP now emerged as a distinctly left-of-centre formation – a point of articulation of numerous social movements.

The crafting of Narendra Modi

It is only with this background in mind that we can make any sense of the way in which the candidature of Narendra Modi was turned into a veritable propaganda blitz by the media in the last few months of the campaign.

As we have mentioned, right from 2009–10, the corporate sector had been trying to put in place a dispensation that would give them unrestrained access to and control over land and the natural commons. The real turning point in Modi's relationship with the corporate sector came in October 2008 – as far as his makeover from 'a militant Hindutva politician' to a 'pro-business development man' was concerned. This was the moment when the Tatas, forced to withdraw from West Bengal and close operations on the much-hyped Nano car plant in the face of massive resistance from farmers, were looking for an alternative site. Modi immediately swung into action and provided land in Gujarat for the Nano factory (Jose 2012). It was suddenly as if the corporate sector had found the leader and mascot they were looking for.

It should be underlined that even though the UPA had maintained a 7.6 percent growth rate over the ten years of its rule, the corporate sector and the bourgeoisie at large were not happy. The reason for their unhappiness was that UPA was unable to give them free play for their profit-making, hamstrung as it still was by democratic pressures from mass movements. They were looking for a regime that would set aside democratic pressures and allow them easy access to land and forests for mining and other projects and not let environmental clearances stand in the way. They were looking for a dispensation where labour laws could be further eased in accordance with their wishes and the SEZ idea could be brought back.

Thus it was that they decided to back the candidature of Narendra Modi for Prime Ministership, who had by now acquired the reputation as Gujarat Chief Minister, of taking quick decisions in matters that were important for the corporate sector. There being virtually no opposition worth the name in his state and with the Hindu middle classes tied in a compact to the Development utopia of neoliberal elites, this was not a difficult task.

Modi's corporate supporters realized that for his candidature to be taken seriously his party, the BJP, and the parent organization of the Hindu Right, the RSS, had to be brought on board, which could be a risky enterprise. The BJP was already in shambles, riven with factionalism and dissension and gripped with a general loss of direction. Moreover, old war horses in the BJP, like L. K. Advani among many other leaders, also nursed ambitions of becoming Prime Minister, if the BJP were to ever come into power. The RSS, more concerned with its agenda of militarizing Hinduism, too had been adrift for the last few years, with attendance to its *shakhas* dwindling and the youth generally moving away from it. Moreover, the RSS is militantly nationalist, opposed to globalization and foreign investments and has also been taking an ecological stand on some development projects, from a Hindu perspective of sacred rivers and gods being disturbed by dams and mining (Sharma 2011).

The corporate strategy of making Modi Prime Minister therefore had to be devised independently of both the BJP and the RSS. In addition, Modi's figure was too closely linked to the Gujarat 2002 carnage. His image therefore, needed a complete overhaul.

A global PR company, APCO Worldwide was hired to promote Modi's investment and development showpiece 'Vibrant Gujarat'. The idea clearly was not simply to promote Vibrant Gujarat but also its leader, in the international business community.[14] The campaign for Modi's candidature was thus planned around the idea of the 'Gujarat Model of Development' – and it had the great advantage both of foregrounding the agenda that was so dear to corporate capital, and of being independent of both the BJP and the RSS.

The ground was prepared among the wider Hindu right public outside the BJP and the RSS.[15] For many of the more radical Hindu Right cadres at the local levels, Modi's name boosted their sagging morale. To them Modi was important precisely because he had presided over the mass killings of Muslims; his was the image of a strong man who would not shy away from implementing the Hindutva agenda. Eventually it was the wider support outside these formations, that proved crucial in settling the deal in his favour. And so was forged the shaky and unstable alliance between corporate interests and the Hindu Right public. And yet, it is doubtful if this alliance would have been backed by the media so strongly, had it not been for the fact that the short period of AAP rule gave a glimpse of the potential anti-corporate agenda that might unfold after the elections.

It is from this time that we see a near complete capture of all media space – both electronic and print – by the Modi campaign (Nigam 2014b). An idea of the kind of media blitz that followed can be had from the calculation done by the Centre for Media Studies, which showed that Modi got 33.2 percent of the prime time coverage in various channels as compared to Rahul Gandhi, Manmohan Singh and Sonia Gandi, whose combined figure came to 8.1 percent. Arvind Kejriwal of AAP got 10.3 percent – but almost all of it was highly negative coverage. Over and above this, were the advertisements put up by the party and corporate well-wishers. For over two months, it was Modi's face covering the entire front page of almost every newspaper – one such premium front page advertisement costs around 75 lakh rupees (US$ 124,825 at current rates). Bus shelters, hoardings, television advertisements – Modi's 'brooding face' was everywhere (Kazmin 2014).

It is increasingly clear that this is a Modi government and not a BJP or NDA government, and that the RSS is also going to be very tightly leashed as regards government policy. The BJP for instance, had voted against the UPA on the Indo-US civil nuclear agreement in 2008 (Chapter 7), and also resisted subsequent legislation on civil nuclear liability law which eventually 'deterred nuclear power equipment suppliers from participating in setting up of nuclear power plants in India' (Kaushal and Tiwari 2014). But the President's address to the joint Houses of Parliament after the Modi government was sworn in, stated that the government endorsed the India-US nuclear deal, and promised that the agreement will be operationalised (Kaushal and Tiwari 2014).

Another instance is that the BJP and RSS were among the right-wing political formations that endorsed the Supreme Court judgement in December 2013 that upheld the criminalization of homosexuality through Section 377 of the Indian Penal Code.[16] In doing so, the apex court overturned the historic judgment of the Delhi High Court in 2009 that had 'read down' Section 377, decriminalising adult consensual same sex conduct, drawing on the Constitutional rights to freedom and equality. In January 2104, the Supreme Court refused to review its verdict after hearing petitions filed by rights activists and the Congress government (which had withdrawn from its original position supporting Section 377).[17]

However, after the elections the RSS chief Ram Madhav said in an interview, in response to a question on Section 377, that 'while glorification of certain forms of social behaviour is not something we endorse, the penalising and criminalisation aspects need to be looked into. Whether to call homosexuality a crime and treat it as one in this day and age is questionable' (Kapur 2014).

Probably a corporate-backed Modi-led BJP has little time to waste on homophobia, and the RSS will have to fall in line. What is clear is that there is an on-going tussle over government policy between RSS and corporate-backed Modi.

From 'achhe din aane wale hain' to 'kadvi dava'

Modi's slogan 'Good times are on the way' had become impossible to avoid hearing or seeing for months, and these were the words with which the Prime Minister elect greeted his supporters in Vadodara on his triumphant return after the results were known. Promises to the corporate sector began to be implemented within days of the new government being sworn in. In a week, 'fast-tracking' of 200 'defence-related projects' along the Himalayan border had been announced, over the objections hitherto raised on environmental grounds. Activists are concerned because with the presence of glaciers and pristine forests from where several rivers originate, the hundred kilometre zone from the Line of Actual Control in these states is ecologically crucial, and is the source of water for North India (Sambhav 2014; Paranjpe 2014).

Within ten days, the BJP government of Rajasthan cleared state-level amendments to three critical Central Government legislations – the Industrial Disputes Act, Contract Labour Act and the Factories Act, 'seeking to liberate the corporate sector from the shackles of stringent requirements of the laws' as an enthusiastic news report put it (Iyer 2014). According to the changes, government permission will now not be required for retrenchment of up to 300 workers (up from 100 workers), a three-year time limit has been introduced for raising disputes and the percentage of workers needed for registration as a representative union has been raised from 15 percent to 30 percent.

In three weeks, the Central Government too, announced labour law 'liberalization'. That is, a review of the country's labour laws to 'tailor them to meet the needs of the National Manufacturing Policy with an aim towards boosting growth in the manufacturing sector.' Accordingly, the Labour Ministry proposed changes to the Industrial Disputes Act, 1947, for easier retrenchment of workers in the National Investment and Manufacturing Zones (NIMZs), and to raise the maximum 'overtime' from 50 hours to 100 hours a quarter (Surabhi 2014).

On June 15, in a major speech hinting at the Union Budget, Modi said that he would have to administer 'bitter medicine' and take 'harsh decisions'. He added, 'The medicine may hurt some of you but I ask for your support at this time.'[18]

Clearly, the 'bitter medicine' is for the people of the country, and the 'good days ahead' for the corporations. An approving report on what the Narendra Modi victory signals put it quite clearly:

'Conflicts about land, water, the environment and labour will remain, and are likely to even grow sharper, because the struggle to appropriate the fruits of development will always remain, and because development comes with "creative destruction". But the big difference will be that the might of the state will now be squarely with the business lobby.' (Chakravarty 2014).

We ended *Power and Contestation* on an optimistic note in late 2006. Almost eight years down the line, we still believe that contestations to the power of Nation and Capital will continue unabated. For the present, the power of Capital is on the ascendant, and the patrons of Hindu nationalism control institutions of government.

Notes

Introduction

1 "Not losing hope," *The Economist*, April 7, 2005.

2 Interview available at <http://www.pbs.org/newshour/bb/asia/jan-june04/friedman_03-09.html>. Downloaded May 3, 2007.

3 Interview on CNN (April 23, 2006), transcript available at <http:// edition.cnn.com/TRANSCRIPTS/0604/23!le.ol.html>. Downloaded on May 3, 2007.

4 *India Today*, January 15, 1990.

5 *India Today*, April 15, 1989, pp. 102–3.

1 The recalcitrance of caste

1 The term "Nehruvian era" is being used here to refer to an era that actually extends far beyond the person of Jawaharlal Nehru himself – almost up to the beginning of the 1980s, when the terms of political discourse and practice were still articulated within a secular-nationalist framework that was put in place by the Nehruvian leadership.

2 See *Lok Sabha Debates*, Sixth Series, XXII (1), Lok Sabha Secretariat, Febuary 23,1978, pp. 340–3. The *Manusmriti* is one of the central texts of what is now called Hinduism, which lays down, among other things, a rigorous fixation of occupations in line with caste and gender status.

3 The term "Dalitbahujan" is a recent coinage that refers to the broad spectrum of lower-caste groups ranging from the "Untouchable" outcastes, that is Dalits, to the other lower castes or non-Brahmins, generally referred to as Shudras in the language of the *chaturvarna* caste system.

4 The term Shudraatishudra has the same meaning as Dalitbahujan.

5 For details, see "Organised killings of Dalits in Khairlanji village, taluka Mohadi, district Bhandara: a report under the SC-ST (Prevention of Atrocities Act 1989), commissioned by Nodal Officer, SC-ST (PoA 1989), investigated by Dr Baba Saheb Ambedkar Research and Training Institute, Department of Social Justice, Government of Maharashtra and Centre for Equity and Social Justice, Yashada, at <lass.cs.umass.edu/~purukulk/yashada_khairlanji.pdf>, accessed February 1, 2007.

6 See Chapter 2 for Hindutva's take on the theory of Aryan invasions.

7 Press conference, *The Hindu*, November 28, 1999.

8 News report in *Times of India*, March 9, 1999.

9 Uma Bharati, "Not a woman's world. Case for OBC reservation," *Times of India*, July 17, 1998, p. 12, as told to Vidya Subramaniam. Uma Bharati has since left the BJP.

10 Saheli, Sabla Sangh, Action India, Disha, Women's Center, Forum Against Oppression of Women and Awaz-e-Niswan, *Development for Whom – a Critique of Women's Development Programmes*, 1991.

11 See Chapter 2.

12 There is now recognition on the Left, although it is grudging, that caste is a reality of Indian politics, and has to be dealt with. The CPI(M)'s *Draft of Updated Party Programme* (May, 2000) acknowledges that "The assertion by dalits has a democratic content reflecting the aspirations of the most oppressed sections of society. The backward castes have also asserted their rights in a caste-ridden society." This is, however, qualified by the following: "At the same time, a purely caste appeal which seeks to perpetuate caste divisions for the narrow aim of consolidating vote banks and detaching these downtrodden sections from the common democratic movement has also been at work" (p. 25). The Left engagement with caste is still very uneasy.

2 Politics of Hindutva and the minorities

1 Adivasi gods vary from region to region. In Dangs in Gujarat, for example, they worship Waghdev (a tiger deity), Nagdev (a snake deity), Dongardev (a hill deity), and Satimata, which is today interpreted in the terms of the *Ramayana* as a version of Sita. They also have their own *Ramayana* in which Ram is not the hero (Devy 2005: 9).

2 See Chapter 6.

3 Communalism/communal are the terms used in the Indian subcontinent to refer to exclusivist, religious identity-based politics.

4 "Jhajjar lynching was mistaken identity," *The Times of India*, November 28, 2002.

5 Bajrang Dal means Squad of Bajrang or Hanuman, the most devoted follower of Ram.

6 "Globalization" functions in public discourse as a stand-in for a whole range of negative features such as privatization, trade liberalization and opening up for foreign capital. The complexity of this phenomenon is unpacked over Chapters 3 and 4.

7 A provision under Muslim personal law that enables Muslim men to divorce unilaterally by uttering the word *talaq* three times.

8 This was a case of a Hindu married man converting to Islam in order to marry for the second time. Flavia Agnes points out that the judgment focused entirely on Muslim personal law, avoiding entirely the issue of bigamy by Hindu men, thus deliberately, and wrongly, assuming that the only breach of monogamy among Hindu men is by conversion to Islam.

9 A recent instance is a 2006 judgment by the Supreme Court that if a male member in a Hindu family dies without leaving a will, his share of coparcenary (joint family) property should be divided among his children on the basis of "notional partition," i.e. as if the partition of property was effected just before his death on the basis of the Hindu Succession Act (HSA). Under this act daughters do not have a direct share in ancestral property, they have a right only to the father's individual share of it. Thus this judgment ensured

that instead of the two daughters and one son of the deceased man getting a third each of his ancestral property, the property was to be considered to have first been equally divided between father and son, and only one half (the father's) was divided among the three children. This was a simply reported news item, with neither judges nor the media nor Hindutva forces becoming agitated about gender discriminatory aspects of Hindu religious personal laws. "Hindu law. Notional partition without will," *The Hindu*, October 10, 2006. Available at <http://www.hindu.com/2006/10/10/stories/2006101013200300.htm>.

The HSA was amended in 2005 to give daughters equal share in ancestral property, but this does not apply restrospectively. Nevertheless, while lower courts had evidently accepted the daughters' claim in this case, the Supreme Court judgment chose to interpret the HSA in a gender discriminatory way.

10 For a more extensive discussion of the Uniform Civil Code issue, see Nivedita Menon (2000).

11 Another emotive site for Hindutva politics. See Romila Thapar (2005).

12 "Godhra train fire accidental: Banerjee Report," *The Times of India*, March 4, 2006.

13 "Municipal win perks up Modi," *Telegraph*, July 21, 2004.

14 B. R. Ambedkar, for instance, was labeled by Hindutva votary Arun Shourie as casteist and anti-nationalist for insisting on prioritizing caste oppression.

15 The Waqf is a religious endowment run by theologians and meant to finance religious activities.

16 Sikand (2004b) reports on an important conference in New Delhi, organized at the Jamia Hamdard, "that brought together a number of Muslim women activists from different parts of India, as well as some members of the All-India Muslim Personal Law Board to discuss a range of issues relating to Muslim women." More importantly, newspapers such as the *Milli Gazette* have begun to carry statements issued by the AIMWPLB. See report <http://www.

milligazette.com/IndMusStat/2006a/966-aimwplb12jun06-reservation. htm> for instance.

17 Imrana alleged that she was raped by her father-in-law, and filed a complaint with the police. Following this the ulemas of Darul Uloom, Deoband, issued a fatwa, saying she could no longer stay with her husband as she had had sex with her father-in-law. A major controversy erupted threatening to blow up into a Shah Bano-type polarization. The BJP was of course ready to pounce once again and raise the issue of a uniform civil code, while chief minister Mulayam Singh Yadav came out in support of the clerics' fatwa. The All India Muslim Personal Law Board (AIMPLB) was split over the fatwa. Eventually, the father-in-law was found guilty and sentenced by a criminal court to ten years in prison, a decision welcomed by the AIMPLB. The last known of Imrana before she fell off the news pages is that she's been sent back to her maternal home with her five children, while her husband, a poor rickshaw-puller, has been thrown out of the house. The point is, however, that both she and her husband refused to be cowed by the fatwa.

18 For a history of Ayodhya as a multi-religious center with multiple influences from Buddhism to Islam and Sufism, see the Hindi book *Ayodhya: Sanjhi Sanskriti, Sanjhi Virasat* (Ayodhya: Shared Culture, Shared Traditions) by Vidya Bhushan Rawat, New Delhi: Books for Change, 2005. Book review in English by Yoginder Sikand available at <http://www.indianmuslims.info/books_info/history/ ayodhya_shared_culture_and_traditions_vidya_bhushan_rawat. html?PHPSESSID=42e9f9db38eb87b09a5fcb2fd10997b4>.

19 Prayer to Hanuman, Ram's devoted deputy.

20 For a discussion of this episode, see Chapter 5.

21 See report "Gujarat riot toll: millions of pounds," Rashmee Z. Ahmed, *Times of India*, May 15, 2002, at <http://timesofindia. indiatimes.com:80/cms.dll/articleshow?art_id=9984880>, accessed May 5, 2007. Subsequently, Gujarat has managed to recover from this setback and has been among the foremost state governments in attracting private investment.

3 Globalization I: accumulation by dispossession

1 We have borrowed the expression "accumulation by dispossession" from David Harvey (2003), though our argument takes a very different direction.

2 We are aware of critiques of this study by proponents of big dams, but we do not think that these are able to address the substantial questions raised by the authors. For one such critical review, see A. Vaidyanathan in *Economic and Political Weekly*, December 3, 2005.

3 See report by Independent Media in <http://www.countercurrents.org/hr-im060106.htm>.

4 "Jindal Stainless scouting for buys in Asia, Europe," Mines and Communities Website, August 23, 2006, <http://www.minesandcommunities.org/Action/press1198.htm>.

5 See official site of the External Affairs Ministry, <http://meaindia.nic.in/indiapublication/Special%20Economic.htm>.

6 Editorial, "Mining and industrialization update Orissa," p. 1, available at <http://www.freewebs.com/epgorissa/M%20I%20Update/Final%20Mining%20Update%20-%20October%5B1%5D.pdf>.

7 It may be noted that a book on the rise to power of Dhirubhai Ambani, the founder of the Reliance Group of Industries, by Hamish MacDonald, *The Polyester Prince: The Rise of Dhirubhai Ambani* (Allen and Unwin, 1998) has been made unavailable by the might of Reliance. One single copy is available at the time of writing this, on Amazon at the cost of US $997!

8 "VP Singh arrested on way to Reliance Plant," *The Hindu*, July 9, 2006, p. 1.

9 See also Chapter 5.

10 Explained in Chapter 6.

11 Report available at <http://narmada.aidindia.org/content/view/52/>.

12 The information on industrial closures in Delhi is drawn from a Citizens' Report, *The Order that Felled a City* (Delhi Janwadi Adhikar Manch), of which the authors were a part.

13 Judgment on PIL of Almitra Patel etc., February 16, 2000. Cited in Delhi Janwadi Adhikar Manch, *How Many Errors Does Time Have Patience For? Industrial Closures and Slum Demolitions in Delhi*, Delhi, 2000, p. 21.

14 *Tehelka*, May 27, 2006.

15 This aspect of the "opening up" of satellite towns is invisible for instance to Suketu Mehta, who in *Maximum City* (2004: 131) partly attributes the "tragedy of Bombay" to the failure to shift offices to Navi Mumbai, while the tragedy of the original inhabitants of Navi Mumbai and the inevitable ripple effects of this pattern of urbanization remain unnoticed.

16 From Alternative Law Forum, "Claiming the city – module from illegal citizen course," on the ALF website, <http://www.altlawforum.org/ EDUCATIONAL%20INITIATIVES/claiming>.

4 Globalization II: new economies of desire

1 Gurcharan Das (2000).

2 *Sunday Express*, August 10, 2003, p. 11.

3 As Manuel (2001) observes, "piracy has been the nemesis of the cassette industry from its inception" (p. 78). He goes on: the very "ease of duplication" that fueled the industry's growth now made possible "the emergence of a vast, parasitic 'unorganized' sector of the music industry which has bled many legitimate producers to bankruptcy" (ibid).

4 *India Today*, May 15, 1988, p. 145.

5 This certainly causes immense anxieties among both corporate interests and state elites and moves to regulate the cable operators were already afoot in 2003. A new system known as Conditional Access System (CAS), pushed by the Supreme Court, has now been put in place that seeks to eliminate the small operators, ostensibly in the name of the consumer. A CAS is a system that restricts electronic transmission through cable, and makes it available only to subscribed clients, as the signal is encrypted and is unavailable for unauthorized reception. A set-top box containing a conditional access module is

required in the customer premises to receive and decrypt the signal. For an early debate, see "Should CAS be introduced?," Rediff.com at <http://inhome.rediff.com/money/2003/may/28cas.htm>, accessed February 2, 2007.

6 We have extended the metaphor used by Pachauri here but the sense remains largely his.

7 *Navbharat Times*, December 19, 2006, front page.

8 Political movements around this dimension are discussed in Chapter 5.

9 A traditional community of male-to-female transgender people.

10 In (Prasad 2004), he cites the following from the *Communist Manifesto*: "The bourgeoisie, wherever it has got the upper hand, has put an end to all feudal, patriarchal, idyllic relations."

11 All the citations are from the two-page invitation letter for the party issued by Chandra Bhan Prasad.

12 See the *Bhopal Document*, Government of Madhya Pradesh, 2002. Also see Aditya Nigam (2002).

13 One of the present authors has dealt with this aspect in a separate paper, Aditya Nigam (unpublished) "Heterotopias of Dalit politics: becoming-subject and the consumption Utopia," presented at the Shelby Cullom Davis Center for Historical Studies, Department of History, Princeton University, April 27, 2006.

5 Old Left, New Left

1 See Chapter 2 for details.

2 Finally, the BJP was called in by the president to form the government and was given two weeks to prove its majority on the floor of the parliament. It is a measure of the BJP's political isolation, following the Babri Masjid demolition, that even in 1996, there were few who were willing to join it in government. The government lasted for just thirteen days and was soon replaced by a United Front government (see Chapter 2).

3 For Caesarism, see Antonio Gramsci, *Selections from the Prison Notebooks*, <http://www.marxists.org/archive/gramsci/prison_notebooks/state_civil/ch02.htm>, downloaded May 1, 2007.

4 For details on the revolt of lower castes, see Chapter 1.

5 See Chapter 3.

6 The Trinamool Congress is a breakaway party from the state Congress.

7 A number of fact-finding teams and groups have made their investigation reports public that corroborate this. Many of these reports, especially those produced by the Association for the Protection of Democratic Rights (APDR), Paschim Banga Khet Majoor Samity (PBKMS), and the National Alliance of People's Movements (NAPM), are available on the web. See especially <www.kafila.org>, <www.sanhati.com>, and <www. sacredmediacow.com>.

8 "Kerala CPM takes on indiscipline," DH News Service, *Deccan Herald*, December 29, 2006, <http://www.deccanherald.com/deccanherald/dec292006/national23281720061228.asp>. See also "CPM's Kerala secy signals to CM: can't follow party line? Then, leave," *Indian Express*, December 29, 2006, front page.

9 The term "mainstream Left" refers here to the formerly pro-Soviet Communist Party of India (CPI) and the Communist Party of India (Marxist) (CPI[M]). The former had become much more a part of the establishment during the Soviet days, thanks to the USSR's close relationship to the ruling Congress Party. Lately, however, the CPI has shown greater openness to other radical currents and has to that extent been less part of the establishment. It is not, however, really a force of any consequence anywhere in the country. We shall therefore not deal with the CPI here and focus only on the CPI(M), which plays for much greater stakes.

10 The Central Committee review of the 1996 elections noted, for instance, that "... we are not able to go beyond our existing areas and increase our electoral strength ... At the organizational level, it must be examined why despite the considerable range of mass activities and movements conducted by the Party ... they have not found reflection

in terms of the expansion of the mass strength of the Party." For details, see *Political Organizational Report Adopted by the 16th Congress of the CPI(M)*, New Delhi: CPI(M).

11 This term denotes land held in somebody else's name, usually to circumvent land ceiling laws.

12 A Marathi word meaning "to search out critically."

13 Kothari summarized it thus: "(I)ssues and arenas of human activity that were not so far seen as amenable to political action – people's health, rights over forests and community resources, even deeply personal and primordial issues as are involved in the struggle for women's rights – get defined as political and provide for arenas of struggle" (Kothari, B. 1984: 219–20).

14 The project was shelved due to the intervention of Prime Minister Indira Gandhi in 1979. The controversy, however, had already unleashed a major debate within the party, especially the intellectual circles associated with it, on the entire question of environmental sustainability of development.

15 Guha Niyogi began his political career in the late 1960s when he joined the Bhilai Steel Plant as a worker and formed a union called the "Blast Furnace Action Committee." After being thrown out of the job for "security reasons," he left Bhilai and went to work in the forests of Bastar. Learning the local tribal languages, Gondi and Halbi, he did odd jobs ranging from trading in goats to fishing while he was there (Sail 1998: 18). When the Naxalite revolt took place, he briefly joined the movement, but basically continued to work where he was and in the way he was. After a brief association, he broke with the Naxalite group he was associated with because he had sharp disagreements with their attitude to trade union work, which its members thought was "economism" and "reformism" (Singh, N. K. 1977: 40–1). After the Emergency, he returned to Durg and worked in the Dani Tola mines near Dalli-Rajhara, where he began his experiments in "trade unionism with a difference" (Sail 1998: 18).

16 It should be stated here that it is not the "reality" of the Cultural Revolution that is relevant here; rather, the popular appeal

of China's "struggle against revisionism" of the USSR, among younger communists drew directly from the Mao's idea that class struggles would continue even under socialism.

17 Charu Mazumdar, the most important leader of the movement, had declared that the 1970s would be the decade of liberation.

18 Later, many of the latter shifted their loyalties to the backward-caste politics of Laloo Yadav once he became chief minister.

19 This should not be read, of course, as something exceptional to an Oriental society such as India's. On the contrary, seen through the lens of the Indian experience, as also the post-colonial experience in general, it will reveal that even in the secular West, radical as well as liberal politics continues to be so structured by community and religion.

20 The distinguishing parts of the names of most groups, like "Liberation" or "People's War," were actually names of the newspapers or journals brought out by the group.

21 We distinguish such forums from what are called "human rights organizations," many of which are funded organizations that work in tandem with internationally evolving agendas. The latter we would place under the rubric of "NGOs."

22 Not to be confused with the various communist-led outfits of the cold war period, like the All India Peace and Solidarity Organization (AIPSO), which were not ever autonomous peace movements.

23 See <http://www.anawa.org.au/india/jaduguda.html> and <http://www.wise-uranium.org/umopjdg.html>, last accessed May 3, 2007.

24 The contempt in which citizens' knowledge of these issues is held by the government's Department of Atomic Energy is evident in a response of the DAE to a protest letter sent to it by the local population. The DAE argued that by mining and taking uranium away, it would be removing a source of radiation from the area! See "Uranium mining. Questionable decision," *Economic and Political Weekly*, November 11, 2000, p. 3984.

6 When was the nation?

1 Here we use the well-known title of the book by Sunil Khilnani, *The Idea of India*, Penguin Books, 2003.

2 Of course, the classic process even in Europe was forceful and authoritarian. French historian Eugen Weber starkly terms it as "akin to colonialism." This is how he describes the "acculturation" process in the nineteenth century by which the inhabitants of the area that became France were made "French": "the civilization of the French by urban France, the disintegration of local cultures by modernity and their absorption into the dominant civilization of Paris ... Left largely to their own devices until their promotion to citizenship, the unassimilated rural masses had to be integrated into the dominant culture as they had been integrated into an administrative entity. What happened was akin to colonialism ..." (Weber 1976: 486).

3 "Princely states" were kingdoms, many of ancient lineage, and with a long history of exercising political power. It was British colonial terminology that referred to the rulers as "princes." While the quasi-independent status they enjoyed under British rule made them hostile to the anti-imperialist nationalist movement, some of these kingdoms had enlightened rulers with agendas that were in many cases more progressive than that of the British government.

4 It was an LITE suicide bomber who assassinated Prime Minister Rajiv Gandhi in 1991.

5 We are thankful to M. S. S. Pandian for a conversation on this last point.

6 ULFA is the United Liberation Front of Assam and NSCN-IM is the National Socialist Council of Nagaland (Isaac-Muivah). Both organizations are discussed in more detail later in the chapter.

7 See homepage of ULFA <http://www.geocities.com/CapitolHill/Congress/7434/ulfa.htm>, downloaded December 10, 2006; and homepage of NSCN <http://www.nscnonline.org/nscn/index-2.html>, downloaded December 25, 2006.

8 From the homepage of ULFA <http://www.geocities.com/CapitolHill/Congress/7434/ulfa.htm>, downloaded December 10, 2006.

9 Translation of ULFA leaflet, "*Ahombashi Purbabangiya Janaganaloy*," Sanjukta Mukti Bahini Ahom, 1992, by Bhibhu Prasad Routray, "ULFA. The 'Revolution' comes full circle," available at <http://www.satp.org/satporgtp/ publication/faultlines/volume13/Article6.htm>.

10 It would be misleading not to recognize that the ULFA has been responsible for other violent acts directed at non-combatant individuals who were not representatives of the state. In 1997 an NGO activist Sanjoy Ghose was kidnapped by ULFA. The coalition of NGOs with which he worked was accused of "promoting corporate culture" and of being "enemies of Assamese nationalist aspirations," and was asked to leave Assam, which it did within twenty-four hours of the ultimatum. Ghose remained missing while ULFA issued conflicting statements on his health. Eventually his dead body was recovered, and in the face of mounting outrage from all sections, including those sympathetic to the legitimate demands of ULFA, and opposed to measures such as the AFSPA, ULFA claimed that Ghose had died accidentally. See "Activist Sanjoy Ghose dead, confirms ULFA," *Rediff on the Net*, available at http://www.rediff.com/news/aug/o7ghose.htm>.

11 Meiteis are the largest ethnic group in Manipur, the majority having converted to Hinduism around the seventeenth/eighteenth centuries, while the rest practice other religions, including an ancient Meitei religion.

12 See Note 1, Chapter 2, for a discussion of the term "tribe."

13 The Inner Line was introduced by the British in 1873, separating the plains from the hills, in order to govern activities by British entrepreneurs whose reckless expansion for raw rubber and tea plantations was endangering the relationship of the Crown with the hill tribes. This new policy led to strict maintenance of boundaries in what had hitherto been "a complex world of interrelationships" (Baruah 1999: 28–9).

14 "Ticking alien bomb," *North East Enquirer*, 2 (10), August 22–September 6, 2003. Available at <http://www.nenanews.com/NEE%20Aug.22%20-%20Sept.6,%2003/Cover%20Story.htm>.

15 Formed in 1964, the Jammu and Kashmir National Liberation Front had offices in several countries including Pakistan. It was renamed Jammu and Kashmir Liberation Front (JKLF) in 1971.

16 The terms "pro-" India or Pakistan must not be understood as necessarily implying the desire to accede to either. The tilt of specific groups reveals only their assessment of which country's support they believe would provide greater possibilities of achieving their own agenda.

17 See homepage of JKLF, <http://www.geocities.com/jklf-kashmir/jklfaims.html>.

18 A form of hijab.

19 A hereditary title of one of Kashmir's important religious seats, and head priest of the Jamia Masjid in Srinagar.

20 The JKLF that is Pakistan-based, however, continues to espouse armed struggle.

21 See, for example, reports by Committee for Initiative on Kashmir, New Delhi (1991, 1993); Human Rights Watch (2006); Balagopal (1996); Ghate (2002).

22 News report "First for Valley," Express News Service (2006).

23 There was also pressure within the NDA to amend POTA from the MDMK, whose general secretary Vaiko, as we saw earlier, had been arrested under it.

24 Lathis are heavy bamboo poles bound with iron used by Indian police.

7 India in the World

1 See Chapter 6 for a detailed discussion of these positions.

2 See also Chapter 2.

3 Sudheendra Kulkarni (2006) commends both BJP's Arun Shourie and the CPI(M) leader Prakash Karat for having "publicly aired convergent views on an important national issue."

4 See, for instance, *Economic and Political Weekly*, editorial "US designs, India's choices," December 23, 2006, p. 5204.

5 For a more comprehensive articulation of this voice, see also articles by Itty Abraham; Achin Vanaik; M. V. Ramana; and R. Rajaraman, Z. Mian, and A. H. Nayyar in *Economic and Political Weekly*, November 20–6, 2004, pp. 4997–5026.

6 See also Chapter 6.

7 "India, Iran and Pakistan gas pipeline talks continue in Teheran," domain-b.com, 25 January, 2007, at <http://www.domain-b.com/industry/oil_gas/20070125_pipeline.html>, accessed January 29, 2007.

8 "Iran, India and Pakistan agree on peace pipeline price formula," Iranian Students News Agency, Teheran, <http://www.domain-b.com/industry/oil_gas/20070125_pipeline.html>, accessed January 29, 2007. It is worth stating here that the United States of America had been quite unhappy about this pipeline agreement, especially, though not only, because of Iran's defiance on the nuclear issue. For details see Voice of America report by Patricia Nunan (2005).

9 It is important that this bloc came into existence at the time of the right-wing NDA regime in June 2003, and represents, thus, a larger logic than simple party/ideological considerations. See <http://www.tribuneindia.com/2003/20030608/world.htm#1>, accessed January 30.

10 In 1974, ignoring the protests of Bangladesh, India constructed the Farakka barrage to divert the waters of the river Ganga (Ganges), ostensibly to prevent silting of the Calcutta port. The barrage severely limited the access to the river of the Bangladeshi population of the lower Gangetic plain. Apart from this, the ecosystem of the plain was also adversely affected.

11 Insurgency in the north-east of India is discussed in Chapter 6. Please note that Myint refers to "Burma" rather than "Myanmar" in the article cited here.

Conclusion: a heterogeneous present

1 Zee News Bureau Report, "India's GDP to surpass UK by mid-next decade: Goldman Sachs," January 31, 2007 at <http://www.

zeenews.com/znnew/articies.asp?aid=349683&sid=BUS&ssid=50>, accessed January 31, 2007.

2 See special issue of *Social Scientist*, 33 (9–10), September–October 2005, pp. 388–9, for the critique of the new National Curriculum Framework by Left historians close to the CPI(M). For a response to this critique, see Menon (2005).

3 See "Land unsettled," *Down to Earth*, January 31, 2007, <http://www.downtoearth.org.in/ful16.asp?foldername=20050531&filename=news&sec_id=4&sid=2>, accessed January 31, 2007.

4 "National consultation on the draft Forest Rights Bill," Asian Centre for Human Rights, <http://www.achrweb.org/DFRB/Forest_Bill.htm>, accessed January 31, 2007.

5 "Court stays proceedings against MF Hussain," Legal correspondent, *The Hindu*, May 9, 2007, front page.

6 For details of this judgment see Nivedita Menon "Contempt of democracy: time for judicial reform," at <http://www.kafila.org/2007/03/01/contempt-of-democracy-time-for-judicial-reform/>.

7 Meena Menon, "Opposition to SEZ pays dividends for PWP, Sena in Raigad," *The Hindu*, March 28, 2007, p. 1.

8 Special Correspondent, "Kerala traders threaten to boycott reliance products," *The Hindu*, May 20, 2007, p. 8.

9 See Introduction.

Epilogue June 2014

1 "BJP activists resort to vandalism, attack Masjids amidst celebrations," *Coastal Digest* http://coastaldigest.com/index.php/ls-polls-2014/64664-bjp-activists-resort-to-vandalism-attack-masjids-amidst-celebrations, accessed June 19, 2014. "Chicken stall owner beaten up in Hoode," *The Hindu* May 18, 2014.

2 "Muslims in Pune avoid skull caps, Pathani suits after techie killing," *Trans Asia News Service*, June 8, 2014, <http://transasianews.com/asia/52-india/2153-muslims-in-pune-avoid-skull-caps-pathani-suits-after-techie-killing>.

3 "Communal clashes in Narendra Modi's Ahmedabad on eve of his swearing in ceremony," *DNA*, Tuesday, May 27, 2014.

4 "Communal clash near Gurgaon injures 15," *The Times of India* June 9, 2014.

5 "How Amit Shah Delivered Uttar Pradesh For the BJP," <http://www.ndtv.com/elections/article/election-2014/how-amit-shah-delivered-uttar-pradesh-for-the-bjp-524828>

6 "Documentary sheds light on Amit Shah's link in Muzaffarnagar riots," *The Indian Express*, Ahmedabad, March 19, 2014

7 See for instance, Jyotika Sood, "Supreme Court Upholds Land Rights of People Affected by Infrastructure Projects," *Down to Earth*, November 7, 2012, <http://www.downtoearth.org.in/content/supreme-court-upholds-land-rights-people-affected-infrastructure-projects>, accessed June 17, 2014), and "Land Owners Score in First SC Verdict," *The Free Press Journal*, January 26, 2014, <http://freepressjournal.in/land-owners-score-in-first-sc-verdict>, accessed June 17, 2014.

8 In February 2012, the Supreme Court of India cancelled all the 122 2G Spectrum licenses that had been issued during Raja's tenure. The court held the allocation of licenses to be "wholly arbitrary, capricious and contrary to public interest apart from being violative of the doctrine of equality" to "favour some companies at the cost of the public exchequer." See <http://timesofindia.indiatimes.com/india/2G-verdict-A-Raja-virtually-gifted-away-important-national-asset-says-Supreme-Court/articleshow/11728003.cms?referral=PM>, accessed June 10, 2014.

9 'Some Telephone Conversations – The X-Tapes', *OPEN Magazine*, November 20, 2010, <http://www.openthemagazine.com/article/nation/some-telephone-conversations>, accessed June 18, 2014.

10 See, for instance, *Outlook*, Web edition, December 10, 2010, <http://www.outlookindia.com/article/800-New-Radia-Tapes/268618> and <http://www.outlookindia.com/article/ 4718881902620090522161 405/268625>, accessed June 10, 2014.

11 See, for instance, the report in *India Today* "Coal Scam: How India Lost Rs 1.86 Lakh Crores," at <http://indiatoday.intoday.in/gallery/

coal-scam-how-india-lost-rs-1.86-lakh-crores/1/7610.html#photo3>, accessed June 10, 2014.

12 See, for instance, "Day-to-day trial in CWG scam case as per SC verdict," *Times of India*, April 27, 2014. <http://timesofindia.indiatimes.com/india/Day-to-day-trial-in-CWG-scam-case-as-per-SC-verdict/articleshow/34282535.cms>; "CWG scam: Oppn tears into govt, pins OC blame on PM, Sonia," *Times of India*, August 10, 2011, <http://timesofindia.indiatimes.com/india/CWG-scam-Oppn-tears-into-govt-pins-OC-blame-on-PM-Sonia/articleshow/9547862.cms>; and Vishal Kant, "FIR Against Shiela in CWG Scam," <http://www.thehindu.com/news/cities/Delhi/fir-against-sheila-in-cwg-scam/article5661469.ece>, accessed June 10, 2014.

13 See the site of the National Campaign for People's Right to Information <http://righttoinformation.info/974/list-of-rti-activists-killed/>

14 Appu Esthose Suresh, "The Modi Machine: Makeover Gurus," *The Indian Express*, October 20, 2013, <http://archive.indianexpress.com/news/the-modi-machine-makeover-gurus/1184809>, accessed June 18, 2014

15 One can get an indication about at how late a stage both these organizations ultimately 'agreed' to support Modi's candidature from the following reports: "RSS Sets Four Conditions for Backing Modi's PM Candidature," *India Today Online*, September 10, 2013, <http://indiatoday.intoday.in/story/narendra-modi-rss-rss-conditions-for-modi-bjp-pm-candidate-ayodhya/1/309155.html>, accessed on June 18, 2014); and Marya Shakil, "Narendra Modi as PM Candidate: Has RSS-BJP Reached a Consensus," *IBNLive*, September 9, 2013, <http://ibnlive.in.com/news/narendra-modi-as-pm-candidate-has-rssbjp-reached-a-consensus/420686-37-64.html>, accessed on June 18, 2014.

16 "Supreme Court right in sticking with 377: RSS," <http://www.newsx.com/national/nation/item/15150-supreme-court-right-in-sticking-with-section-377-rss>, accessed June 19, 2014.

17 "Supreme Court sets aside the High Court decision on anti-sodomy law: Huge setback for LGBT rights, activists vow to continue the fight," Lawyers' Collective <http://www.lawyerscollective.org/

updates/supreme-court-sets-high-court-decision-anti-sodomy.html>, accessed June 19, 2014.

18 "Ahead of Union Budget, PM Narendra Modi hints at 'bitter medicine'," <http://economictimes.indiatimes.com/articleshow/36589234.cms?utm_source=contentofinterest&utm_medium=text&utm_campaign=cppst>, accessed June 19, 2014.

Bibliography

Adeney, Katharine and Lawrence Saez (eds) (2005) *Coalition Politics and Hindu Nationalism*, London and New York: Routledge.

Agnes, Flavia (1994a) "Women's movement within a secular framework: redefining the agenda," *Economic and Political Weekly*, XXIX(19).

— (1994b) "Triple *talaq* judgement: do women really benefit?," *Economic and Political Weekly*, May 14.

— (2002) "Affidavit," in *Of Lofty Claims and Muffled Voices*, Flavia Agnes (ed.), Bombay: Majlis.

Ajith, S "Lokpal and Lokayuktas Act: A Commentary," *Live Law. in*, March 1, <http://www.livelaw.in/lokpal-lokayuktas-act-commentary/>.

Akoijam, Bimol A. (2006) "Ghosts of colonial modernity: identity and conflict in the eastern frontier of South Asia," in Prasenjit Biswas and C. Joshua Thomas (eds), *Peace in India's North-East. Meaning, Metaphor and Method*, New Delhi: Regency Publications.

Akoijam, Bimol A. and Th. Tarunkumar (2005) "Armed Forces (Special Powers) Act 1958: disguised war and its subversions," *Eastern Quarterly*, 1, April–June.

Alvares, Claude and Ramesh Billorey (2006) *Damming the Narmada. India's Greatest Planned Environmental Disaster*, Dehradun: Natraj Publishers.

Amin, Samir (1993) "Social movements in the periphery," in Ponna Wignaraja (ed.), *New Social Movements in the South. Empowering the People*, New Delhi: Vistaar Publications, pp. 76–100.

Bibliography

Amte, Baba (1990) "Narmada Project. The case against and an alternative perspective," *Economic and Political Weekly*, April 21, pp. 811–18.

Anonymous (1996) "Women. Invisible constituency," Commentary in *Economic and Political Weekly*, May 18.

Anwar, Ali (2005) *Masawat Ki Jung* (trans. Mohd Imran Ali and Zakia Jowher), New Delhi: Indian Social Institute.

Appadurai, Arjun (2011) "Our Corruption, Our Selves," *Kafila*, August 30. <http://kafila.org/2011/08/30/our-corruption-ourselves-arjun-appadurai>.

Arora, Satish Kumar (1956) "The reorganization of the Indian states," *Far Eastern Survey*, 25(2), February, pp. 27–30.

Awasthi, Neeraj, Shalini Joshi, Govindan Kutty, Nivedita Menon and Anjali Sinha (1998) Report of the team investigating the events of April 22–3, 1998, at the Maheswar dam site, village Jalud, Madya Pradesh.

Awasthi, Puja (2007) "Muslim women: our own personal law board," May 8, 2007, *India Together*, <http://www.indiatogether.org/2006/sep/womaimwplb.htm>.

Bachman, Monica (2002) "After the fire," in Ruth Vanita (ed.), *Queering India. Same-sex Love and Eroticism in Indian Culture and Society*, New York and London: Routledge.

Balagopal, K. (1996) "Kashmir: self-determination, communalism and democratic rights," *Economic and Political Weekly*, November 2.

— (2006) interview with Vijay Simha, *Tehelka*, January 21, p. 27.

Banerjee, Parthasarathi (2006) "West Bengal – land acquisition and peasant resistance at Singur," *Economic and Political Weekly*, November 18, pp. 4718–20.

Banerjee, Sumanta (1984) *India's Simmering Revolution: The Naxalite Uprising*, New Delhi: Select Book Service Syndicate.

Banerjee, Surabhi (1997) *Jyoti Basu: The Authorized Biography*, New Delhi: Penguin (Viking), excerpted in Rediff on the Net, at <http://www.rediff.com/news/mar/28basu.htm>.

Barbora, Sanjay (2002) "Ethnic politics and land use. Genesis of conflict in India's north-east," *Economic and Political Weekly*, March 30.

— (2006) "Rethinking India's counter-insurgency campaign in north-east," *Economic and Political Weekly*, September 2.

Baruah, Sanjib (1989) "Minority policy in the north-east. Achievements and dangers," *Economic and Political Weekly*, September 16, pp. 2087–90.

— (1999) *India Against Itself. Assam and the Politics of Nationality*, New Delhi: Oxford University Press.

— (2005a) "Nations within nation-states," *Hindustan Times*, October 13.

— (2005b) *Durable Disorder. Understanding the Politics of Northeast India*, New Delhi: Oxford University Press.

Basu, Amrita (1996) "Mass movement or elite conspiracy? The puzzle of Indian nationalism," in David Ludden (ed.), *Contesting the Nation. Religion, Community and the Politics of Democracy in India*, Philadelphia: University of Pennsylvania Press.

Basu, Jyoti (2002) "Twenty-five years of Left Front government: people made history," *People's Democracy*, 26(24), June 23.

Basu, Tapan, Pradip Datta, Sumit Sarkar, Tanika Sarkar and Sambuddha Sen (1993) *Khaki Shorts, Saffron Flags*, Delhi and Hyderabad: Orient Longman.

Baviskar, Amita (1995) *In the Belly of the River. Tribal Conflicts over Development in the Narmada Valley*, Delhi: Oxford University Press.

— (2003) "Between violence and desire: space, power, and identity in the making of metropolitan Delhi," *International Social Science Journal*, 55(175), pp. 89–98.

— (2005) "Adivasi encounters with Hindu nationalism in MP," *Economic and Political Weekly*, November 26, pp. 5105–13.

Baxi, Upendra, Vasudha Dhagamwar, Raghunath Kelkar and Lotika Sarkar (1979) "An Open Letter to the Chief Justice of India, in Mary E. John (ed) *Women's Studies in India: A Reader*, Penguin 2008.

Behar, Amitabh (2002) "Peoples' social movements: an alternative perspective on forest management in India," Draft Working Paper, Overseas Development Institute, London, <http://www.odi.uk/livelihoodoptions/papers/draft%20177.pdf>, downloaded February 9, 2005.

Behera, Navnita Chadha (2000) *State, Identity and Violence. Jammu, Kashmir and Ladakh*, New Delhi: Manohar.

Benjamin, Solomon (2000) "Governance, economic settings and poverty in Bangalore," *Environment and Urbanization*, (12)35, available at <http://eau.sagepub.com/cgi/content/abstract/12/1/35>.

Beteille, Andre (2004) "Race and caste," in Sukhdeo Thorat and Umakant (eds), *Caste, Race and Discrimination. Discourses in International Context*, Jaipur and New Delhi: Rawat Publications

Bhan, Gautam (2006) "Whose Delhi is it anyway?," *Tehelka*, October 7.

Bhattacharya, Buddhadeb (2007) "Thousands of young people want jobs ... they will shape the country's future," *Indian Express*, January 19, 2007, p. 11.

Bhattacharya, Rajeev (2006) "Nagalim will not be part of India, says Muivah," *Indian Express*, December 22, p. 3.

Bhushan, Prashant (2000) "People be damned," *Hindustan Times*, October 20.

Bidwai, Praful (2002) "Portents from the Kashmir polls," <http://www.antiwar.com/bidwai/bi092002.html>, September 20, downloaded December 29, 2006.

— (2006) "Nuclear disadvantage," *Tehelka*, July 15, 2006.

— (2007) "Drifting into nuclear blunderland," South Asians Against Nukes. Available at <groups.yahoo.com/group/SAAN_/message/999>.

Bidwai, Praful and Achin Vanaik (1999) *South Asia on a Short Fuse. Nuclear Politics and the Future of Global Disarmament*, New Delhi: Oxford University Press.

Biswas, Nilanjana (2007) "The loan that looms over Kerala," *Tehelka*, January 27, Edit page.

Biswas, Soutik (2004) "Storm over Indian women's mosque," BBC Online, January 27, <http://news.bbc.co.uk/2/hi/south_asia/3429695.stm>.

Brass, Paul (2006) *Forms of Collective Violence. Riots, Pogroms and Genocide in Modern India*, Gurgaon: Three Essays Collective.

Butalia, Urvashi and Tanika Sarkar (eds) (1995) *Women and the Hindu Right*, Delhi: Kali for Women.

Brass, Thomas R (2006) *Forms of Collective Violence. Riots, Pogroms and Genocide in Modern India*, Gurgaon: Three Essays Collective

— (2005) *The Production of Hindu-Muslim Violence in Contemporary India*, Seattle: University of Washington Press.

Candland, Christopher (n.d.) "New social and new political unionism: labour, industry and the state in India and Pakistan," *Global Solidarity Dialogue*, <http://www.antena.nl/~waterman/candland.html>, downloaded February 18, 2005.

Centre for Education and Communication (CEC) (1998) *On a Rainbow in the Sky: The Chattisgarh Mukti Morcha*, New Delhi.

Chatterjee, Manini (2004) "Sangh rushes in to mine Muslim population data," *Indian Express*, September 8, p. 1.

Chakravarty, Manas (2014) "Election results a victory for Indian capitalism", <http://www.livemint.com/Opinion/rccwjo8IwotZaCbSioNZFP/Election-results-a-victory-for-Indian-capitalism.html?utm_source=copy, accessed June 19, 2104.

Chakravarti, Uma (1983) "Rape, class and the State," PUCL Bulletin, September. <http://www.pucl.org/from-archives/Gender/rape-class.htm>.

Chatterjee, Partha (2011) "Against Corruption = Against Politics," *Kafila*, August 28, <http://kafila.org/2011/08/28/against-corruption-against-politics-partha-chatterjee/>.

— (1994/1998) "Secularism and toleration," in Rajeev Bhargava (ed.), *Secularism and Its Critics*, New Delhi: Oxford University Press.

Chiriyankandath, James and Andrew Wyatt (2005) "The NDA and Indian foreign policy," in K. Adeney and L. Saez (eds), *Coalition Politics and Hindu Nationalism*, London and New York: Routledge.

Chowdhary, Rekha (2000) "Debating autonomy," *Seminar*, 496, December. Committee for Initiative on Kashmir (1991) *Kashmir: A Land Ruled by the Gun*, New Delhi.

— (1993) *Kashmir War Proxy War*, New Delhi.

Citizens' Report (2013) "In the relief camps of Muzaffarnagar and Shamli," *Kafila*, September 24. <http://kafila.org/2013/09/24/in-the-relief-camps-of-muzaffarnagar-and-shamli/>, accessed June 19, 2014.

Communist Party of India (Marxist) (1998) *Political Organizational Report Adopted by the 16th Congress of the CPI(M)*, New Delhi.

Corbridge, Stuart and John Harris (2000) *Reinventing India: Liberalization, Hindu Nationalism and Popular Democracy*, Cambridge: Polity.

Das, Gurcharan (2000) *India Unbound*, New Delhi and New York: Viking.

Das, Prafulla (2004) "A murky deal," *The Hindu*, December 4, 2004.

Dasgupta, Biplab (1974) *The Naxalite Movement*, New Delhi: Allied Publishers.

Datta, Polly (2005) "The issue of discrimination in Indian federalism in the post-1977 politics of West Bengal," *Comparative Studies of South Asia, Africa and the Middle East*, 25(2), pp. 449–64.

Delhi Janwadi Adhikar Manch (1997) *The Order That Felled a City*, Delhi.
— (2001) *How Many Errors Does Time Have Patience For? Industrial Closures and Slum Demolitions in Delhi*, Delhi.
Deshpande, Satish (2002) *Contemporary India: A Sociological View*, New Delhi: Penguin India.
Deshpande, Satish and Yogendra Yadav (2006) "Redesigning affirmative action: castes and benefits in higher education," *Economic and Political Weekly*, 41(24), June 17, 2006.
Devy, Ganesh (2005) "Myth to capture the Dangs," interview with Mahesh Langa in *Tehelka*, October 15.
Dharmadhikary, Shripad, Swathi Sheshadri, Rehmat (2005) *Unravelling Bhakra: Assessing the Temple of Resurgent India. Report of a Study of the Bhakra Nangal Project*, Manthan Adhyayan Kendra, Badwani. Pdf version may be downloaded at <http://www.manthan-india.org/article19.html>.
Dietrich, Gabriele (1994) "Women and religious identities in India after Ayodhya," in *Against All Odds*, Kamla Bhasin, Ritu Menon and Nighat Said Khan (eds), New Delhi: Kali for Women.
Dixit, Kanak Mani (2007) "Finally South Block seems enthusiastic about the region," *Himal Southasian*, 20(3), March.
Dixit, Neha (2014) "Rape in India: Reading between the lines," *Aljazeera America*, June 15, <http://america.aljazeera.com/articles/2014/6/15/rape-in-india-readingbetweenthelines.html>, accessed June 19, 2014.
D'Monte, Darryl (1989) "'Green' at the Grassroots," *Seminar 355*, March 1989, pp. 16–20.
DN (1991) "Kashmir and India," *Economic and Political Weekly*, August 24.
Dubey, Abhay Kumar (1991) *Kranti ka atmasangharsha: naxalvaadi andolan ke badalte chehre ka adhyayan*, Delhi: Vinay Prakashan.

— (2005) "Footpath par Kaamsutra – Nayee Sexy Dilli," pp. 115–39, in *Deewan-e-Sarai 02*, Delhi: Sarai-CSDS and Vaani Prakashan.

Dubey, Muchkund (2006) "Emerging political equations in Nepal," *Economic and Political Weekly*, XLI(42), October 21–7, pp. 4414–17.

Egreteau, Renaud (2006) *Instability at the Gate: India's Troubled Northeast and Its External Connections*, CSH Occasional Paper, Publication of the French Research Institutes in India, 16.

EPW Editorial (2014) "Anger, Aspiration, Apprehension," *Economic and Political Weekly*, Vol. XLIX, No. 21, May 24.

Express News Service (2006) "First for valley: a religious dialogue," *Indian Express*, December 29, p. 6.

Fernandes, Walter (2004) "Limits of law and order approach to the northeast," *Economic and Political Weekly*, October 16, pp. 4609–11.

— (2006) "Shortages, ethnic conflicts and economic development in northeastern India," in C. Joshua Thomas (ed.), *Engagement and Development. India's Northeast and Neighbouring Countries*, New Delhi: Akansha Publishing House.

Frankel, Francine R. (2005) *India's political economy 1947–2004*, New Delhi: Oxford University Press.

Free the Narmada Campaign (2001) *Who Pays? Who Profits?*, <www.narmada.org>.

Gandhi, Nandita and Nandita Shah (1992) *The Issues at Stakes*, New Delhi: Kali for Women.

Gangoli, Geetanjali (1996) *The Law is on Trial: The Debate on the Uniform Civil Code*, Bombay: Akshara Women's Resource Centre.

Geetha, V. and S. V. Rajadurai (1998) *Towards a Non-Brahmin Millennium: From Iyothee Thass to Periyar*, Kolkata: Samya.

Ghatak, Maitreesh, Parikshit Ghosh and Ashok Kotwal (2014), 'Growth in the Time of UPA: Myths and Reality', *Economic and Political Weekly*, Vol XLIX, No. 16, April 19.

Ghate, Prabhu (2002) "Kashmir: the dirty war," *Economic and Political Weekly*, January 26.

Ghosh, Anjan (1989) "Civil Liberties, Uncivil State," *Seminar 355*, March 1989, pp. 34–7.

Ghosh, Bishwanath (2000) "BJP endorses RSS swadeshi call," *Asian Age*, October 18.

Ghosh, Shohini (1999) "The troubled existence of sex and sexuality: feminists engage with censorship," in Christiane Brosius and Melissa Butcher (eds), *Image Journeys: Audio-Visual Media and Cultural Change in India*, New Delhi: Sage.

— (2003) "From the frying pan to the fire: dismantled myths and deviant behaviour," in Vijaya Ramaswamy (ed.), *Researching Indian Women*, Delhi: Manohar.

Gill, S. S. (2006) "What the Mandal Commission wanted," *Indian Express*, April 13, available at <http://www.indianexpress.com/story/2343.html>.

Greenspan, Anna (2004) *India and the IT Revolution – Networks of Global Culture*, New York: Palgrave Macmillan.

Gudavarthy, Ajay (2005) "Dalit and Naxalite movement in AP: solidarity or hegemony?," *Ecomonic and Political Weekly*, December 17, XL(51), pp. 5410–18.

Guha, Ramchandra (1989) "The Problem," *Seminar 355*, March 1989, pp. 12–15.

Guha Thakurta, Paranjoy, Subir Ghosh, and Jyotirmoy Chaudhuri, *Gas Wars, Crony Capitalism and the Ambanis* (2014) published by Paranjoy Guha Thakurta.

Gupta, Anish (1990) "Red star over Assam: is ULFA a Maoist organization?," *Sunday*, June 3–9.

Gupta, Charu (2001) *Sexuality, Obscenity, Community. Women, Muslims and the Hindu Public in Colonial India*, Delhi: Permanent Black.

Gupta, Shekhar and Bhaskar Roy (1989) "Stunning manoeuvre," *India Today*, August 15.

Hansen, Thomas Blom (2001) *Wages of Violence. Naming and Identity in Postcolonial Bombay*, Princeton, NJ: Princeton University Press.

Hardgrave Jr, Robert L. and Stanley Kochanek (1993) *India – Government and Politics in a Developing Nation*, Philadelphia, PA and New York: Harcourt Brace Jovanovich College Publishers.

Harvey, David (2003) *The New Imperialism*, New York: Oxford University Press.

Hazarika, Sanjoy (1995) *Strangers of the Mist. Tales of War and Peace from India's Northeast*, New Delhi: Penguin Books.

— (2000) *Rites of Passage. Border Crossings, Imagined Homelands, India's East and Bangladesh*, New Delhi: Penguin Books.

Heitzman, James (2004) *Network City: Planning and the Information Society in Bangalore*, New Delhi: Oxford University Press.

Hoodbhoy, Pervez (2006) "South Asia needs a bomb-less deal," *Economic and Political Weekly*, April 15.

Human Rights Watch (2006) *"Everyone Lives in Fear." Patterns of Impunity in Jammu and Kashmir*, September, 18(11) (C).

Hussain, Wasbir (2002) "Ominous signs in the northeast," *The Hindu*, September 9, p. 9.

Ilaiah, Kancha (1997) Interview with Chris Chekuri and Biju Mathew, *Ghadar*, 1(2), November 26, <http://www.foil.org/resources/ghadar/v1n2/ilaiah.htm>.

— (2003) "Cultural globalisation," *The Hindu*, February 22.

Isaac, T. M. Thomas and Richard W. Franke (2002) *Local Democracy and Development: The Kerala People's Campaign for Decentralized Planning*, Lanham, NY, and Oxford: Rowman and Littlefield Publishers.

Isaac, T. M. Thomas and Michael P. K. Tharakan (1995) "Kerala – the emerging perspectives: overview of the International

Congress on Kerala Studies," *Social Scientist*, 23(1–3), January–March.

Iyer, Ramaswamy R. (2002) "Linking of rivers. Judicial activism or error?," *Economic and Political Weekly*, November 16.

Iyer, Vaidyanathan (2014) "Rajasthan shows way in labour reforms," *The Indian Express*, June 8.

Iype, George (2000) "It makes sense for us to secede from India," at *rediff.com*, <http://www.rediff.com/news/2000/oct/09tamil.htm>, downloaded January 6, 2007.

Jaffrelot, Christophe (1996) *The Hindu Nationalist Movement and Indian Politics*, New Delhi: Penguin Books.

— (2003) *India's Silent Revolution: The Rise of the Low Castes in North Indian Politics*, Delhi: Permanent Black.

Jana, Naresh (2007) "Mobilization and mayhem – hitmen and motive," *Telegraph*, January 8, at <http://www.telegraphindia.com/1070108/asp/bengal/story_7233809.asp>.

Jayaraman, T. (2006) "Journey from Pokhran II to Hyde Act," *Economic and Political Weekly*, December 23.

Jeelani, Mehboob (2011) "The Insurgent," *The Caravan*, September 1, <http://caravanmagazine.in/reportage/insurgent>.

Jha, Prashant (2006) "Gujarat as another country. The making and reality of a fascist realm," *Himal South Asian*, October. Available at <http://www.himalmag.com/2006/october/cover_story.htm>.

Jha, Vinay and Rajeev Bhattacharya (2006) "Another shot at Naga peace," *Indian Express*, December 19, p. 4.

Jodhka, Surinder S. (2006) "Beyond 'crises': rethinking contemporary Punjab agriculture," *Economic and Political Weekly*, XLI(16), April 22.

John, Mary and Tejaswini Niranjana (1999) "Mirror politics: 'fire', Hindutva and Indian culture," *Economic and Political Weekly*, 34(10, 11), March 6–19, pp. 581–4.

Jose, Vinod K (2012) "The Emperor Uncrowned: The Rise of Narendra Modi," *The Caravan*, March 1, <http://caravanmagazine.in/reportage/emperor-uncrowned>, accessed June 18, 2014.

Joshi, Arun (2002) "A long history of rigged elections," *Hindustan Times*, May 19.

Joshua, Anita (2004) "Revised data shows drop in growth rate of Muslims," *The Hindu*, September 9, p. 3.

JTSA (Jamia Teachers Solidarity Association) (2010) "Back to Batla House," *Outlook* (Web), February 8, <http://www.outlookindia.com/article/Back-To-Batla-House/264179>, accessed 17 June 2014.

Kalpavriksha (1988) *The Narmada Valley Project. A Critique*, Delhi.

Kannabiran, Vasanth, Volga and Kalpana Kannabiran (2004) "Women's rights and Naxalite groups," *Economic and Political Weekly*, XXXIX(45), November 6, pp. 4874–7.

Kapur, Manavi (2014) "The strength of RSS lies in adapting to change: Ram Madhav," *Business Standard*, June 14.

Kapur, Ratna (1999) "A love song to our mongrel selves: hybridity, sexuality and the law," *Social and Legal Studies*, 8(3).

— (2000) "Too hot to handle: the cultural politics of fire," *Feminist Review*, 64, Spring, pp. 53–64.

Karat, Prakash (1985) "Naxalism today: at an ideological dead-end," *The Marxist*, 3(1), January–March, pp. 42–65.

Kashyap, Samudra Gupta (2006) "Indians main migrants, evict them, Bangladeshis could go later, says ULFA," *Indian Express*, December 19, p. 6.

— (2007a) "Day after security review, ULFA back: 15 migrants killed," *Indian Express*, January 6, p. 1.

— (2007b) "ULFA kills and struts," *Indian Express*, January 7, p. 1.

— (2007c) "Poll: 95 pc people reject ULFA sovereignty demand," *Indian Express*, January 6, p. 8.

Kaul, Jawaharlal (2007) "Makapa ka dvandvatmak bazarvaad," *Jansatta*, Edit page.

Kaushal, Pradeep R. and Ravish Tiwari (2014) "Mandate for hope is plan for change: Modi government outlines ambitious agenda," *The Indian Express*, June 10.

Kaviraj, Sudipta (1994) "On the structure of nationalist discourse," in T. V. Sathyamurthy (ed.) *State and Nation in the Context of Social Change*, Volume I, New Delhi: Oxford University Press.

— (1995) "Democracy and development in India," in Amiya Bagchi (ed.), *Democracy and Development*, London: St Martin's Press.

— (1996) "Dilemmas of democratic development in India," in Adrian Leftwich (ed.), *Democracy and Development. Theory and Practice*, Cambridge: Polity Press.

— (2000) "Democracy and social equality," in Francine Frankel, Zoya Hasan, Rajeev Bhargava and Balveer Arora (eds), *Transforming India*, Delhi: Oxford University Press.

Kazmin, Amy (2014) "Narendra Modi rode wave of money to Indian victory," *Financial Times*, May 19.

Khan, Ayesha (2007) "Student in jail, Chancellor is upset but the V-C rules," *Sunday Express*, 13 May.

Khan, Sona (2004) "Veil of ignorance: Muslim women's talaq trap," *Indian Express*, August 24, <http://www.expressindia.com/fullstory.php?newsid=35361#compstory>.

Khanna, Rohit (2007) "Nandigram ready for siege," *Indian Express*, January 5, p. 5.

Kishwar, Madhu and Ruth Vanita (eds) (1984) *In Search of Answers: Indian Women's Voices from Manushi*, London: Zed Books.

Kohli, Atul (ed.) (1988) *India's Democracy: An Analysis of Changing State–Society Relations*, Princeton, NJ: Princeton University Press.

Kohli, Kanchi (2006) "Mine? What mine? Ah, yes, the mine," <http://indiatogether.org/2006/dec/env-whatmine.htm>, downloaded December 27, 2006.

Kothari, Rajni (1984) "The Non-Party Political Process," *Economic and Political Weekly*, February 4, 19(5), pp. 216–24.

— (1988) *State Against Democracy: In Search of Humane Governance*, Delhi: Ajanta Publications.

Kothari, Smitu (1996) "Whose nation? Displaced as victims of development," *Economic and Political Weekly*, June 15, pp. 1476–85.

Kulkarni, Sudheendra (2006) "Accepting America's nuclear hegemony," *Indian Express*, December 24.

Kumar, Pradeep (1994) "A stock-taking," *Seminar*, 417, May.

Kumar, Radha (1993) *The History of Doing*, Delhi: Kali for Women.

Kuppuswamy, C. S. (2006) "India's look-east policy – more aggressive, better dividends," South Asia Analysis Group, <http://www.saag.org/%5Cpapers17%5Cpaper1663.html> , accessed January 29, 2007.

Lakshmanan, C. (2004) "Dalit masculinities in social science research.revisiting a Tamil village," *Economic and Political Weekly*, March 6.

Liang, Lawrence (2005) "The other information city," World-Information.Org, available at <http://world-information.org/wio/readme/992003309/1115043912>.

Ludden, David (1996) "Introduction. Ayodhya: a window on the world," in David Ludden (ed.), *Contesting the Nation. Religion, Community and the Politics of Democracy in India*, Philadelphia: University of Pennsylvania Press.

McGuire, John and Ian Copland (eds) (2007) *Hindu Nationalism and Governance*, Delhi: Oxford University Press.

Malkani, K. R. (1994) "Understanding the BJP," *Seminar*, 417, May.

Mamdani, Mahmood (2007) "The politics of naming: genocide, civil war, insurgency," *London Review of Books*, 29(5), March 8.

Bibliography | 243

Mani, Mohan (1995) "New attempts at workers' resistance," *Economic and Political Weekly*, October 7.

Mahapatra, Dhananjay (2011) "2G Loss? Govt Gained over Rs 3000 crore: Trai," *Times of India*, Sept 7, <http://timesofindia. indiatimes.com/india/2G-loss-Govt-gained-over-Rs-3000cr-Trai/articleshow/9890803.cms?referral=PM>, accessed 10 June 2014.

Manuel, Peter (2001) *Cassette Culture – Popular Music and Technology in North India*, Delhi: Oxford University Press.

Marx, Karl (n.d.) *Capital, Vol. I*, Moscow: Progress Publishers.

Mazumdar, Ranjani (1996) "Is there a type beyond the stereotype: women in Hindi cinema," *Voices*, 4(2).

— (2002) "Women and the city: fashion, desire and dance in popular Bombay cinema," *Kapital & Karma: Kunsthalle Vienna Catalogue on Contemporary Indian Art*, Hatje Cantz.

Mazumdar, Veena (1997) "Historical Soundings," *Seminar*, 457, September.

Mehta, Suketu (2004) *Maximum City: Bombay Lost and Found*, New Delhi: Penguin/Viking.

Menon, Dilip (2006) *The Blindness of Insight: Essays on Caste in Modern India*, Pondicherry: Navayana.

Menon M. S. (2006) "A win-win approach on Mullaperiyar," *Indian Express*, December 27, p. 10.

Menon, Nivedita (2014) "Two days with AAP in Banaras," *Kafila*, May 4, <http://kafila.org/2014/05/04/two-days-with-aap-in-banaras/>, accessed June 19, 2104.

— (2008) "Mumbai Terror, the Revolt of the Elites and Life Itself," *Kafila*, <http://kafila.org/2008/12/06/mumbai-terror-the-revolt-of-the-elites-and-life-itself/>, accessed 15 June 2014.

— (1998) "State/gender/community: citizenship in contemporary India," *Economic and Political Weekly*, January 31.

— (2000) "State, community and the debate on the Uniform Civil Code in India," in Mahmood Mamdani (ed.) *Beyond Rights Talk and Culture Talk*, Cape Town: David Philip Publishers.

— (2002) "Surviving Gujarat 2002," *Economic and Political Weekly*, July 6–12.
— (2004a) "What does census data on communities prove?," *Economic Times*, September 14, p. 7.
— (2004b) *Recovering Subversion. Feminist Politics Beyond the Law*, Delhi: Permanent Black and University of Illinois Press.
— (2005) "To accommodate the curious mind," *Telegraph*, August 25.
Menon, Nivedita and Adiyta Nigam (2011) "If only there were no people, democracy would be fine...," *Kafila*, August 22. <http://kafila.org/2011/08/22/if-only-there-were-no-people-democracy-would-be-fine/>.
— (2007) "Lambs at the law's guillotine," *Tehelka*, October 7.
Menon, Parvati (2002) "A difficult turn on Cauvery," *Frontline*, 19(21), October 12–25.
Misra, Geetanjali, Ajay Mahal and Rima Shah (2005) "Protecting the right of sex workers: the Indian experience," in Misra Geetanjali and Radhika Chandirmani (eds), *Sexuality, Gender and Rights. Exploring Theory and Practice in South and Southeast Asia*, New Delhi: Sage.
Misra, Udayon (2000) *The Periphery Strikes Back. Challenges to the Nationstate in Assam and Nagaland*, Shimla: Indian Institute of Advanced Study.
Mishra, Vinod (1991) "Mao and his thought," *Frontier*, February 23.
Mohanakumar, S. and R. K. Sharma (2006) "Analysis of farmers' suicides in Kerala," *Economic and Political Weekly*, XLI(16), April 22.
Mohanty, Manoranjan (1995) "On the concept of empowerment," *Economic and Political Weekly*, June 17.
Moon, Vasant (2002) *Growing up Untouchable in India. A Dalit Autobiography* (trans. Gail Omvedt), New Delhi: Vistaar Publications.
Mukherji, Nirmalangshu (2004) "Who attacked parliament?," *Revolutionary Democracy*, X(2), September.

— (2005) *December 13: Terror Over Democracy*, New Delhi: Promilla and Co. and Bibliophile South Asia.

Myint, Soe (2007) "The distasteful Burma–India embrace," *Himal Southasia*, February.

Nagaraj, D. R. (1993) *The Flaming Feet – A Study of the Dalit Movement*, Bangalore: South Forum Press and Institute for Cultural Research and Action.

Nair, Janaki (1997) "An important springboard," *Seminar*, 457, September.

— (2005) *The Promise of the Metropolis: Bangalore's Twentieth Century*, New Delhi: Oxford University Press.

Nandy, Ashis (1994) "Paradox of secularism. The buying and selling of religion," *Times of India*, May 21, p. 10.

— (1985/2003) "Anti-secularist manifesto," *The Romance of the State. And the Fate of Dissent in the Tropics*, New Delhi: Oxford University Press.

Narayan, Badri (2006) "Memories, saffronising statues and constructing communal politics," *Economic and Political Weekly*, November 11.

Narrain, Arvind and Gautam Bhan (eds) (2005) *Because I Have a Voice. Queer Politics in India*, Delhi: Yoda.

Navlakha, Gautam (1996) "Invoking union: Kashmir and official nationalism of Bharat," in T. V. Satyamurthy (ed.), *Region, Religion, Caste, Gender and Culture in Contemporary India*, Vol. 3, New Delhi: Oxford University Press.

— (2006) "Kashmir roundtable conference: turnaround or downturn?," *Economic and Political Weekly*, March 18.

Nigam, Aditya (2014a) "So Who has won the election?", *Kafila*, May 16, at <http://kafila.org/2014/05/16/so-who-has-won-the-election/>.

— (2014b) "Beyond the Elections – Need for a Vibrant and Credible Left," *Kafila*, May 25, 2014, <http://kafila.org/2014/05/25/beyond-the-elections-need-for-a-vibrant-and-credible-left/>, accessed 17 June 2014.

— (2014c) "Xenophobia, Racism and Vigilantism – Danger Signals for AAP", *Kafila*, January 17.

— (2001) "Industrial closures in Delhi," *Revolutionary Democracy*, VII(2).

— (2002) "In search of a bourgeoisie: Dalit politics enters a new phase," *Economic and Political Weekly*, March 30.

— (2004) "Imagining the global nation: time and hegemony," *Economic and Political Weekly*, 39(1), January 3–9.

— (2006a) "Das Kapital in Buddha's Bengal?," *Tehelka*, January 28, p. 19.

— (2006b) *The Insurrection of Little Selves. The Crisis of Secular-Nationalism in India*, Delhi: Oxford University Press.

Noorani, A. G. (2002) "Nehru and linguistic states," *Frontline*, 19(16), August, pp. 3–16.

Noorani, A. G. et al. (2006) *December 13: A Reader. The Strange Case of the Attack on the Indian Parliament*, New Delhi: Penguin Books.

Nunan, Patricia (2005) "US concerned about India–Iran pipeline project," Voice of America, New Delhi, <http://www.payvand.com/news/05/mar/1150.html>, accessed January 29, 2007.

Oinam, Bhagat and Homen Thangjam (2006) "Indian 'nation state,' and crisis of the 'periphery,'" in Prasenjit Biswas and C. Joshua Thomas (eds), *Peace in India's North-East. Meaning, Metaphor and Method*, New Delhi: Regency Publications.

Omvedt, Gail (1990) *Violence Against Women. New Movements and New Theories in India*, New Delhi: Kali for Women.

— (1993) *Reinventing Revolution: New Social Movements and the Socialist Tradition in India*, New York and London: M. E. Sharpe.

Pachauri, Sudhish (2000) *Cyberspace Aur Media*, New Delhi: Praveen Prakashan.

Pachauri, Sudhish and Achala Sharma (2002) *Naye Jan Sanchar Madhyam Aur Hindi*, New Delhi and Patna: Rajkamal Prakashan.

Pandey, Gyanendra (1992) *The Construction of Communalism in Colonial North India*, Delhi: Oxford University Press.

Pandian, M. S. S. (2007) *Brahmin and Non-Brahmin. Genealogies of the Tamil Political Present*, New Delhi: Permanent Black.

Pandit, Ambika and Neha Lalchandani (2014) "Arvind Kejriwal quits over Jan Lokpal bill," *The Times of India*, February 14.

Paranjpe, Shailendra Prakash (2014) "Javadekar to fast track 200 projects, keeps mum on Lavasa," *DNA* June 2. <http://www.samachar.com/Prakash-Javadekar-to-fast-track-200-projects-keeps-mum-on-Lavasa-ogchKvigihh.html>, accessed June 20, 2014.

Patel, Geeta (2002) "On fire: sexuality and its inducements," in Ruth Vanita (ed.), *Queering India. Same-sex Love and Eroticism in Indian Culture and Society*, New York and London: Routledge.

Patil, Bal (2006) "Anti conversion bill in Gujarat, a problem for the Jain minority too," AsiaNews.it, September 25. Downloaded from <http://www.asianews.it/view.php?l=en&art=7308>, October 14, 2006.

Patkar, Medha (1999) Interview with Venu Govindu, <http://www.indiatogether.org/interviews/iview-mpatkar.htm>, downloaded March 3, 2005.

— (2005) Interview with Robert Jensen, <http://www.progressivetrail.org/articles/040226Jensen.shtml>, downloaded March 3, 2005.

— (ed.) (2006) *River Linking. A Millennium Folly?*, Mumbai: National Alliance for People's Movements and Initiatives.

Pederson, Jorgen Dige (2001) "India's industrial dilemmas in West Bengal," *Asian Survey*, 41(4), pp. 646–68.

People's Union for Democratic Rights (PUDR) (1991) *Shankar Guha Niyogi and the Chattisgarh People's Movement*, Delhi.

— (2005) *Halting the Mining Juggernaut. People's Struggle Against Alumina Projects in Orissa*, Delhi (Email: pudrdelhi@yahoo.com).

Pereira, Ignatius (2006) "Mullaperiyar not an inter-state river dispute: minister," *The Hindu*, September 5.

Phadke, Shilpa (2005) "Some notes towards understanding the construction of middle-class urban women's sexuality in India," in Geetanjali Misra and Radhika Chandiramani (eds), *Sexuality, Gender and Rights. Exploring Theory and Practice in South and Southeast Asia*, New Delhi: Sage.

Phukon, Girin (2006) "Politics of peace in north-east India," in Prasenjit Biswas and C. Joshua Thomas (eds), *Peace in India's North-East. Meaning, Metaphor and Method*, New Delhi: Regency Publications.

Polanki, Pallavi (2012) "Bhatta-Parsaul Debacle: Rahul Entered Late, Left Early," *Firstpost*, March 8, 2012, <http://www.firstpost.com/politics/bhatta-parsaul-debacle-rahul-entered-late-left-early-238391.html>, accessed June 17, 2014.

Prabhakara, M. S. (2006) "Talking about talks," *Economic and Political Weekly*, March 4, pp. 777–80.

Prasad, Chandrabhan (2000) "When Dalits walked into an evening of *The Gin Drinkers*," *Indian Express*, November 2, p. 1.

— (2004) *Dalit Diary: 1999–2003. Reflections on Apartheid in India*, Chennai: Navayana Publishing.

PTI (Press Trust of India) (2002) "Kashmiri Pandits, Muslims, meet for first time in 13 years," *Times of India*, March 30.

Punyani, Ram (2002) "Dalits and adivasis: Hindutva's foot-soldiers," *The Dalit*, May–June.

Puri, Balraj (1993) *Kashmir. Towards Insurgency*, Hyderabad: Orient Longman.

Rahman, M., Raghunandan Das and Prabhu Chawla (1989) "Crime, money and politics," *India Today*, August 31.

Raj, Udit (2005a) <http://www.dalitnetwork.org/Documents/Udit%20Raj%2010-20-05.html>.

— (2005b) "United States asked to uplift Dalits," <http://www.nepaldalitinfo.20m.com/news/USAsked.htm>.

Raja Mohan, C. (2003) "An enduring diplomat," *The Hindu*, February 9, 2003, at <http://www.hinduonnet.com/thehindu/mag/2003/02/09/stories/2003020900060400.htm>, accessed January 29, 2007.

Rajeev, P. I. (2006) "All red faces: ADB loan and a divided party," *Indian Express*, December 29, p. 4.

Ram Mohan, T.T. (2014) "Bank Privatization by the Backdoor," *Economic and Political Weekly*, June 7.

Ram, Rahul (1993) *Muddy Waters: An Assessment of the Benefits of the Sardar Sarovar Project*, Delhi: Kalpvriksha.

Ramanathan, Usha (1996) "Displacement and the law," *Economic and Political Weekly*, June 15, pp. 1486–91.

— (2006) "Illegality and the urban poor," *Economic and Political Weekly*, July 22, pp. 3193–7.

Ramkumar, Vivek (2004) "Beyond democratic rights and electoral reform campaign: challenges facing non party political movements," <http://www.freedominfo.org/case/mkss/beyond.doc>, downloaded February 9, 2005.

Rao, Narasimha P. and K. C. Suri (2006) "Dimensions of agrarian distress in Andhra Pradesh," *Economic and Political Weekly*, XLI(16), April 22.

Rashid, Toufiq (2006) "If madrasas produce terror, then Kashmir should be peaceful," *Indian Express*, December 29, p. 1.

Ravindran, K. T. (2007) "Redeveloping Delhi into a compact city," *Hindustan Times*, January 12, p. 5.

Ray, Rabindra (1988) *The Naxalites and Their Ideology*, Delhi: Oxford University Press.

Ray, Shankar (2004) "Fiddling with numbers," available at <http://www.hardnewsmedia.com/oct2004/census2.php>.

Reddy, Sheela (2005) "Labour of hate," *Outlook*, August 8.

Rege, Arati (1997) "A decade of lesbian hulla gulla," in Bina Fernandez (ed.), *Humjinsi. A Resource Book on Lesbian, Gay and Bisexual Rights in India*, Mumbai: Combat Law Publications.

Renan, Ernest (1996) "What is a nation?," in Geoff Eley and Ronald Grigor Suny (eds), *Becoming National. A Reader*, New York and Oxford: Oxford University Press.

Roy, Aruna and Nikhil Dey (2004) "The Redistribution of Power," *Seminar*, 541, August 31.

Roy, Aruna, Nikhil Dey and Shanker Singh (2001) "Demanding Accountability," *Seminar*, 500, June 26.

Roy, Arundhati (2011) "I'd rather not be Anna," *The Hindu*, October 2.

— (1999) *The Greater Common Good*, <http://www.narmada.org/gcg/gcg.html>.

— (2000) "The people vs. the god of big dams," *Times of India*, October 26.

— (2006) "The very strange story of the attack on the Indian Parliament," *Outlook*, October 30.

Roy, Bidyut (2007) "Happy with ADB, Bengal CPM wants VS to back down," *Indian Express*, January 3, p. 7.

Sail, Rajendra (1998) "The man was a machine with a human heart," in *On a Rainbow in the Sky: The Chattisgarh Mukti Morcha*, New Delhi: CEC.

Sambhav, Kumar S (2014) "Defence projects, border roads will not require green nod from Centre: Javadekar," *Down to Earth*, June 13, <http://www.downtoearth.org.in/content/defence-projects-roads-border-will-not-require-green-nod-centre-javadekar>, accessed June 19, 2104.

Samaddar, Ranabir (1999) *The Marginal Nation. Transborder Migration from Bangladesh to West Bengal*, New Delhi: Sage.

Sangari, Kumkum (1999) "Consent, agency, and rhetoric of incitement," *Politics of the Possible. Essays on Gender, History, Narratives, Colonial English*, Delhi: Tulika Press, pp. 364–489.

Sangvai, Sanjay (1994) "'Nation,' 'Nationalism,' and mega projects," *Economic and Political Weekly*, March 5, pp. 537–40.

— (2003) "Emerging politics of just and sustainable development," <http://www.aidindia.org/desh/ep.html>, downloaded June 15, 2004.

Sarkar, Sumit (2007) "A question marked in red," *Indian Express*, January 9, p. 11.

Sarkar, Tanika (1998) "Women, community and nation: a historical identity for Hindu identity politics," in Patricia Jeffrey and Amrita Basu (eds), *Appropriating Gender: Women's Activism and Politicised Religion in South Asia*, London: Routledge, pp. 89–104.

— (2002) "Semiotics of terror: Muslim children and women in Hindu Rashtra," *Economic and Political Weekly*, July 13, pp. 2872–6.

Sathyamurthy, T. V. (1997) "India's international role – economic dependence and non-alignment, 1947–1991," in T. V. Sathyamurthy (ed), *State and Nation in the Context of Social Change. Social Change and Political Discourse in India*, Vol. 1, New Delhi: Oxford University Press.

Sengupta, Shuddhabrata (2014) "The Triumph of the Will(ie): Prasannarajan Anoints Modi in the Open," *Kafila*, May 18, <http://kafila.org/2014/05/18/the-triumph-of-the-willie-prasannarajan-anoints-modi-in-the-open>, accessed June 19, 2104.

— (2011) "Hazare, Khwahishein Aisi: Desiring a new politics, after Anna Hazare and beyond corruption," *Kafila*, August 27, <http://kafila.org/2011/08/27/hazare-khwahishein-aur-bhi-hain-hazare-there-are-things-still-left-wanting-what-is-to-the-left-of-anna-hazare-and-india-against-corruption/>.

Sethi, Aman (2005) "Fighting for relevance," *Frontline*, October 21, pp. 20–1.

Sethi, Harsh (1993a) "Survival and democracy: ecological struggles in India," in Ponna Wignaraja (ed.), *New Social Movements in the South: Empowering the People*, New Delhi: Vistaar Publications, pp. 121–48.

— (1993b) "Action groups in the new politics," in Ponna Wignaraja (ed.), *New Social Movements in the South: Empowering the People*, New Delhi: Vistaar Publications, pp. 230–55.

Sharma, Mukul (2011) *Green and Saffron. Hindu Nationalism and Indian Environmental Politics*. Ranikhet: Permanent Black.

Sharma, Kalpana (2004) "Come back, Yasin Malik tells Kashmiri Pandits," *The Hindu*, January 21, p. 3.

Sharma, R. N. (2003) "Involuntary displacement. A few encounters," *Economic and Political Weekly*, March 1, pp. 907–12.

Shaw, Annapurna (2004) *The Making of Navi Mumbai*, Hyderabad: Orient Longman.

Shimray, U. A. (2004) "Socio-political unrest in the region called north-east India," *Economic and Political Weekly*, October 16, pp. 4637–43.

Shourie, Arun (2006) "Now let the PM square this circle," *Indian Express*, November 28, p. 9.

Sikand, Yoginder (2004a) *Islam, Caste and Dalit–Muslim Relations in India*, New Delhi: Global Meda Publications.

— (2004b) "Muslim women and gender justice," *Countercurrents. org*, October 15, 2004, <http://www.countercurrents.org/gender-sidkand151004.htm>.

— (2006) "Mayhem in Mangalore," October 21, available at <http://communalism.blogspot.com/2006/10/mayhem-in-mangalore.html>.

Singh, N. K. (1977) "Trade Unionism with a Difference," *Economic and Political Weekly*, July 16, reprinted in *On a Rainbow in the Sky*, New Delhi: CEC.

Singh, Ramendra (2014) "First arrest in Muzaffarnagar gangrape cases," *The Indian Express*, January 26.

Singh, Shashi Bhushan (2005) "Limits to power: Naxalism and caste relations in a south Bihar village," *Economic and Political Weekly*, July 16, XL(29), pp. 3167–75.

Singh, Shekhar (2000) "The karma of dams," *Indian Express*, October 25.

Sivaramakrishnan, G. (1989) "S&T: Road to Utopia?," *Seminar* 355, March 1989, pp. 29–33.

Special Correspondent (2006a) "Mullaperiyar: chief minister rejects preconditions for talks," *The Hindu*, October 25.

— (2006b) "Another jawan commits suicide," *The Hindu*, December 19.

— (2006c) "Army plans to recruit 400 psychiatrists. Step intended to tackle stress, suicides and fratricidal deaths among personnel," *The Hindu*, December 30, p. 14.

Sreejith, K. (2005) "Naxalite movement and cultural resistance: experience of Janakiya Samskarika Vedi in Kerala (1980–82)," *Economic and Political Weekly*, XL(50), December 10, pp. 5333–7.

Sridhar, Madabhushi (2007) "Right to information: say no to the new iron curtains," *India Together*, <http://www.indiatogether.org/2006/aug/rtifilenotes.htm>, accessed January 31, 2007.

Sridhar, V. (2006) "Why do farmers commit suicide? The case of Andhra Pradesh," *Economic and Political Weekly*, XLI(16), April 22.

Stein, Arthur (1969) *India and the Soviet Union – The Nehru Era*, Chicago, IL and London: University of Chicago Press.

Subrahmaniam, Vidya (2006) "Varanasi in the time of terror," *The Hindu*, July 26.

Subramanian, T. S. (1999) "New alignments in Tamil Nadu," *Frontline*, 16(13), June 19–July 2.

Surabhi (2014) "Narendra Modi govt working towards liberalising labour laws," *The Financial Express*, June 19.

Suri, K. C. (2006) "Political economy of agrarian distress," *Economic and Political Weekly*, XLI(16), April 22.

Talukdar, Sushanta (2005) "A conflict in Meghalaya," *Frontline*, 22(22), October 22–November 4.

Taneja, Nalini (2006) "Mangalore 'riots,'" *People's Democracy*, October 22.

Teltumbde, Anand (n.d.) "Globalization and the Dalits," <http://ambedkar.org/research/globalisationandthedalits.pdf>.

Thakkar, Himanshu (2006) "The guilt of thirst," *Tehelka*, May 6, p. 23.

Thapar, Romila (2005) *Somanatha: The Many Voices of History*, London: Verso.

Thorat, Sukhdeo and Umakant (eds) (2004) *Caste, Race and Discrimination: Discourses in the International Context*, Jaipur and New Delhi: Rawat Publications.

Upadhyay, Videh (2000) "Changing judicial power. Courts on infrastructure projects and environment," *Economic and Political Weekly*, October 28, pp. 3789–92.

Vajpeyi, Yogesh (2003) "For the oppressed, covered in diamonds – govt plays host at Mayawati birthday bash," *Telegraph*, January 16, front page.

Valmiki, Om Prakash (2003) *Joothan: A Dalit's Life* (trans. Arun Prabha Mukherjee), Kolkata: Samya.

Vanaik, Achin (1995) *India in a Changing World*, Tracts for the Times 9, New Delhi: Orient Longman.

Vardarajan, Siddharth (ed.) (2002) *Gujarat: The Making of a Tragedy*, New Delhi: Penguin Books.

— (2007) "Blame the police, not the messenger," *The Hindu*, May 11.

Vasuki, S. N. and Shiv Taneja (1990) "A buoyant mood," *India Today*, January 15.

Venkatesan, J. (2004) "Tirumangalam speech calculated to whip up secessionist sentiments," *The Hindu*, March 6.

Venu, M. K. (2007) "Look east policy and multilateralism," Times News Network, 23 January, 2007, <http://economictimes.indiatimes.com/articleshow/1386800.cms>, accessed January 29, 2007.

Watt, Romeet K. (2002) "Jammu: denial, delay and dereliction," Guest Column in South Asia Analysis Group Paper no. 550, available at <http://www.saag.org/papers6/paper550.html>, downloaded December 29, 2006.

Weber, Eugen (1976) *Peasants into Frenchmen*, Stanford, CA: Stanford University Press.

Yadav, Yogendra (1999) "Electoral politics in the time of change. India's third electoral system, 1989–99," *Economic and Political Weekly*, August 21–8.

Index

13 December 2001 attacks on Parliament, 126–7, 164

Abdullah, Farooq, 155, 156, 160, 161
Abdullah, Sheikh, 152, 154–5
Achuthanandan, V.S., 107
Adivasis, 38–9, 75
Advani, Lal Krishna, 23, 49
agriculture, 63–4, 105, 111, 151
AIDS, 91; awareness of, 129–30; epidemic, 129; prevention work, 95
AIDS Bhedbhav Virodhi Andolan, 129
Akoijam, Bimol, 150
Akshardham temple, 79
alcoholism, 73
Ali, Ejaz, 56
All India Anna Dravida Munnetra Kazhagam (AIADMK), 26, 50, 138
All India Backward Muslim Morcha (AIBMM), 56
All India Institute of Medical Sciences, 34
All India Kashmiri Pandit Conference, 162
All India Muslim Personal Law Board (AIMPLB), 55
All India People's Resistance Forum (AIPRF), 123
All India Radio, 94
All India Trade Union Congress (AITUC), 117
All Party Hurriyat Conference (APHC), 158
Althusser, Louis, 4
Ambani, Dhirubhai, 11
Ambedkar, B.R., 58, 97, 99, 114
Anamukti organization, 132
Ananda Bazar Patrika, 113
anarchism, 121
Andhra Pradesh, 136
Andhra Pradesh Civil Liberties Committee (APCLC), 125
anti-communal groups, 127
anti-nuclear movement, 132–3
Anwar, Ali, 56
Armed Forces (Jammu and Kashmir) Special Powers Act, 159
Armed Forces Special Powers Act (AFSPA), 141, 146–7
armed struggle, 121–2, 140, 145, 150

Aryans, 37, 38
Asia Social Forum, 134
Asiad workers' case, 74
Asian Development Bank (ADB), 106–7
Asianet, 90
Asom Gana Parishad (AGP), 143–4
Assam, 142–5
Assam Accord, 144
assimilationism, 37–40
Association for the Protection of Democratic Rights (APDR), 125–6
Association of South East AsianNations (ASEAN), 171
Athawale, Indira, 100
Aung San Suu Kyi, 173
automobile: as focus of development, 81; spread of, 92
autonomous workers' movement, 117–18
autonomy, demand for, 140
Awami Action Committee, 155
Azad, Ghulam Nabi, 163
Azad Kashmir, 152

Babri Masjid, demolition of, 5, 23, 36, 43, 48–50, 60, 103, 127
Bahujan Samaj Party (BSP), 21–3, 24–5, 29, 57–8, 179
Bajrang Dal, 43–4, 53, 59
Balagopal, K., 122
Banerjee, U.C., 51
Bangalore: growth of, 81; slum demolitions in, 81
Bangladesh, 139, 143, 147, 153, 167, 175
Bano, Shah, 42, 45–6, 47, 54
Barbora, Sanjay, 150, 151
Basu, Jyoti, 103–5, 111
Baviskar, Amita, 39, 79
Bay of Bengal Initiative, 171
beggars, rounding up of, 81
Behera, Navnita Chadha, 156
benami land, 110
Bharat Jan Andolan, 122
Bharati, Uma, 29–30
Bharatiya Jan Sangh, 42
Bharatiya Janata Party (BJP), 5, 22, 24, 26, 28, 30, 35, 38, 42–3, 44, 46, 48, 50, 53–4, 57, 103, 105, 108, 157–8, 160, 161, 168, 178, 179
Bharatiya Mazdoor Sangh, 44
Bharucha, Justice, 71
Bhattcharya, Buddhadeb, 106, 107, 113
Bhilai steel plant, 166
Bhopal Conference, 100–2
Bhotmange family, killing of, 25
Bhushan, Prashant, 78
Bhutan, 172, 174
Bidwai, Praful, 133, 160–1

Bodos tribal people, 147
Bofors gun deal, 10–11
brain drain, 10
Brass, Paul, 52
Buddhism, 38, 161; conversions to, 59
Burakumin, 20

capital punishment, 164; opposition to, 126, 165
cassette tapes, 85, 86; video, 91
caste, 13, 15–35, 37, 51, 96, 97, 119–20, 131, 178–80; affirmative action, 4; British action on "untouchables", 57; OBC, 7, 15, 25, 31, 38, 49, 56, 104, 120, 138, 179; politics of, 57–8 *see also* Dalits
censorship, 93–4
Chandran, Civic, 121
chastity, 40, 94
Chatterjee, Partha, 13, 19, 76
Chhattisgarh Mine Shramik Sangh (CMSS), 117
Chhattisgarh Mukti Morcha (CMM), 117, 122
China, 152, 169, 174; Cultural Revolution, 118; relations with US, 167
Chipko movement, 116
Chopra, Anil, 85

Christianity, 38, 39; violence against Christians, 39, 44, 179
citizen's initiatives, 115, 124–33
city: celebration of, 83; cleansing of, 76; compact, 82; ordered and zoned, 128
civil liberties, 125
Clinton, Bill, 81, 159
Coalition for Nuclear Disarmament and Peace (CNDP), 133
Coalition of Civil Society, 160
coalitions, building of, 50
coffee plantations, abandoned, 151
cold war, end of, 166–7
Committee for a Fair Trial for S.A.R. Geelani, 126
Committee for a Sane Nuclear Policy (COSNUP), 132
Committee on the Status of Women in India (CSWI), 27
commons, dispossession of, 72
communalism, 52, 53, 57, 155, 161–3
Communist Party of India (Maoist) (CPI (Maoist)), 123–4
Communist Party of India (Marxist) (CPI (M)), 44, 50, 103–19, 133; metamorphosis of, 108

Communist Party of India (Marxist-Leninist) (CPI (ML)), 119
Communist Party of India (Marxist-Leninist) (CPI (ML) Liberation), 120–1
Communist Party of India (Marxist-Leninist) (CPI (ML) Party Unity), 123
Communist Party of India (Marxist-Leninist) (CPI (ML) People's War), 122–3
compact disks, 88
Conference of Autonomous Women's Movements, 131
Confidence Building Measures, 170
Congress Party, 6–7, 8, 15, 45, 46, 50, 111, 112, 119, 136, 155, 163, 168, 176
Constitution of India, 34
consumer durables, demand for, 86
consumerism, 86, 92, 102; celebration of, 95–7
conversion, religious, 38–9, 55; to Buddhism, 59
corporations, private, 64–8
corruption, 10, 15, 1445
courts, role of, 74–5
cow, sacred nature of, 43
cultural pollution, 89

Dalit capitalism, 95–9
Dalit International Conference, 97
Dalit Panther movement, 114
Dalits, 17, 31, 37, 40, 43, 50, 56, 83, 99, 120, 179; conflicts with OBCs, 25–6; segregation of, 20; upsurge of, 19–21
dams: Bhakra Nangal, 68; Hirakud, 68; Indira Sagar, 61, 70; Kuntapuzha river, 116; Maheshwar, funds withdrawn, 68; Mullaperiyar dam, 137; Sardar Sarovar, 69, 70–1 (Supreme Court decision, 71, 74)
Das, Mahant Lal, killing of, 58
dating advertisements, 92
de-industrialization, 111
Debonair sex survey, 91
debt, 147; rural, 64
decentralization, 116
Delhi, 76, 154; as capital of homosexuals, 92; closure of polluting industries, 77; lack of planned development in, 79; massacre of Sikhs in, 127; Master Plan, 179; removal of slums, 78
democracy, 13, 69, 121–2
democratization, of capital, 98, 100

Deshpande, Satish, 16, 35
desire, economies of, 83–102
De Souza, Joseph, 100
development: accelerated, 61–4; ideology of, 116
Devi, Bhanwari, 132
Dharmadhikary, Sripad, 63
diasporic communities, 90
displaced people, 179; rehabilitation of, 71, 72–4; relocation of, 75; struggles of, 123
Dixit, Kanak Mani, 174
Domestic Violence Act (2005), 180
Doordarshan, 89, 94
dowry, issue of, 28
Dravida Munnetra Kazhagam (DMK), 26, 138
Dravidian, use of term, 26
Dravidian movement, 137
dress code, 95; wearing of burqa, 157
Dubey, Abhay, 91, 92
Durbar Mahila Samanwaya Committee, 129

ecomilitancy, 150
Eenadu television, 90
Ekta Parishad (EP), 125
Emergency, 6, 12, 111, 125
eminent domain, 116; principle of, 72

empowerment, use of term, 31
environmental issues, 76, 77, 80, 116; role of courts in, 74–5
ethnic identity, 147–50
existentialism, 121

feminism, 3, 28, 114, 180; NGOization of, 131–2; rethinking of sexuality, 93–5
Fernandes, Walter, 139
Foreigners (Tribunals for Assam) Order, 143
forests, deforestation, 154
Freedom of Religion Act, 38
freight equalization policy, 112
Friedman, Thomas, 1
Friends of the Earth, 70

Gandhi, Indira, 5, 8, 15, 84; assassination of, 7
Gandhi, Mahatma, 140
Gandhi, Rajiv, 15, 46, 70, 71; accession to premiership, 8, 10; assassination of, 4, 173
Garo Students' Union, 149
Garo tribe, 149
gas pipeline, Iran to Pakistan, 172
Gawdakal, killing of civilians, 156
gay and lesbian activism, 59, 130

Geelani, S.A.R., 126–7, 158
gender, 40
Ghosh, Shohini, 93
Gill, S.S., 32
global city, production of, 76–82
globalization, 13, 61–82, 89, 90, 99, 171, 176; cultural, 101; opposition to, 98, 181
Gogoi, Pradip, 144
Golwalkar, M.S., 38
Green Revolution, 63, 64
Greenspan, Anna, 88
growth, economic, 85–6, 176
Guha, Ramchandra, 101
Gujarat, massacre of Muslims, 22, 36, 51–2, 127–8
Gujral, Inder Kumar, 170
Gujral doctrine, 170, 172
Guru, Afzal, death sentence on, 164–5
Gyanendra, King, 174

Haksar, Nandita, 126
Harkat-ul-Ansar, 158
Harsud town, submergence of, 61–2
hazardous industries, location of, 76
Hazratbal mosque, siege of, 158
heteronormativity, 128–9, 130
hijras, 129; harassment of, 95
Hindi: and media explosion, 89–91; cleansing of, 90

Hindi film: circulation of, 87; music of, 86; values of, 94
Hindu Right, 4, 18, 24, 36, 37, 51, 53, 59, 93, 95, 104, 126, 127, 130, 133, 155, 176, 177, 178; organization of, 41–5; rise of, 23
Hindus: in Kashmir, 159, 162; killing of, 157
Hindutva, 13, 25, 30, 36–60, 161, 178–80; in relation to Hindus, 58–60
Hinglish, 90
Hizbul Mujahideen (HM), 157
homophobia, 130–1
homosexuality, 92, 95, 129
Honda Motorcycles and Scooters India, 67
human rights, violations of, 159
hunger strike, 146
Hussain, M.F., 179
Hydari Agreement, 140
Hyde Act, 168–9
Hyderabad, 154; slum demolitions in, 80–1

IBM company, 98–9
Ilaiah, Kancha, 99, 100, 101
imagination, unshackling of, 85–9
immigration, 143, 144; illegal, 149, 175 (citizenship rights, 151)

import-substituting industrialization, 83, 110
Imran case, 55
Independence, 3, 62, 68
India, contested notion of, 135–65
India-Sri Lanka Accord, 173
Indian Independence Act (1947), 152
Indian Institutes of Management, 32
Indian Institutes of Technology, 32
Indian National Congress, 3
Indian Peace Keeping Force (IPKF), 172–3
Indianization, 96
indigenous peoples, 123, 147, 148
Indo-Soviet Friendship Treaty, 167
Industrial Development Corporation of India Limited (IDCOL), 65
industrialization, obstacles to, 112
infant mortality, 109
Instrument of Accession, 153, 154
International Atomic Energy Authority (IAEA), 168, 169
International Fund for Agricultural Development (IFAD), 151
International Monetary Fund (IMF), 4
Internet, 88, 92
Iran, containment of, 168–9
Iraq war, 167
irrigation, 63
Islam, 38, 39, 51, 152, 158; sectarianism within, 162
Islamic National Front, 147
Islamic Revolutionary Front, 147
Israel, 168

Jaduguda, radiation pollution in, 132
Jaffrelot, Christopher, 18, 49
Jagmohan, Governor, 156–7
Jainism, 38
Jalud village, submersion of, 67–8
Jamaat-i-Islami, 162
Jammu and Kashmir, 152–65; elections in, 159–61
Jammu and Kashmir Disturbed Areas Act (1990), 159
Jammu and Kashmir Liberation Front (JKLF), 156–8, 162
Jana Sangh, 6
Janakiya Samskarika Vedi (JSV), 121
Janata Party (JP), 6, 15, 42, 112

Jawaharlal Nehru University, 34
Jeevan Reddy Committee, 146
jhoom lands, 151
jhuggis, demolition of, 75, 78
Jindal Strips Limited, 65
Judge, Paramjit Singh, 120
judiciary, role of, 12–13
Junagadh, 154
Justice Rajinder Sachar Committee Report, 56

Kaga-Kuki conflict, 148
Kaka Kalelkar Commission, 17–18
Kalelkar, Kaka, 18
Kalinganagar tribal peoples, 181; protest movement of, 64–5
Kamani Tubes company, 117–18
Kapur, Ratna, 93
Karbi tribe, 150
Kargil war, 71, 159, 170
Karnataka, 179; incidents in, 53; water dispute in, 137
Kashmir, 136, 166; militarization of, 163 *see also* Jammu and Kashmir
Kashmir Accord, 155, 163
Katiya, Vinay, 59
Katju, Justice Markandya, 78
Kaviraj, Sudipta, 7, 69, 135

Kerala, 120; model of development, 109
Kerala Shastra Sahitya Parishad (KSSP), 116–17
Kerala Sustainable Development Project, 106
Khairlanji village incident, 25
Khan, Sona, 55
Khasi movement, 148
Khasi Students' Union (KSU), 149–50
Kissinger, Henry, 167
Kolkata, eviction of slum dwellers, 80
Konkan railway case, 75
Kothari, Rajni, 116, 126
kothis, 129–30
Krishna, Raj, 85
Kudremukh National Park, relocation of indigenous peoples, 123
Kumar, Krishna, 177
Kumars, S., 67
Kushwaha, Ram Naresh, 17
Kutty, Paloli Mohammed, 108

labor laws, 66, 77
land: acquisition by state, 66, 105–6, 113, 147 (compensation for, 70, 72–4; resistance to, 181); occupations of, 121; redistribution of, 100

land-for-land provisions, 73–4
land reform, 109, 113
landlessness, 105
language, explorations of, 83
Lashkar-e-Jabbar, 157
Latifi, Daniel, 55
Left, New, 3, 14, 103–34; emergence of, 114–15
Left Front (LF) in West Bengal, 66, 105, 110, 112–13
liberalization, resistance to, 104
Liberation Tigers of Tamil Eelam (LTTE), 137, 173
Linguistic Provinces Commission, 136
linguistic reorganization of states, 136
literacy, 21, 109
look east policy of India, 171–2
LPG connections, queues for, 84

MacDonald, Ramsay, 101
Magowa group, 114
Maharashtra state, 45
Mali, Yasin, 158–9
Mamdani, Mahmood, 2
Mandal, B.P., 15
Mandal Commission, 4, 7;
Mandal II, 32–5, 180; Report, 13, 15–35, 49
Manipur, 140, 148, 152

Manipur People's Liberation Front (MPLF), 145
Manorama, killing of, 146
Manuel, Peter, 85, 86–7
Maoism, 115, 118, 121–4, 144, 173
Maoist Communist Centre (MCC), 120, 123
Marumalarchi Dravida Munnetra Kazagham (MDMK), 137
Marx, Karl, *Capital*, 61; with Friedrich Engels, *Communist Manifesto*, 96
Marxism, 97, 107, 114, 118; ecological, 117
Mayawati, political leader, 29, 102, 179
Mazdoor Kisan Sangharsh Samiti (MKSS), 120
Mazdoor Kisan Shakti Sangathan, 177
Mazumdar, Vina, 29
media, role of, 12–13
Meghalaya: identity politics in, 148–9; resistance to mining in, 132–3
Meghalaya Board of School Education (MBOSE), 149
Mehta, Deepa, *Fire*, 130
Mehta, M.C., 76
Mehta, Suketu, *Maximum City*, 1–2

Meitei people, 147, 148
Mekong Ganga Cooperation Project, 171
Menon, Dilip, 58
Menon, Krishna, 136
middle class, 9, 11
migration, 148 *see also* immigration
Mir Baki, 36
Misra, Udayon, 145
Misra, Veer Bhadra, 59
Mizo people, 149
mobile phones, 84–5, 92
modernity, 16, 69
Modi, Narendra, 52
Mohanty, Manoranjan, 30
Morse Committee, 70
mosques, for women, 55
Motilal Nehru Committee Report, 136
Mugdal, Sarla, 47
Mukherji, Nirmalangshu, 164
Mumbai, 79; slum demolitions in, 80
Musharraf, Pervez, 161
music industry, 86
Muslim politics, 54–7
Muslim United Front (MUF), 155–6
Muslim Women (Protection of Rights Upon Divorce) Act, 46, 48, 55
Muslims: alleged population growth of, 41; stereotypes of, 40
Myanmar, 173

Naga National Council (NNC), 140, 141
Nagaland, 141–2, 146, 148; protected status of, 140
Nagarik Ekta Manch, 127
Naidu, Chandrababu, 81
Nair, Janaki, 81
Nandigram, struggles in, 66, 106, 181
Nangla Maachi, 75
Narayan, Badri, 39–40
Narmada Bachao Andolan (NBA) movement, 69, 70, 72, 116
Narmada Hydroelectric Development Corporation (NHDC), 62
Narmada Valley Project (NVP), 61, 63, 67, 69–72, 75, 123
Narmada Water Disputes Tribunal Award, 62
nation state, 116, 154; logic of, 139
National Center for Labor (NCL), 118
National Council of Educational Research and Training (NCERT), 177

National Democratic Alliance
(NDA), 50–4, 66, 143, 168
National Front, 11, 15, 49
National Hydro Power
Corporation (NHPC), 61,
154
National Perspective Plan
(NPP), 27
National Rural Employment
Guarantee Act (2005), 178
National Socialist Council
of Nagaland (NSCN),
142; Isaac-Muivah faction
(NCSN-IM), 142, 146, 148
National Thermal Power
Corporation case, 75
Navbharat Times, 90–1
Navi Mumbai, 79
Naxalites, 105, 114, 115, 117,
118–21, 121–4
Nehru, Jawaharlal, 18, 48, 63,
166
Nehruvian Consensus, 3–5, 15,
104, 128, 177
Nellie, killing of Muslims, 139
neoliberalism, 110–13
Nepal, 124, 173–4
New Left *see* Left, New
New Trade Union Initiative
(NTUI), 118
Niyamgiri Hills, bauxite mining
in, 65–6
Nomani, Abdul Batin, 59

non-governmental
organizations (NGOs),
124–33
non-party movements, 115–18
Non-Resident Indians (NRIs),
10
north east of India, 138–9;
conflict management in,
150–1
North East Students'
Organization (NESO),
149–50
nuclear bomb: India's testing
of, 50, 71, 133, 159;
Pakistan's testing of, 50, 170
nuclear energy, 62, 133; critique
of, 132; deal with US, 168–9
Nuclear Non-Proliferation
Treaty (NPT), 169
Nyogi, Shankar Guha, 117

obscenity, campaigns against,
93
Omvedt, Gail, 99, 114
Operation Barga, 111

Pachauri, Sudhish, 90
Pakistan, 147, 152, 157, 159,
160, 167, 169, 170–1, 175;
India's war with, 71, 153;
television serials, 87, 89
Pakistan India People's Forum
for Peace and Democracy,
171

Pakistan-Occupied Kashmir (POK), 152
Pal, Justice Ruma, 78
Panchayati Raj Institutions (PRI), 27, 29
panchayats, 109, 113
Pandits, 157, 162
Panun Kashmir organization, 162
Parameswaran, M.P., 116–17
Parivartan organization, 178
Patkar, Medha, 105
Pasmaanda Muslim Mahaj (PMM), 55–6
Patil, Sharad, 114
pavement dwellers, 128; rights of, 80
peace movement, 132–3
peasantry, 7, 109, 119–20, 122–3, 125; movements of, 105
Peasants' and Workers' Party, 181
Penal Code, Section 377, 129
pensions for agricultural workers, 109
People to People contact, 170
People's Democratic Party (PDP), 163
People's Forum Against ADB, 107
People's Liberation Army (PLA), 145
People's Plan Campaign (Kerala), 107
People's Union for Civil Liberties (PUCL), 125
People's Union for Civil Liberties and Democratic Rights (PUCLDR), 125
People's Union for Democratic Rights (PUDR), 73, 125
People's War Group (PWG), 122–3
personal law, 46–7, 54; Muslim, 45
Phadke, Shilpa, 94
Phule, Jyotiba, 22
piracy in music market, 87
Pitroda, Satyen Gangaram (Sam), 9
police, revolt of, 6
political society, 13, 19
pollution, 128; fighting against, 77–8
pornography, 91; raid on cyber cafés, 95
poverty, 1, 17, 101
Prasad, Chandra Bhan, 57, 95–9
Prevention of Terrorism Act, 126, 137, 164
Progressive Organization of Women (POW), 114
protest movements, 68–9
Public Interest Litigation (PIL), 74–5, 78, 80

268 | Index

Puri, Balraj, 154, 162

rainforest, 139; submergence of, 116
Raj, Udit, 100
Rajshekhar, V.T., 99
Ram, Kanshi, 22
Ramasamy Naicker, E.V.R., 22
Ramjanmabhoomi movement, 40, 42, 43, 48–50, 58–9, 127
Rao, Narasimha, 171
rape, 25, 28, 132, 141, 146, 173; definition of, 132, 180; marital, 180; of Muslim women, 40
Rashtriya Janata Dal, 54
Rashtriya Swayamsevak Sangh (RSS), 6, 8, 41–2, 53–4, 58, 161
Rath Yatra, 23
Ravindran, K.T., 81–2
Regional Autonomy Committee (RAC), 161, 162
Rekhi, Kanwal, 88
Reliance Industries, 11, 66, 85
relocation of poor people from cities, 113
reservations, 33, 34, 98–9, 100
Right to Information Act (2005), 177–8
riots, institutionalised production of, 52
Roy, Arundhati, 126, 163–4

Rushdie, Salman, *Satanic Verses*, 156

Samaddar, Ranabir, 165, 175
Samajwadi Party, 23, 29, 54, 179
Sampada Grameen Mahila Parishad (SANGRAM), 129
Sampradayikta Virodhi Andolan (SVA), 127
Sangh Parivar, 50, 103
Sangvai, Sanjay, 116
Sankat Mochan temple, 59
Sarkar, Sumit, 106
Satyashodhak Communist Party, 114
Savarkar, Vinayak Damodar, 36
Savvy sex survey, 91
Sayed, Badar, 55
Sayeed, Mufti Mohammed, 156, 160
Scheduled Tribes (Recognition of Forest Rights) Act (2006), 178
school textbooks, debate about, 177
secularism, 21–6, 36, 57–8, 162; relation to state project, 60
Seven Party Alliance, 173
sex ratio, decline in, 180
sex surveys, 91–2
sexual harassment in the workplace, 131, 180

sexuality, 40–1, 83, 128–30; rethought by feminism, 93–5
Shahabuddin, Syed, 56
Shankaracharya of Kanchi, arrest of, 59
shanty towns, 79; demolition of see *jhuggis*, demolition of
sharecroppers, 66; registering of, 111
shari'a law, 45–6, 47
Sharifa, Daud, 55
Sharma, B.D., 122
Sharmila, Irom, 146
Shaw, Annapurna, 79
Shi'a Islam, 162
Shillong Accord, 141
Shiv Sena, 44–5, 181
shortages of commodities, 84
Shourie, Arun, 169
Simla Agreement, 153
Singh, Arun, 10
Singh, Digvijay, 100
Singh, Hari, 152, 154
Singh, K.P., 96–7
Singh, Manmohan, 80, 146
Singh, V.P., 15, 16, 18, 23, 49, 103, 104
Sitaramaiah, Kondapalli, 122
slum dwellers, criminalization of, 79
South Asian Association for Regional Cooperation (SAARC), 174
Southasia, 172–5
sovereignty, issue of, 169
Special Economic Zones (SEZ), 64–8, 106
Sreejith, K., 121
Sri Lanka, 4, 172–3
Staines, Graham, killing of, 44
state, issue of, 93–4
States Reorganization Act (1956), 136
Stephen, C.M., 84
student movement, 6
Sufism, 157
Sugathakumari, poet, 116
suicides of farmers, 63, 64, 181
Supreme Court, 72, 73, 103, 143, 165, 178, 179; known as Green Bench, 76; role of, 74–5; Sardar Sarovar judgement, 71, 74; stay of Mandal II, 180; Vishakha judgement, 131–2, 180
surrender schemes, 150
Swadeshi Jagran Manch (SJM), 44
Swadhin Asom, 145

talaq, 47
Tamil Nadu, 137–8, 180; water dispute, 137
Tata Iron and Steel Company (TISCO), 64, 65, 105
taxation, exemptions, 65

Tehri Hydropower Corporation, 75
Telecom Commission, 9
telecoms, public call offices, 9
Telegraph Group, 113
telephones, acquisition of, 84
television, 87; cable/satellite, 88–9
Teltumbde, Anand, 99
Thomas Isaac, T.M., 108
trade unions, 6, 44, 118; attacks on, 123; resistance to, 67
tribal peoples, 147
Trinamool Congress, 105

UN Conference on Racism and Related Forms of Discrimination, 20
UN resolutions, India's voting in, 167–8
underground economy, 150
Uniform Civil Code (UCC), 31, 45–8
Union of Soviet Socialist Republics (USSR), 166; collapse of, 5, 110, 113, 167, 171
United Front (UF), 103, 110, 119
United National Liberation Front (UNLF), 145
United National Liberation Front of Assam (ULFA), 144–5, 148

United Progressive Alliance, 66, 176, 177, 180
United States of America (USA), 159, 166; diversity programs, 98; relations with China, 167; relations with India, 168
Uranium Mining Corporation of India, 132
urban space, 80; struggles over, 128
Urdu language, 89, 90
Uttar Pradesh, elections in, 179

Valentine's Day, attacks on couples, 95
Vedanta Alumina Limited, 65
video-taping of television, 87–8
violence, against women, 28, 93, 132, 180
Vishakha judgement of Supreme Court, 131–2, 180
Vishva Hindu Parishad (VHP), 43–4, 48–9

wages, minimum, 74
War on Terror, 126, 168
water, 154; access to, 106; disputes over, 137; mining of groundwater, 63; privatization of, 178
West Bengal, 109, 110–13, 133
Winfrey, Oprah, 101

women, 28–32, 59;
empowerment of, 30;
mobilization of, 40; Muslim,
55 (rights of, 46); quotas-
within-quotas, 29, 32;
viewing of pornography, 91
Women's Development
Programme (Rajasthan), 31
women's movement, 3, 31, 47,
129, 130–2; second wave of,
28
Women's Reservation Bill,
27–32, 131
World Bank, 4–5, 30, 115, 178;
reduces dam funding, 70

World Social Forum, Mumbai
meeting, 133–4
World Trade Organization
(WTO), 44

Yadav, Mulayam Singh, 23, 24,
29
Yadav, Yogendra, 28, 35
Yamuna river, cleansing of,
78–9
Yaypayee, Atal Behari,
11

Zee television, 90
Zoroastrians, 38